Patronage Politics in Egypt

Between the military takeover of 1952 and the collapse of the Mubarak regime in 2011, the political system of Egypt depended upon a variety of mechanisms and structures to establish and consolidate its power base. Among these, an intricate web of what could be described as 'patronage politics' emerged as one of the main foundations of these tools.

Throughout the post-1952 era, political patrons and respective clients were influential in Egyptian politics, shaping the policies implemented by Egypt's rulers, as well as the tactics orchestrated by the wider population. On a macro level, *Patronage Politics in Egypt* examines the activities of the National Democratic Party (the ruling party from 1978 to 2011) and its opposition, the Muslim Brotherhood. On a micro level, the book uses the geographical area of Misr al-Qadima as a case study to examine the factors that have ensured the durability of patronage networks within the Egyptian polity.

By examining how the local links into macro-level politics, this book portrays the socioeconomic and political contexts that set the stage for the January 25 revolution. This topical study will be an invaluable resource for students, scholars and researchers of the Middle East and Islam, as well as those with a more general interest in politics.

Mohamed Fahmy Menza earned his PhD in Arab and Islamic Studies, specializing in political economy and sociology, from the Institute of Arab and Islamic Studies at Exeter University, UK. He has previously taught courses in political economy and development at Exeter University and the American University in Cairo (AUC), and currently teaches Arab and Global South Dialogue at the Core Curriculum, AUC. His research interests lie within the field of Middle East politics and society in general, with a special focus on state–society relations, informal and patronage politics, and the political economy of development.

Routledge Studies in Middle Eastern Politics

Patronage Politics in Egypt

The National Democratic Party and
Muslim Brotherhood in Cairo

Mohamed Fahmy Menza

Routledge
Taylor & Francis Group

LONDON AND NEW YORK

First published 2013
by Routledge
2 Park Square, Milton Park, Abingdon, Oxon OX14 4RN

Simultaneously published in the USA and Canada
by Routledge
711 Third Avenue, New York, NY 10017

Routledge is an imprint of the Taylor & Francis Group, an informa business

British Library Cataloguing in Publication Data
A catalogue record for this book is available from the British Library

Library of Congress Cataloging in Publication Data
Fahmy Menza, Mohamed.
Patronage politics in Egypt : the National Democratic Party and Muslim
Brotherhood in Cairo / Mohamed Fahmy Menza.
    p. cm. – (Routledge studies in Middle Eastern politics)
    Includes bibliographical references and index.
    1. Patronage, Political–Egypt. 2. Hizb al-Watani al-Dimuqrati (Egypt)
3. Jam'iyat al-Ikhwan al-Muslimin (Egypt) 4. Egypt–Politics and
government–1981- I. Title. II. Series: Routledge studies in Middle Eastern
politics.
    JF2111.F35 2012   324.262'083–dc23
    2012024762

ISBN: 978–0–415–68623–5 (hbk)
ISBN: 978–0–203–07666–8 (ebk)

Typeset in Times New Roman
by Bookcraft Ltd, Stroud, Gloucestershire

MIX
Paper from
responsible sources
FSC
www.fsc.org   FSC® C004839

Printed and bound in Great Britain by
TJ International Ltd, Padstow, Cornwall

Contents

List of figures

List of tables

Preface

This book is not about the January 25 revolution. The bulk of the fieldwork upon which this writing depends was conducted in the few years that preceded the inception of the popular uprisings that brought an end to the Mubarak regime. In fact, as the events of what was later referred to as the 'revolution' unfolded, I started questioning the validity of this research as a whole, now that the regime, with the National Democratic Party (NDP) at its core, was clearly collapsing under the pressure of the continuous protests that spread like wildfire all over the country. However, on second thoughts and as one started contextualizing the events of the 18-day period of protests after which Mubarak was deposed, the relevance of the propositions, observations and findings that this writing portrays was somehow reinforced.

First, the quasi-anarchy that the whole country went through after the collapse of the police apparatus on 28 January, in addition to the relative swiftness that characterized the downfall of this seemingly brutal apparatus in itself, supported observations regarding the fragility of the foundations upon which the Mubarak regime had been based. These events also confirmed assumptions pertaining to the weakness of the neoliberal state that reduced its existence and displays of legitimacy to the use of force as exercised, or rather manipulated, by the over-inflating and rent-seeking state apparatus known as the 'police'. Afterwards, 2 February's 'Camel Battle' and the role that was played by the *baltagiya* (thugs), who were mobilized by the lesser notabilities in a multitude of Cairo's popular quarters, in instigating acts of violence reinforced the assumptions relating to the power and influence of the lesser notabilities within the popular communities. This showcased their ability to infiltrate such communities and gain access to the massive networks that enabled them to, literally, mobilize tens of thousands of people in a few hours. Furthermore, the predominance of clientelistic politics, even after the collapse of the Mubarak clique, refutes the supposition that political patronage is primarily dependent upon vertical relationships between the apex of the regime and the subjects beneath, and emphasizes the crucial role played by horizontal networks of *shillal*. This goes to show that patronage is a socioeconomic phenomenon that is embedded within the social fabric of the community rather than an exogenous institution that is maintained solely by the ruling regime.

I revisited the writing in an attempt to update the research after the revolution. Fortunately, and to my surprise, I did not have to change much, apart from the timely developments that had to be mentioned regarding certain people or events. So, after all, this book mainly aims to examine the networks of political patronage that operate within the urban setting of contemporary Egypt. In particular, it looks at the activities of the ex-ruling NDP and the opposition Muslim Brotherhood and how the local links into macro-level politics; in doing so, it portrays an array of the socioeconomic and political conditions that set the stage for the January 25 revolution. The book also traces the impact of the neoliberal policies on the lives of the people in the popular quarters of Cairo, highlighting the role of the lesser notables, those intermediaries who flourish at the lower levels of the Egyptian polity.

Throughout the post-1952 era, political patrons and clients existed in Egyptian politics, shaping, to a great extent, the policies implemented by Egypt's rulers at the apex of the political system, as well as the tactics orchestrated by the populace within the middle and lower echelons of the polity. Dissecting the geographical area of Misr al-Qadima as a case study example of Cairo's popular quarters, this book also aims to analyse the factors that ensured the durability of patronage networks within the Egyptian polity, focusing primarily on the sort of sociostructural reconfiguration that has been taking place in the popular communities of Egypt at the beginning of the twenty-first century.

Acknowledgements

The writing of this book was made possible due to the substantial support of the University of Exeter, which was generous enough to sponsor me as an Exeter Research Scholar. I am also very grateful for the love and support of my friends and companions, without whom the finalization of this writing would have been next to impossible.

In the realm of academia, Dr Kamil Mahdi has been the prime source of academic as well as personal guidance, support and encouragement during the years that I have spent in Exeter. He has been patient and kind enough to bear with the seemingly never-ending process of drafting and enhancing the writing in every way possible. Dr Salwa Ismail was tremendously supportive during my first year at Exeter, and it is no exaggeration to say that she was an inspiration who helped to crystallize the subject matter of the research. Ahmed Abu Zayed and many friends as well as the staff, faculty and students of the Institute of Arab and Islamic Studies (IAIS) at the University of Exeter made this sometimes bumpy ride often quite pleasant. In Cairo, I had the pleasure and honour of having extensive discussions and sometimes lengthy research ventures with Dr Nigel Parsons and Dr Samer Soliman, and this has benefited me greatly in shaping and further developing a number of the arguments that this study puts forward. The efforts that Lina Attalah and Jano Charbel exerted as they went through several drafts of this research were also crucial in improving the writing and bringing it up to the standard to which they aspire as proficient writers and journalists.

I have also to thank all my family, particularly my parents and sister, and, of course my wife, Omneya Ragab, who had to put up with some impossible hours of working and writing, particularly at the time when our new arrival, Ali, was expected. In the course of developing this writing from a dissertation to a book, I was lucky to be part of the families of CARE Egypt and the Core Curriculum of the American University in Cairo, and I must mention the magnificent encouragement and support I received from all my dear friends in these two places. Last, and most definitely not least, it is to the late Ahmed Rozza and the people of Misr al-Qadima that I dedicate this book, in the hope that it will help shed some light on the everyday activities and interactions within Cairo's oldest quarter.

Some of the material in this book has been previously published in the following article: Mohamed, Menza (2012) 'Neoliberal Reform and Socio-Structural Reconfiguration in Cairo's Popular Quarters: The Rise of the lesser notables in Misr Al Qadima', *Mediterranean Politics*, 17(3): 322–39. We are grateful for permission to reproduce it here.

1 Introduction, theoretical framework and methodology/ approaches

Aims and objectives

In the light of the ever-expanding literature dealing with an encompassing conception of state–society relations that goes beyond the definition of the state as a sheer amalgamation of 'formal' institutions, there seems to be a need to revisit the concept of political patronage and try somehow to fit it within this larger sketch of state–society relations. This book aims to analyse the conditions that give rise to patronage in the Egyptian polity. In doing so, it ventures into dissecting some of the recurrent features of this patron–client web in order to examine the main factors that have affected the prevalence of patronage politics in Egypt, particularly throughout the Mubarak phase. Emphasizing the upcoming research questions, this study seeks to provide a better understanding of the factors that have ensured the durability of these patronage networks until the present day. This will be achieved primarily by tackling the issues of transition and liberalization associated with the sort of sociostructural reconfiguration that has been witnessed in the Egyptian polity since the beginning of the twenty-first century.

The main focus of this research will be dedicated to examining the socioeconomic and political roles of the 'lesser notables' as intermediaries in the realm of state–society relations.[1] In the course of this writing, the term 'lesser notables' refers to those middle-level patrons and clients who have flourished at the lower levels of the Egyptian polity and whose sociopolitical agency appears to have been comparatively discarded in the literature pertaining to Middle East politics. The lesser notables constitute an essential segment of the operative cadres in the Muslim Brotherhood (MB) and were also present within the ranks of the former National Democratic Party (NDP), which was dissolved by court order in 2011 in the aftermath of the January 25 revolution.

Research questions

With the seeming mobilization of societal echelons and sociopolitical classes that has taken place in the Egyptian polity in the first decade of the twenty-first century, there is indeed a new realm of relevant political actors who clearly differ from the ones prevalent in the previous periods. For example, the 1980s and 1990s witnessed the rising importance of the political agency of the business community as opposed to the military and the technocratic classes, which had been rather dominant during the socialist heydays of Nasserite Egypt. To what extent has this alteration empowered new classes or echelons of patrons and clients? And can one identify a certain set or sets of neo-patrons and clients who are as a result on the rise in the Egyptian polity? What are the parameters of the socioeconomic and political agency of the lesser notables, those middle-range patrons and clients who play a sizeable role in shaping the dynamics of the popular communities? And what are the major commonalities and differences between those of them who adhered to the ex-ruling NDP in comparison to others who allied with the MB? What role was played by the lesser notabilities in the January 25 revolution, and what are their prospective socioeconomic and political roles in the post-Mubarak phase?

Literature review

Taking into account the informal nature of the majority of the socioeconomic and political activities that this book attempts to scrutinize, primary testimonies from relevant personnel in the dissolved NDP and the MB constitute an essential part of the resources used in this research. As will be elaborated on later in this chapter, the information derived from these sources will be augmented and verified, whenever possible, by data and facts. In order to introduce the subject matter of the research, the literature review will be divided into two sections. The first covers the theoretical framework of postulations dealing with patronage politics and relevant applications to the Egyptian case and, building on that, the second section discusses the major writings that contribute to the methodology and approaches that helped to shape the structure and content of this research.

Theoretical framework

In general, patronage politics could be considered to be an existent theme within almost all political systems. Some analysts have indeed argued that patronage is expected to flourish further in those political systems that are more dependent upon personal rule in their dynamics. 'It is a dynamic world of political will and action that is ordered less by institutions than by personal authorities and power … but without the assured mediation and regulation of effective political institutions' (Jackson and Rosberg, 1981: 12).

However, for this aim to be achieved, a series of collaborations and alliances between the ruling powers and several other actors has to take place to make this process of consolidation of power a mutually beneficial course of action that is advantageous to the various parties involved. This is actualized through patronage, which is a complicated web, usually consisting of several patron–client networks (Jackson and Rosberg, 1981). Here, an amalgamation of mutual beneficiaries that expands vertically throughout the system in a top-down approach is evident, and subsequently co-option, rather than coercion, becomes more widespread as an essential medium for exercising political power.

John Martinussen (1997: 193) expands upon this notion by portraying the roles of the patron and the respective client(s) in actualizing the scheme of patronage networks:

> The system of patronage ... works by the [patron] doling out generously from the public resources and benefits he controls. This patronage is extended to his own clan members and also to a selection of clan leaders whose political support is deemed necessary. The clan leaders can then, at their level within the power hierarchy, use some of their resources in a similar manner to ensure political backing from certain lower-placed clan leaders – and so on, until crumbs from the tables of the mighty eventually fall on the small-scale farmers and other poor people.

The term 'clan' refers here to political alliances and interest groups. Martinussen elaborates that the machinations by which patron–client ties extend from the apex of the political system to its base are best described by the milieu of webs and networks that work their way in a top-down approach. Figure 1.1 shows a generic network of patron–client relations. Of course, sub-patrons and clients eventually emerge as the network approaches the bottom of the hierarchy/polity.

Patronage politics and informal networks

With the inception of the post-1952 phase, the Egyptian polity became a vivid arena for patronage politics whereby informal groups of relatives and friends played a more important role than formal ones in patron–client networks (Moore, 1977). Generally speaking, with the advent of patron–client networks as a primary medium for facilitating political power, the majority of Egyptians, i.e. the common people or the *Sha'b*, gradually developed a sense of scepticism towards their rulers, along with a conviction of the inefficiency of the formal or official seats of government:

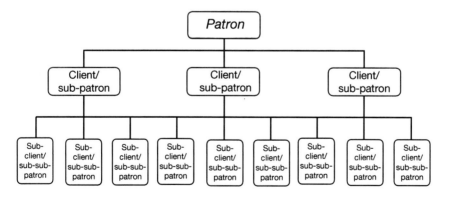

Figure 1.1 The patron–client model.

> The *Sha'b* understand the high costs of participating in formal politics and
> thus develop other institutions to serve their needs ... Elites structure poli-
> tics so that most people cannot participate in the system or their participation
> is not much more than a charade.
>
> Singerman, 1995: 9

So, on the one hand, the *Sha'b* have been suspicious of the government and its
intentions, but, on the other, they have been more concerned with the concept of
'*shillal*' or cliques. For them, the importance of the *shilla* surpasses the importance of any formal sort of union. Henry Moore notes that these *shillal* or cliques
were somehow encouraged in order to form conglomerate units, which was
promoted by the growing bloat of the public sector in the 1960s:

> The more heavily bureaucracy weighs upon the society; the more likely
> it is that vertical patron-client networks give way to horizontal *shillal*. In
> Egypt, corruption appears to be extensive yet decentralized. As bureaucracy
> becomes heavier, it is likely to become more corrupt, especially near the top,
> in the absence of effective political coordination and supervision.
>
> Moore, 1977: 271

More recently, contributors such as Diane Singerman have paid special attention to the concept of informal networks and the sizeable role that such networks
have as alternative venues of political participation, especially for those within
the lower-middle and lower classes in the Egyptian polity. In what could be
described as a relevant anecdote and a potential starting point with regard to
the subject matter of the writing at hand, Singerman asserts that little attention
has been given to those societal forces in the conventional literature tackling
Egyptian politics:

> While there are classic works on elite politics in Egypt, its political economy,
> class formation, interest groups, the bureaucracy, and the military, the poli-
> tics of the common people or the *Sha'b* have received little attention. Their
> political demands, actions, and grievances remain of secondary interest to
> elite analysis. It has been anthropologists, historians, and sociologists who
> have told us about the politics of the common people while the "high poli-
> tics" of the elite ... remained the domain of political scientists. However, if
> one truly wants to consider state-society relations, it seems only natural to
> try to link up these two arenas of interests.
>
> Singerman, 1995: 5

In addition to the fact that these classes have been, more or less, discarded in
the conventional analysis of Egyptian politics, Singerman asserts also that, in
practice, such classes are highly influential and have an actual role to play in the
overall portrait of the Egyptian polity.

Here, it is also worth noting that informal politics are not exclusively the
domain of the lower-middle and lower classes of Egyptian society. In fact, the

Egyptian elite also utilize the machinations of informalities, mostly to penetrate the formal structure of the official institutions, yet the end result is to serve some economic or political benefit. Therefore, it is safe to say that the essence of informal networks somehow infiltrates the hierarchy of the Egyptian polity as well. Hence, Singerman says that, when it comes to the lower echelons, those informal networks which were primarily expanded as a result of the lack of formal or official avenues of political participation are in fact open arenas for patrons and clients to flourish:

> The *Sha'b* have turned exploiting the government into a fine art. People in the community who had a particular talent for dealing with bureaucrats or a wide range of connections to elite politicians and officials were sought after and valued ... The government was something to "take from", an outside external force to be patronized.
>
> Singerman, 1995: 39

The characteristics of those people who are capable of connecting with and benefitting from state institutions are actually congruent with the features of what Salwa Ismail described as the *biytkabarluh* figures in the popular quarters of Cairo. The portrayal of Hajj Saleh, a strongman in Bulaq, exemplifies this: 'The ethos of someone *biytkabarluh* involves rights and obligations on the part of the person occupying the position. Moral deference toward [this] figure derives from relations of kinship, regional origin, and the moral standing of the person' (S. Ismail, 2006: 64) On the one hand, Hajj Saleh's active participation in charitable work gives him the image of a 'man of good', whereas, on the other, his links with the police reaffirm his status as a 'man of power'. Consequently, the Hajj is regularly used by the state apparatus as an influential intermediary with the local community (S. Ismail, 2006). Indeed, here the profile of Hajj Saleh fits the persona of the 'lesser notables', described by Ismail as the political powerhouses of Cairo's popular quarters. Interestingly, these lesser notabilities are characterized by an amalgamation of pragmatic and moral statures. These notables in fact constitute the focal point of this research.

January 25: potential implications regarding popular politics in post-Mubarak Egypt

It might still be too early to outline definitive conclusions regarding prospective alterations in popular politics in the post-Mubarak phase. Indeed, the power-houses of the elite circle of patrons were somewhat disintegrated in the aftermath of January 25, and that was brought about with the dissolution of the NDP and the imprisonment of some of its most influential leading cadres, including Gamal Mubarak. Yet the fact remains that the conglomerate of alliances and networks that constitute the interconnected network of political patronage is somehow embedded within the socioeconomic and political fabric of the middle and the lower echelons of Egyptian society. The prospective changes that will occur with regard to these patronage networks will probably be shaped by the alterations in the political and socioeconomic outlook of the Egyptian state post-Mubarak.

Henceforth, the scope and magnitude of the overall reformulation of the structure of state–society relations is likely to determine the prospects of change concerning patron–client networks. For example, the nature of the social contract between the state and society, exemplified by the socioeconomic policies adopted by the state post-Mubarak, and the degree of empowerment acquired by the populace in terms of participation in the official venues of political decision-making are among the relevant factors here. Such potential reconfigurations may prospectively influence the power dynamics embedded in state–society relations, subsequently redefining the features of patronage politics within the Egyptian polity in the post-Mubarak phase.

The trap of cultural arguments

Patronage politics is not of course a natural ingredient that is embedded solely in the Egyptian or the Arab political culture per se. In fact, similar features of informal politics can be traced in other polities over the globe. Nazih Ayubi prudently notes that:

> Although patronage and clientelism have a long history and an elaborate vocabulary in the Middle East ... they are not the inevitable outcome of certain essential and permanent cultural traits. They are in reality behavioral correlates to articulated modes of production and attitudinal accompaniments of a stage of transition that requires a higher degree of intermediation between the rural and the urban, between the local and the central, between the public and the private. The study of patron-client relationships, cliques, cronies and informal networks ... can be useful and indeed very interesting. Their validity will be constrained however if they are viewed as being exclusively culturally specific, rather than socially and politically contingent.
>
> Ayubi, 1995: 168

Thus, bearing in mind the considerable impact of the prevalent modes of production on the political beliefs and attitudes within a human polity, it is essential to avoid any sort of cultural essentialism that would signify patron–client networks as a peculiar feature of the Arab polity at large, or the Egyptian one in particular. Accordingly, Ayubi states that, for instance regarding the *shilla*, a concept that was mentioned earlier as an important unit of analysis introduced mainly by H.C. Moore and others, '*Shillas* and other types of cliques and informal networks should not be regarded as a Middle Eastern peculiarity: we know increasingly more about their presence in countries such as Italy, Japan and even the United States' (Ayubi, 1995: 168).

But here we are faced with an analytical dilemma. If, as stated earlier, patron–client networks actually appear and flourish in a wide variety of human polities, despite the clear differences such polities might show in terms of governing systems and the modes of production that have prevailed in them, can we still make use of such a concept in understanding any polity at all? Once again, the challenge is to make the proper linkage between the micro and macro levels of analysis:

> It is this analytical shift, however, from micro to macro politics that represents the most challenging conceptual difficulty with clientelism. Given the intellectual history of a concept drawn from anthropology and applied without much theoretical adjustment to complex political systems, it is not surprising that the concept loses much of its explanatory power as one moves from interpersonal relationships to clientelistic structures (i.e. corporate clientelism) at the local or the national level.
>
> Ayubi, 1995: 169

Therefore contextualization, in terms of historical factors and political/economic circumstances, is essential if we are to trace patron–client bonds and potentially attempt to reach observations or findings pertaining to the realities of one human polity or another. In fact, Ayubi ventures through this dilemma by analysing the historical context in which patron–client networks developed in the Middle Eastern polity, as will be shown in Chapter 2.

Putting patrons and clients in context: the rise of the lower echelons

The rise of a powerful group of commercial agents within the Egyptian middle class took place after the *Infitah*, or the Open Door policy, which had been instituted by President Anwar Sadat in 1974:

> Although on a global level the group does not own the means of production it does fulfill the function of global capital through its activity, and is simply placed on the lower echelons of the global bourgeois hierarchy. Locally the group very definitely partly owns and controls the means of production, both through its membership in the ascendant new bourgeoisie as well as its connections with the state bourgeoisie still controlling the state property. The group's class position is therefore quite complex ... linking class structures of both peripheral and metropolitan societies. These groups ... provide the access points for foreign economic entry and political influence.
>
> Zaalouk, 1989: 144

In a sense, these groups represent some of the horizontal *shillal* born out of lower level alliances formed to deal with the state's cumbersome bureaucracy. Indeed, their influence was further enhanced as fillers of the market and the space vacated by the state in the prime of the *Infitah* era. Overall, one can safely argue that what could be dubbed as a new class of patrons and clients was in the making in the post-*Infitah* era. Shortly after occupying their position on the socioeconomic map, the commercial agents emphasized by Zaalouk (1989) were in fact the reserves that were drawn upon by the ex-ruling NDP's neoliberal clique in order to formulate Egypt's new class of patrons, i.e. the business society, as will be discussed in Chapters 5 and 6.

It is indeed essential to assess the structural reconfiguration that took place within the Egyptian polity leading up to the rise, or perhaps the re-emergence, of particular categories of patrons or clients and the demise of others. The re-emergence here actually refers to the fact that, despite the seeming domination that the state had over the modes of production in most of the Arab world at the beginning of the post-colonial era, this has not been always the case. Over most of the Islamic dynasties that spanned large areas of the Middle East after the Arab conquest, commercial agents had played an important role as viable societal actors and sometimes mediators between official authorities and informal/popular groupings, as will be shown in Chapter 2. Moreover, and even during the 'modern' era:

> The expansion of home market, the export of agricultural commodities and the distribution of imported goods all provide a basis for a rapid increase in the 'circulation function' and for an economic strengthening of the role of members of the merchant class, who essentially act as 'linkmen' between modes of production or divisions of labor.
>
> Ayubi, 1995: 171

Practically speaking, the gradual retreat of the state from the public sphere that accompanied the implementation of the *Infitah* policy meant that the field was more or less open for the popular political forces to operate there, and one prime popular force was that of the Islamic movement. Mainstream Islamists

> such as the Muslim Brotherhood have developed a parallel network of Islamic institutions including private clinics, mosques, schools, banks, and investment companies. Moreover, beginning in the 1980's, Islamists have won control of the executive boards of professional syndicates and university faculty clubs.
>
> Wickham, 1994: 508

Interestingly, the MB had to rely upon a scheme of patronage politics that was quite similar to that of the Egyptian regime in order to establish its foundational networks: 'Islamic activists have cultivated ties of patronage with employees at the lower rungs of the state bureaucracy, as well as with elected members of local municipal councils, enabling them to bend existing rules and evade control efforts from above' (Wickham, 1994: 508).

Indeed, within the popular urban and rural quarters, the Municipal Councils constitute a prospective venue for establishing networks and alliances between political groupings such as the MB on the one hand, and the popular notabilities on the other, as will be shown in Chapters 4 and 5. Thus, an overview of the system of local governance in Egypt is in place. The snapshot of the municipalities given below is essential because it paves the way for scrutinizing the role of lesser notabilities as state–society intermediaries taking part in patronage politics at the local level. The current research is especially concerned with the role that the municipality plays as a venue of formal politics that opens the door for lesser notabilities to practise political patronage and infiltrate the 'formal' state institutions in the process.

A note on the Municipal Councils and the characteristics of the local system of governance in Egypt

At a local level, there are 4496 village and 199 town municipalities in Egypt. Municipalities are controlled by their elected councils, which have relatively little power (World Bank and Maghrib Center, 2008). Municipal elections took place in April 2002 and were delayed from 2006 before being held again in 2008, when roughly 70 per cent of the then ruling NDP's candidates ran unopposed. The NDP eventually won 97 per cent of the municipal seats (World Bank and Maghrib Center, 2008). In June 2011, in the aftermath of the January 25 revolution and as a result of the lawsuits claiming that these councils represented one of the remaining corrupt political institutions associated with the dissolved NDP, the Supreme Administrative Court issued the decision to dismantle all the municipalities nationwide.

In terms of local finance and fiscal decentralization, the municipalities have often suffered from insufficient resources and a negligible say in the management of their own budgets. They receive the majority of their financial resources from central government in the form of annual subsidies. Within each governorate, the Municipal Council is expected to exercise governance at the local level of the village or the town. These councils have been largely disempowered and somewhat overshadowed by the governor, whose actual jurisdictions are also quite limited when compared with the powers of the central government in Cairo (Abdalla 2007).

Despite the variations in economic systems adopted by the government throughout the post-1952 phase, the lack of emphasis upon decentralization as a national policy was a recurrent theme within these various economic systems. The Ministry of Local Development, which was delegated the authority to supervise the process of decentralization at the local level, has received minimal budgetary allocations. In 1981/82 its share of the total government expenditure was 1.8 per cent, whereas in 1997/98 this share was even reduced to 1.5 per cent of the total budget (World Bank and Maghrib Center, 2008). In addition, despite the increasing dependence of the local municipalities on the allocations coming from central government, these state allocations were reduced, or at best remained stagnant, in a way that was not able to cope with the growing needs of these administrations (World Bank and Maghrib Center, 2008). In recent years, however, and almost coinciding with the advent of its neoliberal program, the NDP has appeared more fixed on adopting a scheme of decentralization that will give the municipalities some autonomy in managing the affairs of the localities within which they operate. As will be argued in Chapter 5, it is safe to assume that one of the main factors that led to the NDP's determination to revitalize the municipalities was, in practice, the potential role that could be played by these municipalities as power bases of the party in the face of the MB.

The politics of popular quarters

It is noteworthy that the popular classes do play a meaningful role in Egyptian politics. Salwa Ismail draws attention to the socioeconomic structure of Cairo's haphazard (*'ashwa'iyyat*) areas and outlines the context that nurtured the development of informal networks within these neighbourhoods as a pattern of effective organization and governance (Ismail, 2000). This contribution is relevant to this research as it sheds light on the particular dynamics that characterize the dealings of the typology of the middle patrons and clients that the study at hand is concerned with.

With a sizeable portion of their population residing in informal or haphazard slums, Egypt's major cities, such as Cairo and Alexandria, act as open venues for an array of informal politics, and it is apparent that the MB and other Islamists have capitalized upon the already existing socioeconomic structure of such areas to further strengthen its position. According to Ismail:

> The Islamists anchor themselves in oppositional spaces already formed or in the process of formation. The terms of this opposition are spatial, social, cultural, economic, and political ... These neighborhoods propose a reformulation of the popular city, recovering the social role of the street.
>
> Ismail, 2000: 379

A good exemplar of the stratagem adopted by the MB occurred after the October 1992 earthquake when a variety of charitable societies (*Gam'eyat*) affiliated to the MB expanded their network of beneficiaries to the low-income communities that needed food and shelter at the time. This ultimately added points to their credibility and popularity, and subtracted quite a few from that of the state apparatus and the regime associated with it.

The popular social forces that emerged in the aftermath of the Open Door/ liberalization policies can be defined as follows:

> Popular is defined in opposition to the dominant forces – the political and economic elites. It also refers to the economic and social position of a number of classes or fractions of classes which, because of the blurring of boundaries, are not easily distinguishable. The fluidity and blurring of lines has to do with occupational mobility and the fact that members of these classes hold more than one job simultaneously. A common feature between them, however, is the predominance of informal economic activities. This applies to artisans, petty traders, low-level service sector workers, construction workers, and craftsmen.
>
> Ismail, 2000: 375

Logically speaking, the relative absence of the state at the street level left room for popular and informal networking to operate as an alternative outlet for political action:

State disengagement from welfare provision and the residents' efforts at creating self-sufficiency, in social and economic spheres, point to a significant change in state–society relations. The social or moral contract defining these relations in the 1950's and 60's has weakened, if not dissolved.

S. Ismail, 2006: 131

The playground for popular networking was subsequently open for the Islamic movements to dominate. This was reflected in the ballot box in 2005, with 88 MB candidates winning their seats in parliament. The fact that there was virtually a minimal presence of the NDP and the other secular parties at the popular level, as opposed to the Islamic popular movements that were present at street level, gave room for the MB to score its biggest parliamentary victory so far, despite the irregularities that were imposed by the regime in its attempts to halt the MB's widespread electoral success.

Approaches/theoretical framework

The Weberian paradigm: benefits, problems and limitations

Political patronage is a socioeconomic/political phenomenon that is scrutinized in several intellectual approaches/perspectives. The research here will aim to reflect upon and use different aspects of such perspectives in an attempt to enrich the arguments postulated. These various approaches are not mutually exclusive, and some of them can be jointly utilized in order to analyse political patronage – as a social phenomenon – from a multiplicity of angles.

The elite theory, for example, argues for the occurrence of patronage because of the discrepancies in access to resources among the various societal segments within the populace. The elite classes are often the main beneficiaries of such discrepancies, which grant them some sort of preferential treatment. Regardless of the changes that might take place within the political system in terms of ideology or policies, political power is likely to remain in the hands of the elite classes, among which the circles of patronage are likely to rotate (Schwartzmantel, 1987). In the Egyptian case, this explanation holds some truth that should not pass unnoticed. It is indeed realistic to say that the 'big' political patrons usually belong to certain socioeconomic classes, as was the case during the Nasser and the Sadat eras, and even under Mubarak. However, the stature of these so-called elite classes varied across these different phases. For example, as will be reviewed in the course of this study, the socioeconomic and cultural backgrounds of the 'big' patrons in the Nasser era differed to a considerable extent from those who appeared during the Sadat years and so forth.

On the other hand, liberal/pluralist analysis states that political patronage takes place due to the lack of proper democratization and openness in political arenas such as the Egyptian polity, and believes that, with the actualization of a properly implemented pluralist political process that allowed participants equal opportunities, political patronage would most probably wither away (Schwartzmantel, 1987). Despite the fact that the current research does not adopt this perspective, it is sometimes useful to look at patron–client networks as a deviation from the bureaucratic/institutional prototype that is usually associated with the 'modern' nation-state model. This helps in understanding and scrutinizing the intricacies of the popular communities and the entirety of the Egyptian polity at large, by comparing the actual realities lived and the actions undertaken by the populace with the expectations to which they are subject to as citizens of a modern state. By contextualizing the actions of those in the popular polity of a city such as Cairo, one notes that what is often considered to be an improper or illegal act in one of today's modern nation-states can be perceived as mundane or ordinary in the popular community. The examples cited in this study suggest that, in the everyday dealings of the Egyptian polity, value-laden issues such as 'corruption' and public–private divides are, by and large, context-based.

In addition, certain elements of the Weberian approach could be useful in the course of this research. Weber viewed large institutions, including the military, the bureaucracy and other political input structures, not as cohesive political actors but rather as venues within which patrons and clients can flourish (Springborg and Bill, 2000). This perception will be presented as this study delves into scrutinizing the various formal institutions of the Egyptian state, i.e. the NDP, the cabinet, the parliament, etc., and shows that, more often than not, there is no unitary logic governing the actions of such institutions and making them cohesive political actors. Instead, one finds that there is an ongoing process of tension and competition between contesting entourages of patrons and clients within such state venues, which determines to a great extent the politicoeconomic orientation of and subsequent policies adopted by such institutions, as exemplified in the case of the former ruling NDP.

Gellner and Waterbury (1977) use elements of the aforementioned Weberian approach, as they showcase a wide variety of contributions on patronage in theory and practice, with a special focus on Mediterranean societies. In the course of their writing, they provide a gist concerning some of the dominant theories that deal with patronage and political power. In doing so, Gellner and Waterbury pinpoint the fact that patronage networks usually go through a continuous process of reformulation that alters the powerful or relevant patrons and clients, in accordance with the socioeconomic and political contexts prevalent at various junctures. This point is essential in our quest to analyse the potential of sustaining patronage politics in Egypt post-Mubarak, as will be shown in subsequent chapters.

As one attempts to scrutinize political patronage as a sociopolitical phenomenon, a methodological concern comes to the forefront:

> The problem is, firstly, a methodological one. On what grounds do we identify patterns in our data and call them patronage? Do we look at the behavior and the effects of action or do we ask people what they think is happening and how they feel about it? If we do both, is this a matter of summing up diverse kinds of information, or do we 'weigh' them differently? And how do we handle discrepancies in different kinds of information?
>
> Gellner and Waterbury, 1977: 21

In order to deal with these concerns, we need to dissect the interaction between the public and the private spheres and attempt to comprehend the attitudinal tendencies of people by focusing on the economic and political contexts of state–society relations. This can help us to shed light on the infiltrative nature of political patronage, showing how it capitalizes upon the already existing societal and cultural structures of the human polity.

In the case of Egypt, patronage politics capitalized on some embedded tendencies among most Egyptians, primarily the distrust toward the ruling establishment/institution and the conviction that informalities and underground dealings are usually more efficient than government agencies in addressing people's needs. In practice, such tendencies were also very pragmatic in nature for, more often than not, informal networks were more beneficial to the majority of Egyptians than 'formal' ones, especially when it came to realizing economic or political objectives.

Limitations of the Weberian paradigm and relevance of the network approach

We must, however, bear in mind that there are certain limitations when it comes to using the Weberian approach in the context of the Middle Eastern polity. Ayubi (1995: 175) says:

> Both the Marxist and the Weberian paradigms were tried for the study of Middle Eastern societies ... but being basically western paradigms pertaining to capitalist societies, none of them has been found to be fully satisfactory ... In pre-capitalist societies as well as in societies with articulated modes of production, one may find, first, that modes of production are very closely intertwined with modes of coercion and secondly – which is often related to the previous and which is particularly pronounced in the case of the Middle East – that modes of 'distribution' or of 'circulation' are just as important, if not more so, than modes of production.

Thus, with a greater focus on modes of circulation, primarily of goods and services, as opposed to sheer production, Ayubi points out a meaningful limitation of the Weberian and other paradigms when it comes to analysing Middle Eastern polities. Here, the emphasis on modes of circulation is also relevant to the purpose of this study as it highlights the importance of the role of the lesser notabilities, primarily perceived as the commercial agents and the intermediary middlemen who often come into play as the facilitators of such a process of circulation. Other scholars, such as Joel Migdal, have also criticized the Weberian approach, or at least the way it has been utilized, in the context of state–society relations.

The dilemma here arises from the fact that it is the continuous process of struggle and negotiation between state and societal actors that should be the focus of attention if we are to analyse state–society relations:

Weber's definition has the state firing on all cylinders, and, while he certainly did not mean the ideal type to be taken as the normal ... that is precisely what has happened in subsequent scholarship. Of course, in real human society, no state can do all that an ideal-type state can ... Tremendous variation has existed among states in the levelers that their leaders and officials have controlled in order to garner resources and to accomplish a skewed distribution of economic (and other) opportunities ... If real states fell short of the standard ... all sorts of words had to be invented to express the gap between actual ... and the ideal. Terms such as corruption, weakness, and relative capacity implied that the ways things really worked were somehow exogenous to the normative model of what the state and its relations to the society are, or should be.

Migdal, 2001: 14–15

It seems that Weber's definition provided room for other scholars and politicians to consider the ideal state as one conducting 'legitimate' violence, exercising power in a monopolistic manner:

The assumption that only the state does, or should, create rules and ... maintain the violent means to bend people to obey those rules minimizes and trivializes the rich negotiation, interaction, and resistance that occur in every human society.

Migdal 2001: 15

Indeed, such a conceptualization of the state is not necessarily realistic if one is after a functional explanation of state–society relations.

Instead, a plethora of analysts propose a notion of a 'state in society', mainly referring to the dynamism and ongoing interaction between the official locations of state structure and the popular/informal actors within society. Subsequently, two main aspects come to the fore if we attempt to analyse the state in a manner that surpasses a sheer emphasis on the essentiality of state institutions. First is the image of the state, which is signified by the outstanding physical or moral structures of greatness and elevation of the state: city halls, courts, ministries, etc. Second, there is its practice, which is manifested in certain actions, usually channelled via certain actors or agencies:

It must be thought of at once (1) as the powerful image of a clearly bounded, unified organization that can be spoken of in singular terms ... as if it were a single, centrally motivated actor performing in an integrated manner to rule a clearly defined territory; and (2) as the practices of a heap of loosely connected parts or fragments, frequently with ill-defined boundaries between them and other groupings inside and outside the official state borders and often promoting conflicting sets of rules with one another and with the "official" Law. Theories that do not incorporate the two sides of the paradoxical state end up either over-idealizing its ability to turn rhetoric into effective policy or dismissing it as a grab-bag of everyman-out-for-himself, corrupt officials.

Migdal, 2001: 21–2

A similar conclusion is also outlined by Oskar Verkaiik, who identifies, based upon Pakistani popular culture, that distinguishing between the 'state-idea' and the 'state-system', and focusing on how the notion of bureaucratic state power can be used to legitimize as well as discredit the works of the state apparatus, is relevant to the case of the popular conceptualization of the state in Pakistan (Verkaiik, 2004: 9).

Along the same lines, regarding an alternative view of the state as an embedded milieu that interacts with society, other contributors, such as Salwa Ismail, propose a society-in-state model, in which improvization prevails. Based upon observational accounts and extensive fieldwork in the popular urban quarters of Cairo, Ismail says:

> The image of the state that emerges in the account of the market arrange-ments ... underscores a mode of operation that is characterized by improvisation. It would be difficult to prescribe a unitary logic to how local government is managed on daily basis. By the same token, the prop-osition that there is a society that stands outside obscures the coalitions that bring "society in state" to reverse Migdal's (2001) proposition on "the state in society".
>
> S. Ismail 2006: 64

The network approach

Logically speaking, the harsh emphasis on the bureaucratic institutional/ Weberian paradigm that dominated the academic realm in the post-Second World War era had to make its way through to the domain of policy-making. For example, the neoliberal model that was, and probably still is, championed by the Breton Woods institutions, places great importance on a scheme of liberalization that views economic reform as a process dedicated to

> dismantling economic arrangements that served the interests of political power holders, and replacing them with arrangements that reflected the "logic of economics". In this view, liberalization was seen as causing a shift from cronyism, patronage, and rent seeking to transparency, accountability, and well-defined property rights.
>
> Heydemann, 2004: 7

Nonetheless, what took place in reality throughout most of these 'liberaliza-tion' schemes was a process of substitution of particular typologies of patron–client networks for the benefit of others, albeit under the umbrella of economic reform.[2] Hence it could be meaningful to utilize a 'network' approach, instead of depending solely on a rigid view of 'formal' institutions as the primary unit of analysis.

In fact, if we are attempting to dissect patron–client networks, or any other form of informal network, it is essential to solidify a clear conceptualization of what is meant by networks:

> Instead of analyzing individual behaviors, attitudes, and beliefs, social network analysis focuses ... on social entities or actors in interaction with one another and on how those interactions constitute a framework ... that can be studied and analyzed in its own right.
>
> Heydemann 2004: 25

This proposition is relevant in the course of this research as it endeavours to address the socioeconomic and political patron–client networks embedded within Egyptian society. For instance, as will be discussed in Chapter 4, the focus on networks provides us with an opportunity to contextualize the relatively sizeable set of socioeconomic and political networks maintained by the MB in Egypt. Instead of focusing solely on the MB as the main unit of analysis pertaining to the sociopolitical phenomenon of political Islam in Egypt, it is important to situate the group's project within a larger state/society structure containing an overarching web of socioeconomic and political patronage networks that have been partially created and sustained by the MB.

So, provided that one succeeded in outlining the boundaries of particular networks in action, how could such a configuration regarding networks be used in the context of a schematic or, put differently, macro-level analysis? As mentioned earlier, Nazih Ayubi and others have warned of the challenging nature of making a linkage between the micro and the macro levels of analysis. This is one of the most problematic issues of studying social phenomena such as patronage. Perhaps a potential solution could be offered via the analysis of networks:

> A central item on the network agenda is to bridge the gap between the micro- and the macro- order ... One way that network analysis provides a "bridge" between the micro- and macro- orders is that successive levels are "embedded" in one another. Individual relational ties are the crucial components of dyads; dyads constitute triads; triads are contained in higher order subgraphs; and all are embedded in complete networks ... The beauty of the network analysis is that it allows a researcher to tie together so many interdependent parts that constitute micro- and macro- social orders.
>
> Heydemann, 2004: 27

By definition, a social network is an amalgamation of human groupings and ties. Perhaps the study of some networks does not necessarily offer us compelling linkage with macro orders, for instance due to the geographical exclusivity or regional nature of some social networks. Yet in the case of patronage politics, which we are interested in here, the formulation offered by Heydemann, Wasermann and Galaskiewicz, among others, seems to be quite useful and potentially beneficial. This is because networks of political patronage, as will be argued later in this study, do pose an interesting amalgamation of relationships that require a certain set of vertical as well as horizontal linkages to, first, exist, and then survive. In fact, the preliminary definition of patron–client networks that was given earlier in this chapter overlaps with the conceptualization of networks as introduced in the quotation above.

Second generation of analysts: contextualizing patrons and clients within state–society relations

It could be argued that the contributions of Joel Migdal (2001) opened the door for the emergence of a second generation of analysts who tackled the issues relating to informal networks and politics from an interdisciplinary perspective. If we tentatively place the works of John Waterbury, H.C. Moore and Robert Springborg – whose contributions were meaningful and illuminating in shedding light on several elements of political patronage in the Middle East – within a categorical first generation of analysts who dealt with the conceptualization of patron–client networks, the following analysts could be probably classified as the second generation. First, it is useful to take a look at a variety of scholars who tackled the issue of informal politics in the context of state–society relations in different regions over the globe, if we are to sketch a generic synopsis of patronage politics. Next, by moving on to the specificities of the Middle East, a closer scrutiny of the scholarly contributions relating to the Middle East will be also made.

Contextualizing it all: how do we link patrons and clients to state–society relations?

As mentioned earlier, viewing the state as a multifaceted actor intersecting with society on a wide variety of echelons helps to shed light on the pervasive nature of and important role played by informal networks. More often than not, these networks operate as interlocutors between these two entities, or conceptualizations, of state and society.

To begin with, a primary issue regarding any perspective on state–society interaction is indeed the concept of 'sovereignty' and how it is perceived and practised within a polity. According to Thomas Hansen and Finn Stepputat, state sovereignty is not as solid and well defined as many observers believe:

> The state finds itself in constant competition with other centers of sovereignty that dispense violence as well as justice with impunity – criminal gangs, political movements or quasi-autonomous police forces that each try to assert their claims to sovereignty. In such situations, the state is not the natural and self-evident center and origin of sovereignty, but one among several sovereign bodies that tries to assert itself.
>
> Hansen and Stepputat, 2005: 36

The findings postulated by Hansen and Stepputat were predominantly derived from a body of research that dealt with various developing as well as developed countries including Malaysia, China, India, South Africa and the quasi-state of Northern Cyprus. For example:

> the shock and feelings of vulnerability vis-à-vis the huge but strangely anonymous forces of global finance capital are palpable in countries like India

and South Africa that until the early 1990's had sheltered their economies behind high tariffs and heavily interventionist economic regimes.

Hansen and Stepputat, 2005: 32

Sovereignty then becomes an arena of contestation, and societal or informal actors also tend to develop their own scheme of sovereignty. For instance, in urban India:

> Those who define and wield informal sovereignty often are accomplished business people, activists, local politicians, as well as criminal figures. They have managed to capture, privatize or make semi-autonomous territories, institutions, identity forms, and practices in the interstices of the frag-mented configuration of sovereign power in the modern city-spaces. India's dynamic democracy has enabled these men to present themselves as popu-list heroes, representing manly virtues (*mard*) and defending neighborhoods and community life ... A similar phenomenon in Africa [is] the ubiquitous "trickster" ... an enduring cultural model of the daring, creative, and highly mobile individual – physically and socially – who may end up as a respected businessman or political figure.
>
> Hansen and Stepputat, 2005: 31

Interestingly, there is a seeming resemblance between the figures of '*mard*' in India, the 'trickster' in Africa and the '*futuwwa*' on the Arab street. Such figures are historically situated in the social and cultural mosaics of certain societies, yet are versatile enough to reshape and adapt to the realities of the modern-day polity.[3]

Another persona of a local strongman with similar sociocultural features is present when one dissects the characteristics of the phenomenon of 'bossism' in Southeast Asia. Focusing on the case of the districts of Cavite and Cebu in the Philippines, John Sidel notes that, acknowledging the analytical potency of the concept of patronage with regard to understanding the machinations of informal politics in the provinces of the Philippines, there is more to the concept of 'bossism' than the co-optation and endowment of resources that are usually prevalent with patronage politics. Coercion also plays a role in the tactics imple-mented by the bosses:

> Local politicians in the Philippines have indeed maintained patron–client relationships, but they have also long relied heavily upon vote-buying, fraud, intimidation, and violence to win elections. In localities where bosses succeed ... monopoly over coercive means, access to scarce resources and state office also seriously compromise the terms of exchange that lively electoral compe-tition is assumed to dictate to patrons in need of loyal client supporters.
>
> Sidel, 1997: 961

Despite the fact that these cases of provincial politics in the Philippines are not necessarily representative of the entirety of a complex polity as such, there are several similarities in the way in which analogous strongmen operate elsewhere within the polity of the Philippines and in Southeast Asia at large. Some of these strongmen are state-based; some are exposed to coercion and receive no private economic benefit; and others do in fact establish their own economic dynasties. Similar typologies exist with relative variations in countries such as Burma, Thailand, Malaysia and Indonesia (Sidel, 1997).

Therefore, a portrait of various analogous features could be still drawn with regard to the phenomenon of 'bossism' in these different South-Asian localities:

> Bosses have emerged and entrenched themselves when and where the commanding heights of the local political economy have lent themselves to monopolistic control. Insofar as such monopolistic control over the local economy has hinged on state-based derivative and discretionary powers, bosses have depended heavily upon super-ordinate power brokers, whose backing has underpinned their emergence, entrenchment, and survival, and whose hostility has spelled their downfall or death. Insofar as control over the local economy has rested upon a solid base in proprietary wealth outside the purview of state intervention ... bosses have withstood the hostile machinations of super-ordinate power brokers and successfully passed on their empires to successive generations in dynasty form.
>
> Sidel, 1997: 962–3

Overall, Sidel's analysis draws one's attention to some useful observations concerning patron–client networks and informal polities in general. Importantly, the degree of reciprocity that exists within a patron–client relationship, and subsequently whether such a relationship could be signified as a patron–client bond or a variation of that, seems to be an essential theme in his writing.

Patron–client networks, as described earlier, are mainly established upon a notion of mutual benefit and exchange of resources between the patron(s) and a respective set(s) of clients. These could be financial, administrative or other typologies of resources, and this interaction takes place in exchange for political support and loyalty from the client. However, and in line with the nature of a mostly vertical relationship between different agents with varying degrees of power, reciprocity is not always guaranteed and is indeed pretty much dependent upon the supply and demand of available patrons and clients. For example, the bargaining power of a certain patron could vary if there were several patrons competing for a particular or limited group of clients, and vice versa. Logically, if there were only a limited supply of patrons who could provide a certain service or exploit a specific set of resources, the power they held, in comparison to that of their respective clients, would be quite sizeable, and the space for exercising such power by manipulating the client(s) would increase. Here, the boundaries between co-option and coercion become somewhat blurry and difficult to distinguish.

Any attempt to contextualize the phenomenon of patronage/clientelism has to take into consideration the element of 'space'. For example, Bayat speaks of a certain notion of 'street politics' that is mainly derived from the daily interaction of societal forces on the streets in a plethora of so-called 'Third World' polities. Based on research conducted in Iran, South Korea and the Latin American countries of Chile and Brazil, he describes such politics as:

> A set of conflicts and the attendant implications between a collective populace and the authorities, shaped and expressed episodically in the physical and social space of the 'streets'– from the alleyways to the more visible pavements, public parks or sports areas. The 'street' in this sense serves as the only locus of collective expression for, but by no means limited to, those who structurally lack any institutional setting to express discontent.
>
> Bayat, 1997: 63

Within this milieu of street politics, social networks do exist and are mostly passive, although potentially active. An essential element in shaping such street politics is:

> the passive network among the people who use public space. Any collective political act – mobilization – requires some degree of organization, communication and networking among actors. For the most part, this is constituted deliberately either formally or informally.
>
> Bayat, 1997: 64

Hence atomized yet common individuals exist in street politics with shared goals and objectives, and they could possibly be mobilized for joint action. The degree and frequency of such mobilization and the interaction between these networks and the state apparatus are usually very complicated processes that are primarily contingent upon the socioeconomic and political contexts within which they prevail. So even if states sometimes succeed in restricting demonstrations or rallies, they remain 'incapable of prohibiting street populations from working, driving or walking – in short, from street life. The more open and visible the public place, the broader the operation of passive networks and therefore the wider the possibility of collective action becomes' (Bayat, 1997: 63). Indeed, what is described here as 'street politics' is somewhat applicable to the case of the popular quarters of an urban conglomerate like Cairo, where such networks are arguably active and effective in accomplishing the economic, and sometimes political, needs of the populace, or *Sha'b*, as portrayed earlier and, as will be illustrated later in this chapter, in the contributions of Singerman and Ismail.

Street culture

In relation to the concept of 'street politics', several analysts have noted that informal politics are actually the product or producer of a wide array of attitudinal and conceptual tendencies that constitute a collective street or popular 'culture'. For example, based on fieldwork focusing on the Muhajir social movement (MQM) in the popular neighbourhoods of Pakistan, Oskar Verkaiik draws a vivid image of the street culture of modern-day Pakistan and how it is echoed in the ethos and dynamics of this movement. A variety of factors come into play concerning the context within which such features are formulated, and more recently the forces of globalization, exemplified via a plethora of actors from the mass media to the international economic institutions, have become one of these decisive factors:

> A picture of street culture emerges that is more violent, less organized, more racially and ethnically biased, and more excluded from mainstream society than early-modern working-class culture ... such a street culture is "a complex and conflictual web of beliefs, symbols, modes of interaction, values, and ideologies that have emerged in opposition to exclusion from mainstream society." It is not a coherent, conscious universe of political opposition but, rather, a spontaneous set of rebellious practices that in the long term have emerged as an oppositional style ... The homogenizing tendencies in the field of economics, international politics, and mass media do not necessarily lead to an uniformization in cultural styles and expressions. They instead intensify the production of locality and local identity in cultural terms.
>
> Verkaiik, 2004: 7

In fact, this portrayal also resonates with other sketches of popular culture elsewhere in the developing world. Very similar features of this street culture are present in the attitudinal tendencies of the *Sha'b* or the common people of Cairo's popular quarters.

So, with the continuous erosion of the state's capacity to be a welfare entity, the distrust of the state within inner-city areas increases with

> state power abuse, human rights violation, extra-judicial persecution, and the omnipresence of secret intelligence services ... The public imagines itself increasingly in opposition to a state captured by corrupt politicians.
>
> Verkaiik, 2004: 9

The aforementioned somehow explains the public support for the notion of 'politics beyond politics'. Whether it is in the shape of ethnic purity, an Islamic revolution or even, as sometimes displayed by the military when portraying itself as the only institution capable of establishing order and integrity, a military takeover, as was illustrated in the case of Pakistan in 1997 and in Egypt after the January 25 Revolution, this denotation of 'politics beyond politics' is quite palpable. Again, there have been similar occurrences in the popular quarters of a variety of developing countries regarding an alternative sort of politics, separate and distinguishable from the mainstream venues of politics. The typology of street culture that has existed on the Arab street, even prior to the outburst of the Arab Spring, can be considered to be a precursor that set the stage for the social movements that spearheaded the Arab uprisings, and is yet another manifestation of the meaningful role played by societal actors as agents of resistance *vis-à-vis* the dominant sociopolitical order.

Overall, the above-mentioned contributions aim to revisit the modes of state–society interaction in various polities, emphasizing the increasingly important role played by patrons and clients in the human polity. With the incremental retreat of the formal or official state apparatus, there was an inevitable rise in the prowess of a variety of societal actors at the street level. Several versions of what could be described as patronized notables appeared, and in certain cases re-emerged, as pivotal sociopolitical forces. The agency of these key players is closely linked to the politicoeconomic roles ascribed to them. Whether it is the bosses of Southeast Asia, the tricksters in South Africa, or the re-emerging Arab *futuwwas*, the capacity to have access to and circulate resources among potential clients has been a main determinant in shaping the scope and magnitude of the sociopolitical agency enjoyed by these neo-notables.

Finally, before focusing on contributions dealing with informal networks and patronage politics in the Middle East, some light needs to be shed on the notion of institutionalization and its role in battling corruption. In this case, consider patron–client networks in bureaucracy, for instance, as the form of corruption that is to be targetted. The problem here lies in the fact that, in most of the developing countries that are usually targetted in the process of administrative reform, patron–client networks are embedded within a grassroots level that goes deeper than the outer surface of the bureaucracy, entrenched within the socioeconomic and political echelons of the society. In line with what was outlined earlier in this chapter regarding the negligible effect that the neoliberal policies of institutionalization and reform had on embedded patron–client bonds, economists such as M. Khan believe that there are, in practice, powerful structural reasons why such reform is not likely to achieve its aim:

> Economic characteristics of developing countries make patron–client politics both rational for redistributive coalitions and effective as strategies for achieving the goals of powerful constituencies ... The organization of personalized patron–client factions is driven not by the absence of democracy but, rather, by the structural features of the economies of developing countries that make modern welfare driven redistributive politics unviable.
>
> Khan, 2005: 704–21

Thus, unless such structural features change, it will be unrealistic to anticipate an actual shift in the machinations of political patronage within the polities targeted with these reform schemes.

The Arab Spring and the 'new' scholarship of the Middle East

As stated in this chapter, the call to pay closer attention to the politics of the people, as opposed to focusing mainly on issues relating to the processes of democratization or the politics of the elite state institutions has existed in Middle East scholarship for quite some time, albeit often overshadowed by mainstream scholarship that has predominantly examined assumptions relating to the persistence of authoritarianism. The wave of uprisings that swept the region in what became known as the Arab Spring by and large shows that it is important to pay more attention to the politics of the common people in order to understand how citizens interact with the socioeconomic and political structures they experience in their everyday lives. Regardless of the outcome that may ensue as a result of the Arab Spring and the plethora of socioeconomic and political upheavals associated with it, the wave of massive protests that the region witnessed from its outbreak in the spring of 2011 confirms the idea that there is nothing peculiar about the culture or history of the Middle East that makes collective political action unlikely to occur there.

The politics of the informal that this book aims to scrutinize represents one of the many facets worthy of closer investigation in the attempt to dissect the intricate details of the complex mosaic of the Middle Eastern polity. Although mostly produced before the beginning of the Arab Spring, the contributions cited in this writing, as portrayed by the group of scholars who dealt with themes pertaining to the struggles of the urban poor and street resistance, referred to as the second generation of analysts, are tremendously revealing when it comes to studying the Middle East in the post-revolutionary phase.

Enter the Middle East: patronage politics in a different light?

In the course of outlining the essential role played by informal political networks as alternative venues of political participation, Diane Singerman (1995) was one of the main contributors who tackled the issue of informal networks in Middle Eastern societies. Singerman belongs to a second generation of Middle East scholars who attempted to shift the focus characterizing the majority of scholarly contributions on Middle East politics from elitist politics to a consideration of the popular forces of the *Sha'b*, or common people:

> The [political] party itself functions in a clientelistic manner, providing services and "the spoils of the system" to faithful party supporters in exchange for vote and loyal support. "Party-directed patronage is typically directed to 'entire categories, coalitions of interests, groups of employees,' ... and consists of 'mass favors' granted no longer at the administrative level alone but also at the legislative level". Machine politics operate in a similar fashion, where politicians succeed in "privatizing" public goods, "that is, by using the immense resources of the state for purposes of private, productive generosity". Yet networks can be a vehicle for those who are not supported by the immense resources of the state, to protect and further their interests in a more subtle, subterranean way, without attracting the notice of the state.
>
> Singerman, 1995: 136

Here, the important role played by horizontal or reciprocal networks in shaping the machinations of the *Sha'bi*, or popular, polity of Cairo is outlined. These networks in fact serve and provide for a huge array of needs of the Egyptian populace: employment, health care and educational facilities, among other services of course.

The role played by informal networks in managing the affairs of various Middle Eastern polities was also emphasized by analysts such as Janine Clark (2004), who, based upon work in Jordan, Yemen and Egypt, asserts that the prevalence of such networks is one of the most valid reasons for the rise of Islamist politics in these countries. Adopting a social movement theory approach, Clark focuses on the networks perpetuated by Islamic social institutions (ISIs), describing them as 'middle-class networks bringing Islamists and non-Islamists together ... expanded and strengthened via ISIs'. Moderate Islamism, such as that of the MB, seems to be a 'movement of the marginalized, educated middle class' (Clark, 2004: 941). As echoed by Ben Nefissa and others, patron–client relations seem to be present in the political machinations of the MB as well as the ex-ruling NDP.

By and large, in popular Cairo, informal networks can be more precisely described as reciprocity networks rather than exploitative patron–client relations. 'In Cairo networks provide not only economic but political security. An understanding of networks as both a political resource and a political institution for the *Sha'b* moves beyond the negative connotations surrounding clientelism' (Clark, 2004: 941). Thus, in short, although political patronage does exist, perceiving it as a main explanatory tool, and disregarding the reciprocal nature of informal networks that predominates, for example, in the popular quarters of Cairo, will be misleading in any attempt to contextualize political patronage in the Egyptian polity.

What I shall try to convey in the context of this writing, however, is the observation that these two aspects – the set of horizontal networks and the amalgam of vertical patron–client bonds – both exist within the Egyptian polity and are not actually mutually exclusive but rather interconnected. Indeed, one could argue that vertical and horizontal networks, more often than not, do collude and interact within the various echelons of the Egyptian polity. If patron–client relations assume a 'vertical' notion of a hierarchical allocation of resources from patron(s) to clients, their survival and dispensary nature cannot be maintained without the presence of effective 'horizontal' networks that are pervasive enough to cut across groups of various individuals, communities and socioeconomic classes. For example, the existence of particular patrons and respective clients within a certain state bureaucracy, be it a party, a ministry or an educational institution, is usually associated with the presence of informal horizontal networks, or *shillal* in the case of Egypt, through which the allocations are disbursed horizontally. The Egyptian polity, with its lesser notables arising in the popular quarters of Cairo, is perhaps a case in point.

Along the same lines, Salwa Ismail dissects the emergence, or re-emergence, of the lesser notabilities in the popular quarters of Cairo. Dealing with the patterns of interaction in Cairo's informal communities, she traces the development of a particular form of patron–client network, namely those relations established between the old and new settlers of such communities. 'Clientelistic relations exist between early settlers and followers and between "contractors" and small buyers. They also exist between residents and powerful figures from outside the community, who are involved in appropriating large plots of land' (S. Ismail, 1996: 123).

Another figure presented also by Ismail in later contributions on the Egyptian polity is that of the *biytkabarluh*. The interesting thing about such a figure is that it is quite widespread and perhaps even celebrated within Egyptian popular culture, yet is rarely presented or displayed as a viable social or political actor in the literature pertaining to the Middle East. The lesser notabilities of Cairo's popular neighbourhoods are mostly workshop owners, real estate contractors and wholesale-retail traders. 'They come from a social stratum whose ranks have expanded with the economic liberalization and privatization policies [and] share some common socioeconomic features. Some belong to merchant families that have been in business for two or three generations' (S. Ismail, 2006: 49).

The upcoming story is a revealing one that shows the sociopolitical machinations of this typology of lesser patrons. Although the figure portrayed here as the 'patron' is in fact a politician, he still belongs to a lower echelon of notability that is somewhat immersed in the neighbourhoods of the *Sha'bi* communities:

> The ties between the "patron" and the supposed "client" were very close and reciprocal. The "client" received loans from the politician, gifts of food and clothing for her family, publicly subsidized apartments, employment for her and members of her family, assistance with bureaucratic problems and a great deal of information and knowledge which the "client" then utilized to support her personal and familial networks. Through this relationship, the "client" developed a powerful base within the community, building on her family's already strong ties to the merchant community. At election time, the client returned these services by organizing the election campaign and marshaling local political support in the district. This relationship was extremely well publicized and promoted by both the politician and the local leader.
>
> Singerman, 1995: 170–1

In a sense, this tale re-emphasizes the fact that, as stated earlier, vertical patron–clientelism within Cairo's popular quarters seems to be operating in conjunction with horizontal networks.

Placing patron–client networks of political entrepreneurship within the social structure, pyramidal patron–client bonds are likely to materialize as a rational form of organization for societal leaders. 'Faction leaders promise rewards to their clients based on their organizational support, who in turn mobilize those below them, all the way down to foot soldiers who may only be mobilized during elections, strikes, riots, and other political events' (Khan, 2005: 719). Indeed, this pyramidal web is utilized by the 'lesser notables' who, in turn, reproduce their notability in accordance with the resources, privileges and networks at their disposal.

One of the main objectives of this research is to build upon the contributions of this second generation of analysts who have called for an alternative perception of the dynamics of informal networks. The special focus of this book, being the lesser notabilities of the Egyptian polity in specific, pays some attention to the ideas of those who dealt with the informal networks of Egyptian politics at the ascent of the twenty-first century. The produce of this second generation portrays a group of lesser patrons whose political agency is still in the making. The socio-political modes of action of the lesser notabilities and the possible roles they may play in local and national politics in Egypt in the post-Mubarak phase are indeed worthy of close scrutiny. The chapters that follow will also shed some light on the prospects of the sociopolitical agency of these lesser notabilities after the events of the January 25 revolution.

Methodology

In the course of this study, I have conducted fieldwork in the areas of Cairo's popular urban quarters (*Al-ahyaa' al-sha'biyya*) in order to trace the socioeco-nomic and political dynamics of lesser notabilities within the lower echelons of the Egyptian polity. Therefore, for the purpose of this research, the verification and authentication of resources are important due to the usage of a multitude of primary sources such as interviews and personal accounts. During the course of this research, I made use of Ansari's (1986) methodology of verification, which basically depends on the contextualization of the primary sources in accordance with the realities of the time and place subject to investigation, as a procedural tool.[4] Ansari categorically states the difficulties faced when collecting his data owing to the highly informal nature of the structures he dealt with in his the case study of the village of Kamshish, around which he forms the focus of his book. Access to primary sources, mainly direct interviews with villagers and officials, formulated the basic pool of information that was utilized by the author. This technique will be used in the course of the current book as well.

My particular focus is on the area of Misr al-Qadima (Old Cairo), which is arguably the oldest residential quarter in contemporary Cairo. This particular area was selected for two main reasons, the first being the surveys and statistics available on the scope and magnitude of political mobilization and participation in Cairo's popular quarters, through data on party membership, voter turnout, etc. Some of this information was made available via the Central Authority for Public Mobilization and Statistics and Al-Ahram Center for Political and Strategic Studies.

The second factor was the plausibility of conducting fieldwork and research in such an area. I initially aimed to pinpoint seven or eight areas or quarters that could serve as viable examples of Cairo's popular communities, with the intention of focusing on two or three of them afterwards, depending on the availability of informants and middlemen who could act as linkages to such quarters. Eventually, Misr al-Qadima's two main quarters (the relatively recently-constructed 'Ain al-Sirra and the older quarter of Misr al-Qadima proper) were the areas I focused upon in this book, as will be outlined in the chapters that follow. In the context of the field research, the role of informant – highlighted in similar areas of research by Verkaiik (2004), S. Ismail (2006) and Singerman (1995) – was crucial as informants are likely to function as the links and facilita-tors of the transfusion of information between the researcher and the area within which he or she operates.

In conducting my fieldwork, I primarily depended on what is usually referred to as a 'snowball sampling' technique, a process that depends on utilizing the sources of information available as they come across from the respondents. Existing respondents were able to put me in contact with their circles of acquaintances, and these circles were also useful in order for the researcher to connect with other circles, and so forth. Open-ended interviews that allowed respondents the room to talk relatively openly with a considerable degree of ease, and without a specifically prescribed topic of discussion, were also utilized. This was pivotal in order to allow for greater ease and fluidity when it came to the respondent expressing a viewpoint or telling a certain story that might be of relevance. In such an approach, the mission of the researcher, then, becomes one of the assessment and analysis of information, depending on the particular subject he or she is concerned with. This is actually quite similar to an oral history approach, which attempts to generate research areas and foci depending, as much as possible, on the raw or uninterrupted narratives of respondents (W. Ismail, 2006).

However, here I also tended to utilize a participant/observer approach that allowed me to take part in the interactive dealings of the individuals being studied while observing and monitoring the way these dealings functioned. Again, this approach could be beneficial for the researcher because being solely perceived as an outsider alienated from the area of study could potentially hinder the openness and connectivity with which the people of such areas would receive the researcher, especially in a comparatively intimate socioeconomic/cultural setting such as that of Cairo. Despite the fact that I have been a resident of Cairo for most of my life, and that I could subsequently claim to have some fair knowledge of a number of its quarters, the truth remains that, in order for me to undertake the kind of research outlined here, this factor could only be a bonus that required much additional fieldwork and research to build upon.

After sketching a prospective set of features for the 'lesser notable' in Chapter 2, I shall present, in Chapter 3, an overview of Misr al-Qadima as a popular polity. Chapters 4 and 5 deal with the sociopolitical agency of the lesser notabilities and their affiliations with the MB and the dissolved NDP in an attempt to scrutinize the scope and magnitude of the role played by the lesser notabilities in the Misr al-Qadima area. Chapter 6 reflects on the sociopolitical and economic implications of the January 25 revolution regarding the modes of action of the lesser notabilities and other figures of local authority in Cairo's popular communities. It also offers a set of conclusions and findings relating to the current and prospective politicoeconomic roles of the lesser notabilities in the Egyptian polity in the post-Mubarak phase.

2 Who are the lesser notables?

Historical background and modes of production and circulation, affiliations, and political roles

This chapter aims, first, to outline some of the features of what could be dubbed a typology of notables within premodern Middle Eastern/Muslim society, with a particular focus on the Mamluk and Ottoman periods. It then ventures into displaying some of the socioeconomic and political characteristics of the lesser notabilities of Cairo in the contemporary period. In doing so, the text does not attempt to draw direct and necessary linkages between the notables of the Mamluk and Ottoman eras and those of today. Given the remarkably different socioeconomic, political and historical contexts, such an exercise is likely to be of minimal benefit. Instead, the aim is to trace some examples of the figures who were referred to as 'notables' in the literature on the Middle East, and portray the implications pertaining to the socioeconomic and political roles ascribed to those notables within urban and rural settings. In the process, striking similarities as well as crystal-clear differences between the category of Middle Eastern notability in the past and its contemporary counterpart will become clear.

The Muslim city

A glimpse into the Islamic city during the early caliphates of the Umayyads and Abbasids is perhaps important if we are to sketch some of the common features of urban life at the time. Arguably, the mechanisms by which the Muslim city came into being resemble, in essence, those which led to the construction of most civic conglomerates in the medieval period. In essence, both the village and the town needed each other, the town depending on the food produced by the farmers and sold in urban markets. 'The basic unit of Near Eastern society was the "agro-city", the urban conglomeration together with the rural hinterland' (Hourani, 1970: 16).

Indeed, a plethora of scholars have suggested that there emerged a certain set of commonalities among various Middle Eastern cities with the ascent of Islam. For example, based upon an extensive study of North Africa, George and William Marcais noted that the shape of the Islamic city was determined only in part by the exigencies of power, determining where and how the citadel, the city walls and the gates were placed, for instance. Yet in part the character of the city was also largely influenced by being Islamic or, in other words, by constituting an essential aspect of the Islamic caliphate. The congregational mosque in the heart of the city, the religious schools associated with it, the order of *suqs*, the suburban quarters with their confessional/ethnic solidarity, and the scared shrines and cemeteries, all existed and were erect in their particular locations owing to the fact that the city was a Muslim one (Hourani, 1970).

The religious or ethnic distribution of quarters was evident in medieval Muslim cities. Taking the example of Damascus, Ira Lapidus (cited in Hourani, 1970) states that the quarters in practice reflected a sense of communal homogeneity:

> Jews and Christians, and the various sorts of each, had their own districts. Among the Muslims different ethnic groups – Arabs, Kurds, Turkomans – lived apart. So too in the Arab Muslim majority, population affiliation with the different Muslim schools of law was the basis for district quarters, as were common or presumed ancestry, clan ties, or common village origin.
>
> Hourani, 1970: 197

There was also a socioeconomic basis for the division of quarters. Some were based on the clienteles of notable families, whereas others were specialized in terms of certain economic activities, such as tanning, weaving and other manufacturing processes. By and large, these were whole communities composed of notables and commoners and divided on the basis of distinctive socioeconomic classes, religious sects and ethnic groupings (Abu-Lughod, 1987).

There was an evident socioeconomic dimension that played a role in the physical and moral construction of the Muslim city. This was shown via the mounting importance of the professional corporations or guilds. The guilds, in fact, acted at times as 'a convenient vehicle of control by the state over professional and social activities in the city' (Ayubi, 1995: 76). Nevertheless, such corporations also established the foundations of urban society in the Muslim city as they formed the pivot of the ethos of solidarity and individual self-respect (Hourani, 1970). In the eyes of many historians, urban Muslim society was relatively corporate in nature, thanks to the guild system. As such, urban Muslims were able to organize themselves and maintain their communal existence *vis-à-vis* the predominant political order.

The guilds

The example of the political relevance of the commercial guilds could be viewed as one of the early manifestations of a commercial–political relationship within the milieu of the medieval Muslim City. However, other historians noted that this corporate nature of guilds within the Muslim city was not as predominant as portrayed by some. According to this line of thought, championed by C. Cahen and S.M. Stern among others, the guilds of the early Muslim city were not actually guilds in the medieval European sense. These guilds were sometimes instruments of state domination, and it is indeed questionable whether the guilds that existed throughout the Ottoman provinces were even that autonomous. In fact, one can argue that they hardly existed in a fully articulated state of self-control

(Hourani, 1970). Overall, there seems to be a disagreement among historians with regard to the scope and magnitude of the political role played by those commercial agents at the time. Logically, the scope of such a role had to be contingent upon a multitude of socioeconomic and political factors relating to the context within which these guilds operated (Pearson, 1982).

It is highly likely that the associational professional institutions that already existed prior to the Muslim conquest of the Middle East made their way through to the period of the Islamic caliphates. This trend also continued with the beginning of the age of the smaller Muslim states or dynasties. The earliest records marking the presence of a guild system in the medieval Middle East date back to the twelfth century. These earliest texts were the references 'in twelfth century treatises of the *hisba* both in the East and in Spain to foremen of trades' (Hourani, 1970: 14). These foremen were responsible for ensuring that the tradesmen under them would carry out the *muhtasib*'s orders. 'Similar evidence is also forthcoming from the Mamluk period ... The role of the foremen, as assistants of the various delegates of the government, is a constant factor in the history of the organization of the crafts and trades in Islam' (Hourani, 1970: 44).

The guild system has nonetheless witnessed various phases of rise and fall that somehow coincided with the politicoeconomic policies of the Muslim dynasties prevalent during the lifetime of the guilds. In practice, the ascent of the guild system was associated with the rise in the role of the artisans as viable economic actors in the milieu of the Muslim city. With the 'decline in conquests and in the recruitment of Arabs into the army, growing numbers of Arabs started to move into the productive sectors' (Ayubi, 1995: 76).

> Under the Sunni rule, the guilds were persecuted [and] deprived of any legal rights. There was a legal functionary, the *muhtasib*, whose main duty was to supervise the guilds and to [halt] any attempt at independent action ... Quite different was the position of the guilds under the Fatimids, where they enjoyed great prosperity. Recognized by the state, they seem to have possessed considerable privileges, and to have played an important part in the commercial revival that took place under Fatimid rule. It was the Fatimids that founded the guild of teachers which formed the great university of Al-Azhar ... In 1171, Fatimid anti-Caliphate was destroyed by Saladin ... Immediately the guilds were submitted to a very strict control.
>
> Hourani, 1970: 38

It should be noted that other medieval historians would doubt that the degree of control exercised by the Muslim state varied a great deal when comparing the policies of Sunni states with those of Shiite ones. However, regardless of the particular Muslim state that reigned supreme, the role of the *muhtasib* as the supervisor of commercial activities was crucial (Pearson 1982).

The notables: the ulama and the commercial bourgeoisie – patrons and clients

With the demise of the Abbasids around 1248 AD, the relationship between the government and society within the majority of the Muslim Middle East was given shape by two main determinants. First, there was almost a monopoly of political power by politico-military groups of primarily Turkic origin, who were of course Muslim but kept themselves at a distance from the Arabic- or Persian-speaking peoples over whom they prevailed. Second, there was also a close connection between the commercial bourgeoisie and the *ulama*:

> This connection had several aspects: members of the bourgeois families took to learning and the men of learning married into such families. The *ulama* possessed a certain economic and social power through their control of the *awqaf*, and both groups shared an interest in a stable, prosperous and cultivated urban life. Members of the great bourgeois families and of the *ulama* together provided an urban leadership: their wealth, piety, culture and ancient names gave them social prestige and the patronage of quarters.
>
> Hourani, 1970: 17–18

Here, both the commercial bourgeois and the *ulama* formulated a typology of urban notables. The stature of those notables was not merely based on their moral or social roles, as the urban notables had some essential politicoeconomic functions to fulfil as well.

Looking at the class origin of the *ulama*, one finds that, despite the fact that they were the core of the urban elite, the *ulama* came from virtually all walks of life and were thus undifferentiated from the rest of the population. By and large, the door was open to acquire the competencies needed in the kind of religious and judicial knowledge that was required for earning *ulama* status. Subsequently, the professional and class origins of most of these *ulama* were quite mixed: they were merchants, artisans and sometimes even bureaucrats (Hourani, 1970). So, by virtue of these hybrid origins, the *ulama* held firm ties to the various echelons of Muslim society (El Messiri, 1977).

Being the prime interpreters of Islamic law, the *ulama*'s sociopolitical agency was crucial:

> They were the judges and lawyers of the cities. Family life was under their jurisdiction. Commercial transactions, property transfers and contracts in general to be legally binding had to be witnessed and registered by people competent in Islamic law. The regulation of the markets was entrusted to the *ulama* and they were in addition the managers of the cities' educational, religious, and philanthropic institutions. All community interests were thus represented by this unspecialized, multi-competent body which was the religious, professional, commercial, and managerial elite all in one ... the spokesmen, the leaders of the people.
>
> Hourani, 1970: 204

In addition, the *ulama* also helped to create a spectrum of communal cohesion within urban Muslim society as they constituted a higher order of associational life that cut across various social echelons, mainly via the schools of law, which were in practice assemblages of scholars. They were composed of *ulama* study groups in addition to

> teachers, disciples, interested members of the community and patrons; and *ulama* administrative clienteles such as the multitude of deputies, witnesses, orderlies, clerks [who] radiated their influence and were ... an ordering force in the lives of the common people.
>
> Hourani, 1970: 204

Within most of the Mamluk and Ottoman states, there was a ruler (sultan) beneath whom an entire system of control was present: the governor and his household, the secretaries in the government agencies, the *muhtasib*, the *qadi*, etc. But in conjunction with these political actors, there was an important societal spectrum that had to be co-opted by the state, and that is where the political agency of urban notables comes in. As such, these notables, along with the *ulama* and the other leaders of the bourgeois, allied with the government not only as a result of self-interest or fear, but also from a concern with stability and security within the community (Pearson, 1982):

> They were also 'leaders' responsible to the urban population. At times they could use their independent power over it to mobilize urban forces and put pressure on the ruler. This mobilization was carried out through an ancient machinery of contacts between notables of the city and leaders of quarters ... In this process, even those who held posts under the ruler might take part: the *qadi* could become a spokesman for the local *ulama*, the *shaykhs* of quarters or villages could act as clients of local leaders.
>
> Hourani, 1970: 19

In that sense, the urban notables were primarily key players on the streets of the city due to their affluence and capacity to stir the affairs of the street through networking and the exercise of power (Hourani, 1981). More often than not, the political agency of urban notables went in accordance with the already existing political system. Mostly, 'a strong government ruled in close partnership with the bourgeois and their leaders, and the influence of the leaders was thrown on the side of the existing order' (Hourani, 1970: 204).

Practically speaking, the notables could not replace the rulers owing to their extreme diversity and lack of an organizational institution that could mobilize and unite a major part of these networks, possessed by the notables, at a particular point in time. By nature, these networks were fragmented and lacked a sense of cohesiveness (Pearson, 1982). The spectrum of organizational control over the local notability and their active networks could be only done by

> the military rulers, hence the long predominance of "Turkish" or Mamluk ruling groups, acting both as rulers and as patrons ... until much later the

decline of Ottoman authority led to the re-emergence of local leaders in the provincial cities.

Hourani, 1970: 20

The phenomenon of *zu'ar* in Mamluk Syria sheds some light on the mechanisms of patronage politics at the time. In Damascus, the *zu'ar* (literally the troublemakers or scoundrels) were present around the late fifteenth century, although some sources note that the phenomenon had existed in previous periods under various names. The *zu'ar* were:

> Self consciously organized groups of young men ... with recognized chiefs, called *kabirs*, some of whom claimed to be descendants of the prophet. They wore uniforms and a distinctive headdress [and] were recruited from the working population ... Carpenters, criers, shopkeepers, and spinners were among them. They were organized by quarter [and] resisted what they regarded as unwarranted or excessive taxation, assassinated abusive Mamluks and tax collectors ... The *zu'ar* were the core of the late fifteenth century and early sixteenth century popular resistance to the Mamluk regime.

Hourani, 1970: 201

Inasmuch as they were sources of opposition for Mamluk domination, the *zu'ar* also had to be co-opted by the Mamluks, who aimed at winning them over, utilizing their organizational capacity to strengthen their rule. The Mamluks utilized the *zu'ar* as clienteles

> whom they protected, armed, paid, and honored by reviews in military village violence. They employed them in wars, in repression of Bedouin or village violence, as personal following in disputes the Mamluks had with each other, and in their efforts to control and extort money from the population of the city.

Hourani, 1970: 201

Overall, it could be argued that, in the Syrian cities of Damascus and Aleppo, as well as in their other powerhouses in Egypt and elsewhere, the Mamluks cultivated several networks of arms and money in dealing with the powerful sociopolitical key players. On the one hand, this strategy helped to create a sort of clientele that played an efficient role in the administration of these cities, while on the other, it maintained a sense of social equilibrium that reinforced the grip of the Mamluk regime over the affairs of the territories it controlled.

The Ottomans: modernization

Indeed, it could be a shortcut to logical deduction or research to try to abbreviate the extended political history of the complex set of provinces that lay under the Ottoman rule into a unified theme of features concerning the political agency of notables. For example, in the case of Egypt, a comparatively extensive period of Ottoman rule roughly lasted from 1517 until 1805, when Mohammed Ali reigned supreme and initiated his own dynasty. However, this section will aim to assess the correlation between the political role played by the notables in the late Ottoman period and the features of the social structure and the political system that accompanied the widespread wave of modernization of the late 1800s, with a special focus on the Egyptian case.

Throughout the various Ottoman provinces, the pattern of political notability that had existed during the Islamic Caliphates continued to prevail. The notables of the Arab cities during the Ottoman period were local men who had earned a certain standing of socioeconomic and political relevance (Abu-Lughod, 1987). Under the Ottoman rule:

> These notables acted as intermediaries between the 'men of sword' and the local Muslim Population. Basically, they were loyal to the Sultan, but they were also leaders of their cities and heirs of urban civilization of Islam. At times they tried to curb Ottoman power or the use of it, and they had the means of doing so: They could mobilize public opinion by making use of preachers, heads of quarters, leaders of popular organizations, and they had some influence through their links with the religious hierarchy throughout the empire.
>
> Hourani, 1981: 11

Such figures were drawn mainly from the traditionally renowned families of 'notables', some of whom played a key role until modern times. Examples include the Khalidis and Alamis of Jerusalem, the Jabiris in Aleppo, the Gaylanis in Baghdad, and the Bakris in Cairo.

Egypt under Mohammed Ali (1805–1848) and the change in modes of production: exit the classical notables ... enter the lesser notables?

With the arrival in power of Mohammed Ali in 1805, it was obvious that the political role of the classical urban notables of Egypt was somehow waning. Along with the diminishing political agency of the notables generally speaking, there was also a virtual void when it came to the political activity of the urban population. Interestingly, there seems to be a vacuum with regard to the presence of any proof of political action of urban notables in Egypt throughout the nineteenth century and perhaps up until the Urabi rebellion in 1881, when the local notables took part in the army rebellion that aimed to confront Egypt's Khedive, Tawfik, who was also Mohammed Ali's great-grandson. In fact, the exposé of Egypt in the nineteenth century is an anomalous one:

> At one end, a gradual increase in the political activity of the urban population ... reaching its height in the period between the first revolt against the French and the movement which carried Mohammed Ali to power; much later in 1870's, a sudden upsurge, and in between virtually nothing, a political vacuum.
>
> Hourani, 1981: 40

In essence, some would argue that the phase of modernization that took place within the Ottoman provinces brought a practical end to the political influence of the notables. Indeed, the reforms of the *tanzimat* period in the Ottoman Empire and the similar attempts in Egypt 'would, if carried to their logical conclusion, have destroyed the independent power of the notables and the mode of political action it made possible', ideally establishing a 'uniform and centralized administration, linked directly with each citizen, and working in accordance with its own rational principles of justice, applied equally to all' (Hourani, 1981: 40). Yet, despite the fact that these reforms met some success, on aggregate they failed to deliver the aspired objectives. The reasons for this minimal success vary but, importantly, the predominant presence of an absolute ruler in most of the cases where such reformations were attempted was one of the factors that hindered these institutional reforms. The ruler was often only willing to apply these alterations in the governing system as far as they did not threaten his supremacy. Instead, most rulers attempted to capitalize on such reformations in order to consolidate their power.

In Egypt, the process of administrative reform was accompanied by the monopolization of political action that occurred with the rise of a paramount ruler, Mohammed Ali, who established an authoritarian scheme of political power, independent of the Ottoman Empire and its policies. Along with this political scheme, there was also an alteration in the modes of production of the Egyptian state:

> With Muhammad Ali's arrival, the move towards a capitalist mode of production began ... State centralization was enforced, while the semi-communal organizations of the countryside, as well as the artisan and commercial guilds and the Sufi orders ... were all dissolved.
>
> Ayubi, 1995: 100

With the abolition of the *iltizam* system, which empowered a certain class of Mamluks and other powerful notables in order to collect taxes from peasants, Mohammed Ali had indeed ensured the demise of any potential political rivalry that could arise from notable figures within Egyptian society:

> By collecting taxes directly, Mohammed Ali ensured that no new class of *multazims* should arise; when, towards the end of his reign, a new class of landowners began to come into existence, they did not at first possess the same means as the Mamluks of putting pressure on the government.
>
> Hourani 1981: 52

It is true that this class of landowners was soon able to attain a position of power within the rural economy, but landownership by itself did not create political power once more until Khedive Ismail began to depend upon the landowners' help and support in the 1870s.

One could of course still argue that there was some political action on the popular level during the Mohammed Ali era, but the outlets for such action were limited:

The tax farms had gone, the associations of the craftsmen remained ... and so did the *turuq*, but the stricter policing of the street and the bazaars made popular action more difficult. In the countryside, the sedentarisation of the Bedouin, and the growth of the power of the *umda*, the government agent in the villages, destroyed other possible means of action. It seems too that Mohammed Ali set himself deliberately to dispense of those popular leaders who, in the period of confusion before he came to power, had served as mobilisers of popular support in favor of the contenders for power.

Hourani, 1981: 52

In fact, Mohammed Ali started his rule with the eradication of the figures who had initially supported him, such as Umar Makram, a local notable who was also an intermediary with a popular following and access to the military.

Towards the end of the nineteenth century, the political agency of the notables was again on the rise. With the considerable increase in the urban population and the revival of Al Azhar as a religious institution under the patronage of Khedive Ismail, political notability once again came to the forefront of the Egyptian polity. Increasingly, and with the expansion of the Egyptian army to meet the aspirations of the newly rising Egyptian state under the Mohammed Ali Dynasty, Egyptians of rural origin gradually became the backbone of the newly established state institutions, particularly the army. The rising leaders were also of Egyptian and Mamluk origin, and they were incrementally accumulating landowning privileges, primarily through the land grants of the ruler. 'Riaz, Nubar, Sharif, Barudi are the new politicians, and behind them one can see in the shadows different groups inside the ruling family' (Hourani, 1981: 54). As politicians, these figures operated in the traditional way, primarily via building up their networks of clients.

After the first shock of British occupation in 1881, the political role of the notables was given a further push. For the most part, British rule was indirect and needed intermediaries. 'In such circumstances, the notables could play a part, and as usual an ambiguous one, supporting the British occupation but also discreetly serving as the focal points of discontent' (Hourani, 1981: 54).

The *futuwwa*: the advent of the lesser notables

As stated earlier, with the decline of the Mamluk and more so of the Ottoman states, it seemed that the waning political agency of the notable patrons – the *muhtasib* and the commercial bourgeoisie – was gradually giving way to the rise of other political actors. In Egypt, Muhammad Ali somehow succeeded in eliminating the political relevance of the traditional Mamluk and local patrons. Despite the rough return of some political notability of sorts towards the end of the nineteenth and in the early years of the twentieth century, there was still a political vacuum to be filled and utilized by the ruling elite. Perhaps here can be found the increasing importance of a certain figure that was predominant in folktales and on the streets of Middle Eastern cities, that of the *futuwwa*. In Cairo, and perhaps up until the mid-twentieth century, each locality in the popular quarters was identified with one or more of these *futuwwas*. The term is usually used to 'denote a strong bold man ... Generally; it has been applied to the masses but occasionally to members of the elite as well. In all cases the element of protection has been seminal to the role' (El Messiri, 1977: 239).

The conceptualization of the *futuwwa* had its roots in the later Middle Ages, when the organization of crafts started becoming more sophisticated, that is, when the ideology of the *futuwwa* was formulated. 'Salman Al Farisi plays a great role in the later traditions of the *futuwwa*, that ideal moral and social code, which also provided ideals and ceremonies to the associations of the craftsmen ... Salman is honored as the patron of the guilds' (Hourani, 1970: 41–5). In Egyptian folktales, the *futuwwa* is depicted as being 'generous, courageous, possessing *muru`a* (manliness). He is also in Egyptian epics, noted for his cleverness, cunning, sense of humor, and verbal skill' (El Messiri, 1977: 241).

Nevertheless, in addition to the moral and personal attributes of the *futuwwa*, there are also some social and politicoeconomic roles that were fulfilled by this type of personage in the milieu of the Egyptian city, mainly as a leader of the urban quarters. This sociopolitical role of the *futuwwas* had become somewhat intensified by the end of the nineteenth century:

> By the middle of the nineteenth century one no longer hears of resistance movements spanning several quarters, but rather of influential personages, including *futuwwat*, operating within quarters. While documentary evidence is scarce, one may nonetheless deduce something of the role the *futuwwat* played within the quarters or *harat*. In many ways these were social entities as well as physical and geographical units, and their inhabitants were often set off from those of the neighboring *harat* ... To some degree interests among *harat* were conflicting, and it was in the context of defending those interests that the nineteenth century *futuwwa* exercised his role as protector.
> El Messiri, 1977: 241

Regardless of the timeframe within which he predominated, a common feature of the *futuwwa*'s dealings with the inhabitants of the neighbourhood, one may assume, was the fact that they were mostly based on intimate contact and personal ties.

The twentieth-century *futuwwa*

At the beginning of the twentieth century, one finds the *futuwwa* aiming to establish himself within the neighbourhood as 'the paragon of all those virtues and qualities that most citizens of old Cairo would like in some measure to claim as their own. Foremost among those qualities ... is physical strength' (El Messiri, 1977: 241). But this scheme of strength must also be accompanied by other qualities, such as bravery and generosity. Such characteristics are quite important in defining the kind of protection and services that are provided by the *futuwwa* to the inhabitants of the neighbourhood in which he reigns as the supreme patron.[1]

In fact, an essential part of the social identity of the *futuwwa* is defined by the network of social and economic activities in which he is involved. In his own neighbourhood, he is conceived not only as the leader and protector, but also as the problem-solver and the dispenser of much-needed services and resources:

> Most of the problems the people bring to the *futuwwa* relate to work situations, or those that emerge from the traditional style of life and the values attached to it. Typically, people interacted on a personal basis with no formal contracts, bills, or receipts. In these arrangements a man was tied by his tongue ... bound by what he had said. In this way if someone had borrowed money from his neighbor without receipt and refused to pay it back or denied that he had borrowed it, the *futuwwa*, after investigation, could force him to return the money. Some clients may take commodities, promising to pay later, and then continually postpone payment or refuse it altogether; the merchant would then seek help from the *futuwwa*. The *futuwwa* might even end a dispute by paying what was at issue himself.
>
> El Messiri, 1977: 244

Logically, with the virtual absence of official institutional venues for the facilitation of the affairs of the populace, the sociopolitical role of the *futuwwa* appears to be crucial as the arbitrator and settler of disputes. In spite of the vigorous process of modernization and institutionalization that overwhelmed the Egyptian state in the ascent of the twentieth century, the formalization of state services could not meet the needs and demands of the urban dwellers (Hunter, 2000), and consequently room was still available for such popular figures to operate efficiently within the popular quarters of Cairo.

The *futuwwa* also played an economic role of extreme importance within the milieu of the neighbourhood. This role connoted a sense of benevolence for the entirety of the community. He would

> supply the *hitta* with scarce commodities, such as oil or kerosene, to spare the people from black market prices. In the economic crisis of 1942, a certain *futuwwa* used to procure the Kerosene allotment of his whole *hitta*, protect it during delivery, and then distribute it equally throughout the *hitta*.
>
> El Messiri, 1977: 241

Of course, such activities did not occur out of mere goodwill: they were also pragmatic practices that reinforced the paramount role of the *futuwwa* as the sole leader and protector of his own neighbourhood.

Therefore the *futuwwa* would work in financially rewarding jobs that would place him above the average wage-earner and help empower his social standing as the patron and leader of the locale within which he operated. For example, Aziza al-Fahla, one of the few examples of renowned female *futuwwa*s in Cairo in the 1930s and 1940s, earned enough from her work as a prominent dealer in foodstuffs to enable her to purchase eight houses in her neighbourhood, in addition to a coffee shop and a few other commercial stores. As the leader and facilitator of various networks, the *futuwwa* does not operate alone, and his, or in this case her, prestige and prowess is further dependent upon the number of supporters he or she acquires. These potential supporters come from all walks of life and are usually referred to as the *shilla* or the clique (El Messiri, 1977).

In summation, one notes that the role of the *futuwwa* in the social structure of the urban masses was more of a protector as well as an alternative to the formal and mostly inefficient state system. This ascribed role has sometimes placed him in confrontation with the ruling elite, yet at other times the *futuwwa* was utilized by these same elites as an intermediary and a potential facilitator of a variety of social, economic and political roles. In doing so, the *futuwwa* partially succeeded in 'minimizing the abuses and exploitation of the authorities' (El Messiri, 1977). Perhaps, even up to today, the Cairene polity still holds a place for the functional role that was conventionally played by the *futuwwa*. As stated earlier and will be shown further in the context of this writing, one could argue that the institutional substitutes for the functions performed by the *futuwwa* have not yet rooted themselves in the popular quarters of Cairo, and that is the main reason why the values associated with the *futuwwa* have been kept alive until today. As will be described in the following chapters, the socioeconomic or political roles ascribed to the *futuwwa* figure resemble to a great extent the functionalities fulfilled by the lesser notabilities in Cairo's popular quarters during the contemporary period.

The 1952 revolution: contextualizing the re-emergence of the lesser notables

If, beginning with the eleventh century, we examine what has happened in France one half-century to another, we shall not fail to perceive that at the end of each of these periods a two-fold revolution has taken place in the state of society. The noble has gone down social ladder, and the commoner has gone up; the one descends as the other rises. Every half century brings them nearer to each other, and they will soon meet. Nor is this peculiar to France ...

Alexis de Tocqueville cited in Amin, 2000: 1

Galal Amin draws attention to an essential factor that played a paramount role in formulating the Egyptian polity in the aftermath of the 1952 revolution – that of social mobility. Despite the fact that most of the sharp alterations pertaining to the Egyptian social structure were clearly observed after the *Infitah* policies in the mid-1970s, the accelerating pace of social mobility that characterized this period had its firm roots in the 1952 revolution. 'Economic liberalization may have itself been one of the main factors accelerating the rate of social mobility, but it has by no means been the only one. Important factors were at work long before the 1970's' (Amin, 2000: 11). Indeed, with the advent of the nationalization and agricultural reform policies adopted by 1952 regime, new types of middle-class professionals and technocrats rose to the forefront as the viable politicoeconomic segments of society, and the regime depended upon such segments as the main constituency of support.

The amalgamation of policies that were adopted by the 1952 regime, contributing to the rise in the rate of social mobility, includes a variety of economic and political measures, such as:

> The successive land reform laws between 1952 and 1961, the nationalization and sequestration measures of the early 1960's, the raising of minimum wages and of the rates of income tax, as well as the very rapid expansion of free education and other social services. To this one must also add the rapid increase in the rate of investment in agriculture and industry from 1957 to 1965, which led to the absorption of large numbers of agricultural surplus labor in irrigation projects … The growth of bureaucracy and of government-created political organizations provided new career ladders for a great number of university graduates who could not be absorbed in agriculture or industry.
>
> Amin, 2000: 15

In the course of this process, the political and economic relevance of the classical notables, primarily the giant landowners and businessmen, who roughly constituted less than 1 per cent of Egypt's population at the time, gave way to this considerably larger middle class, which was gradually growing in terms of relative size and also in terms of the economic strata and political roles ascribed to it (Amin, 2005).

In the 1970s, more sources of income were induced into the Egyptian economy. After a few years of recession after the 1967 defeat, the Open Door policies of Sadat encouraged the absorption of a variety of external sources of income, including foreign loans, increasing revenues from the Suez Canal, oil production, tourism and, most significantly, labour remittances from abroad. Subsequently, Egypt witnessed an unprecedented rate of economic growth that reached 8 per cent in 1979, which enabled certain segments of the society to amass sizable accumulations of wealth as well (Amin, 2005). These were mainly the intermediaries: merchants, real-estate bidders and contractors, and import–export facilitators were among those who benefitted the most from this Open Door craze. 'Sadat used to publicly take pride in the fact that his presidency witnessed an accumulation of wealth due to the surge in the prices of residential apartments, buildings, and land. He practically measured the success of his policies with this indicator' (Amin, 2005: 159). Indeed, Sadat was keen on attracting those newly wealthy classes to the circles of political power, and, eventually, those which were at the apex of commercial and real-estate activities were the newly viable politicoeconomic actors within the Egyptian polity.

Overall, it is safe to assume that the 1952 regime triggered a deeply entrenched process of social mobility that affected the Egyptian polity for decades, empowering various categories of social actor and enabling them to attain certain strata of economic and political dominance during various time periods. This process was actualized in accordance with the socioeconomic policies adopted by the state. For example, during the Nasser years, the ruling regime put emphasis on the role of the newly rising professional and technocratic middle class, which was subsequently empowered via massively subsidized state services. On the other hand, the period of Sadat also witnessed an accelerating rate of social mobility that gave rise to a relatively new prototype of politicoeconomic notability pertaining to the intermediaries:

> For those social groups who have only recently had access to surplus income, investment in industry or agriculture may seem too risky, requiring more capital, a longer gestation period, and greater experience than is required by investment in residential buildings, transportation, tourism, or the import trade. Much of what is regarded by economists as 'unproductive' investment is in the channels preferred by these investors with less experience who are also more anxious to prove their social advancement and less confident in their ability to maintain their newly acquired social status.
>
> Amin, 2000: 20

Arguably, with the widespread acceleration of these relatively new types of commercial activity that ensured rapid profitability, loyalty to the state also diminished. In fact, most of the income accumulated in the 1970s and 1980s could not be attributed to state activities, but rather to its inactivity: 'To the merely passive role of the state in allowing people to migrate, and to its failure to regulate the rate of inflation and pattern of investment' (Amin, 2000: 22).

Hence, in a rough resemblance to, or perhaps continuation of, the political notability of urban and rural intermediaries cited earlier in this research, Sadat era witnessed an increasingly growing socioeconomic and political role for an echelon of socioeconomic actors who could be described as the 'lesser notables'. By and large, the Egyptian state has been comparatively successful in exercising efficient political and economic control over the central locales of the country: the major and relatively developed urban dwellings in Cairo and Alexandria, the avenues and squares in the towns, the checkpoints between governorates, etc. However, within the peripheral urban and rural popular quarters, there exists a sense of self-management that somehow requires facilitation provided by intermediaries:

> The Egyptian state's recurrent problem as a central/centralized state is that of identifying the intermediaries through which it may observe global control over these communities, maintain public order and impose the social items regarding which the regime refuses to negotiate. Under the old regime, the role of the intermediary between central power and the local level was played, in the countryside, by the owners of latifundiae enjoying absolute authority over their villages ... and, in the city, by the notability system and the futuwwa network ... Under Sadat, and more clearly still under Mubarak until the end of the 1980's, the regime attempted to co-opt the Islamist trend for this role ... The point is to know to what extent this redistribution of

roles … will transform fundamentally the ways in which effective power is exercised in Egypt.

Roussillon, 1998: 391

The next section attempts to portray some of the features of this newly rising category of lesser notability that, arguably, had its roots in the scheme of social mobility initiated by the 1952 regime.

The lesser notables in the contemporary period

There is indeed some sound resemblance between the attributes related to the *biytkabarluh* figures of authority in the popular quarters of contemporary Cairo, cited in Chapter 1, and the aforementioned functions of the *futuwwa* figure who was predominant in Cairo and other Middle Eastern cities for hundreds of years. These two categories, the *futuwwa* as well as the *biytkabarluh*, appear to be distinctive from the traditional notables introduced earlier in this chapter:

> In comparison to the Ottoman notables, today's notables are of a lesser social status in the sense that they do not issue from prominent families with a long, established history. Further, their interventions in local communities are not of the same scale as the interventions of the earlier notables. Although a few of the contemporary local notability have managed to enter national politics through elections to the National Assembly, they could not be referred to as national figures.
>
> S. Ismail, 2006: 48

In light of these differences, today's local notables have been described by Ismail as lesser notables.

The contemporary lesser notabilities have also gone through a process of transformation that overwhelmed Cairo since the early twentieth century.[2] A plethora of sociopolitical and economic alterations took place in the milieu of the popular neighbourhood, setting the ground for such transformation. First, there existed an increasingly heterogeneous population as a result of the continuing waves of rural to urban migration directed towards Cairo, which created a sense of tension between those various societal actors with different, and sometimes conflicting, ethnic and cultural backgrounds. Then, with the incremental rise in the overall population and the subsequent overcrowding of the popular quarters of Cairo, there seems to have been a gradual erosion of the role that familial and personal ties play, and the picture seems to be changing with regard to the role expected to be played by the local patron or leader. Another crucial transformation, albeit also subject to radical alterations in the rise of the neoliberal phase in the early 1990s, is the 'increasing intervention of the state in terms of policing and the maintenance of local order', which narrowed the scope of the activities of traditional popular politics (El Messiri, 1977: 252).

However, in spite of these transformations, several taxonomies of lesser notabilities are still operational in the popular neighbourhoods of contemporary

Cairo. A multitude of merchants, real-estate contractors and the owners of small to medium-sized shops have come to the forefront of political notability in the popular neighbourhoods as viable actors, establishing 'their own economic and social networks through which they consolidate their positions in their neighborhoods' (S. Ismail, 2006: 50). There are recurring examples of merchants and real-estate contractors who belong to this category, usually coming from modest social origins and building up their wealth by investing in commercial goods and real-estate ventures. Most of these notables also invest in building their status by forging socioeconomic links with their neighbourhoods: donating to charitable activities inside and outside their quarters, setting up tables for the needy during the month of Ramadan and other social and religious festivities, and organizing other collections of donations for activities in the neighbourhood through local mosques. These activities are considered to be a sign of their goodness and an expression of humility and connectedness with the people of their own locale (S. Ismail, 2006).

Yet, importantly, along with the socioeconomic features of those lesser notabilities, there is also an essential political dimension that is crucial. Most of these figures also seek to cultivate links with the state authorities, 'organizing banquets to which the police commissioner (*ma'mur*), the head of the police investigative unit, and members of the local and national assemblies are invited ... The organization of these activities allows for direct relations with the leadership' (S. Ismail, 2006: 50). Subsequently, through their contacts with the public institutions of the state and their positions in the community, today's lesser notables are sought out by their clients to resolve disputes and sort out problems.

With the incrementally increasing relevance of the lesser notabilities at the political level, it was logical that they would start seeking positions in local and national legislatures, mainly as a strategy for consolidating and further formalizing their political prowess and authority:

> In this respect, the lesser notability could be said to be following in the steps of the commercial bourgeoisie. Over the last decade, large entrepreneurs and business persons have run, in increasing number, in elections to the National Assembly. As a consequence, their share of seats has been rising. In 2000, this entrepreneurial class won seventy-seven seats, accounting for 17 percent of the total ... Merchants and contractors from popular quarters have joined the business class in running for the National Assembly seats. This entry of the lesser notables into national politics should be interpreted as a confirmation of their role as intermediaries with government ... The notability is also active in party politics, as members in the local assembly, and as secretaries in the local secretaries to the ruling party local branches.
>
> S. Ismail, 2006: 50

In fact, it should be noted that the mounting importance of the lesser notabilities stems from their mediating role as state–society intermediaries within their neighbourhoods. In addition to the resources they allocate locally to the citizens of their own quarters, they also maintain a network of ties with the state authorities, which enables them to provide a variety of services to locals, as will be analysed in later chapters.

As mentioned in Chapter 1, perhaps the most vivid portrayal of the lesser notables of Cairo's popular quarters nowadays is exemplified via the *biytkabarluh* personas, observed in a wide spectrum of popular quarters. Indeed, the ethos of the *biytkabarluh* involves a certain set of duties and services that is expected to be provided by such a figure. Quite often, he or she is expected to gain access to state resources and services that would be otherwise very difficult for locals to acquire without the intervention of this particular *biytkabarluh* figure. This corresponds with the increasing blurring of the boundaries between state and society or, put differently, the public and the private, which was inevitable with the advent of *Infitah* policies.

The acceleration of the Open Door policies, along with the gradual retreat of the Egyptian state from the public domain, required the emergence of a new type of societal actor characterized by their capability to master 'administrative codes and procedures and their access to the "informal" decision-making networks within ministries and government-service sectors' (Roussillon, 1998: 377). The profile of Hajj Saleh, a commercial retailer and owner of a medium-sized shoe factory in the popular quarter of Bulaq displays this:

> Acceding to the position of someone *biytkabarluh* is materially inscribed. It is the hajj's visible links to formal institutions that are ultimately acknowledged and validated at times of intervention. The hajj's involvement in charitable work earns him the image of a 'man of good', while his links with the police establish him as a 'man of power'. As someone *biytkabrluh*, the hajj is incorporated by the state apparatus of coercion to mediate in disputes with the local population.
>
> S. Ismail, 2006: 64

Thus, by virtue of their social standing and the political role ascribed to them, individuals such as Hajj Saleh signify a notability of sorts.

In fact, such figures of lesser notability have become so recurrent in the polity of the popular quarters of Cairo that they were depicted in the highly popular novel *'Imarat Ya'coubian* in 2003. In the novel, the author presents the ongoing rivalry and competition between the seemingly pious entrepreneur, Hajj Azam, who owns a wholesale-retail clothes store and also maintains strong ties with the ruling elites, and Hajj Abu Hamidou, a wholesale-retail merchant with Islamist inclinations and alleged links to the Muslim Brotherhood. Ultimately, and through his ties with the ruling elites, Hajj Azam succeeds in overcoming his Islamist rival, securing a seat in the parliament, in addition to various business incentives facilitated via the back channels he gained access to with the aid of his contacts within the regime (S. Ismail, 2006). This tale is quite illuminating if we attempt to observe the political role played by the lesser notables and the potential for them to be co-opted by the dominant political forces.

A political contest over the co-optation of lesser notables?

If we look at the lesser notabilities of Cairo, an essential query poses itself with regard to the linkages they may have with state authorities. If access to the echelons of notability seems to be related to establishing profound networks with the state institutions, what about those elements which stand in opposition to the government, yet maintain a sense of socioeconomic networking that enables them to fulfil the role of the notability? In fact, the prototype that comes to mind is that of the Islamist notables who have met considerable successes in establishing a sizeable web of patronage in a wide variety of urban as well as rural constituencies in Egypt. The Mubarak regime was well aware of the existential threat posed by these networks. In 2007 the Mubarak regime launched a massive campaign against the 'financial arm' of the Muslim Brotherhood all over the country, arresting hundreds of people who were allegedly associated with a variety of commercial activities that funded the activities of the Muslim Brotherhood (*Al-Ahram*, 15 January 2007).

By and large, the process of divorcing the state structure from the Islamist web of networks does not appear to be an easy one, taking into account the fact that, as stated in Chapter 1, those Islamist forces tend to position themselves within the already existing structure of the state system, creating cohesive alliances and networks with state authorities and personnel. Indeed, Islamist commercial and financial networks are inevitably drawn into interwoven relations with the state. 'For example, in 1980's, the Islamic Societies for the Placement of Funds (ISPF) maintained close contacts with high-ranking government officials and prominent sheikhs. For various reasons … the government intervened to put an end to its speculative investments' (S. Ismail, 2006: 52–6). Although the regime proclaimed that its intervention was due to the irregularities exercised by these funds, the fact that it had initially licensed these entities and then clamped down upon them when they started growing considerably, as Islamist alternatives to secular banks, suggests otherwise. Thus, breaking those state–Islamist ties might pose somewhat of a dilemma as it might also involve state and National Democratic Party (NDP) personnel.

In the chapters that follow, this research will attempt to contextualize the machinations utilized by the lesser notable figures that adhered to the dissolved NDP as well as those that appear to be functioning under the umbrella of the Muslim Brotherhood. In doing so, it is important to highlight a significant difference between these two prototypes: that whereas the former are usually co-opted by the state, the latter's roles and actions are 'framed by ideological articulations that challenged state legitimacy'. Indeed the state authorities 'could not tolerate the rise of a contending leadership, but we may also argue that in assiduously co-opting local figures, state authorities seek to inhibit the rise of independent leaders' (S. Ismail, 2006: 56).

Conclusions

Throughout its vast history, the Muslim city has witnessed various schemes of political notability. Cairo is no exception, and the politicoeconomic role of those notables has been quintessential in maintaining civic life by mediating between the locals and the state authorities. Political notability took various shapes and forms throughout the Mamluk and Ottoman periods; however, with the rise of Mohammed Ali to the apex of the Egyptian state in 1805, the grip of the state over socioeconomic and political affairs was tightened, minimizing the role of those mediating notables and allowing for a class of lesser notability to arise. With this, an apparent rise in the importance of the role played by the *futuwwa* was evident within the popular quarters of Cairo. In a sense, the *futuwwa* represents a possible linkage between the traditional figures of popular politics and the lesser notabilities of today.

Within the context of Egyptian state–society relations, the advent of the Mohammed Ali era and the inception of the modern period brought forward a virtual vacuum in the polity. By then, there was more room for a multitude of local (lesser) notables to act as the necessary politicoeconomic intermediaries. In essence, one could argue that on the level of the *Harra* (quarter) or the *Hitta* (neighbourhood), there emerged an increasingly influential political agency for the *futuwwa* in the early twentieth century. There are indeed interesting similarities between the kind of politicoeconomic functions fulfilled by the *futuwwa* and those of the *biytkabarluh* figure, which is predominant in the present-day popular quarters of Cairo, as outlined earlier in Chapter 1. Therefore the *biytkabarluh* figure represents an extension of the legacies of the *futuwwa* and can be considered to be a part of the amalgam of the figures of lesser notability in contemporary Cairo. These notabilities play a crucial role as the mediators and facilitators of various commercial goods and administrative services. They have mostly anchored themselves within occupational vacancies that provide the locals with necessary functions, which has subsequently made them a target of co-option for the viable political forces operating within Cairo's popular neighbourhoods.

This chapter has served as an introductory framework for those that follow as it attempts to outline some of the various historical manifestations of lesser notability figures in the Middle Eastern city since the Islamic Caliphate, focusing mostly on Egypt. In doing so, it has introduced several models of popular figures who all share the characterization of the lesser notability that possesses a considerable degree of socioeconomic and political agency in the urban quarter. Such figures can be considered as the predecessors that set the stage for the reemergence of *ibn al-balad*, the urban lesser notable who actually thrived in the popular quarter in the twentieth century, and whose persona will be scrutinized further in the next chapter as it portrays the emergence of the 'lesser notable' of the twenty-first century.

3 Misr al-Qadima

The popular quarter and the polity of the lesser notable

In between a proud ancient history and huge walls that recite tales as old as mankind, and a crowded present that is full of adjacent houses and people, lies Misr Al Qadima ... The features of this district do in fact draw a picture for the entire country with all its contradictions.[1]

Misr al-Qadima, which translates from Arabic as Old Egypt, is arguably Cairo's oldest quarter. Built on the remnants of other predecessors of the Cairo that the Fatimids had constructed in the eleventh century AD, such as the Ancient Egyptian Memphis, the Roman fortresses of Babylon and the Arabic-Islamic Fustat, this district is now home to more than 500,000 inhabitants from a plethora of social backgrounds and classes who occupy various socioeconomic roles and strata. Today, the area suffers from socioeconomic disparities that make it one of Cairo's poorest districts in terms of income distribution and education. Moreover, and as will be shown later in this chapter, the demographic profile of the area is characterized by a set of socioeconomic and political features that make this district a favourable environment for the emergence of the lesser notables as viable sociopolitical agents. As a prelude, the following introductory section will provide a brief historical synopsis of Misr al-Qadima.

Introduction

The famous gated town of Babylon was located in the district currently called Misr al-Qadima, to the south of Cairo. This city was the dominant urban centre just before the Arab conquest of Egypt and was connected to the Red Sea by a canal (Hussein, 1965). Cairo, as it is now known, had gradually developed over three centuries after the Arab conquest of Egypt and it went through various phases of metamorphosis until it reached its status as the urban conglomerate we know today. The first two precursors of Cairo were Al Fustat, which was the first city to be constructed by Amr Ibn al-'Aas after the Arab conquest of Egypt in 641 AD as a garrison town, and Al-'Askar ('the military' in Arabic), which was built by the Umayyads as the settlement containing the official residence of the Arab governors and their troops. Both of these towns were in essence an extension as well as a progression of the old town of Babylon, and formed the basis for the main city that was to be built by the Fatimids.

In the ninth century, the Egyptian sovereign Ahmed Ibn Toulun reckoned that Al-'Askar and Al-Fustat were overcrowded and unsuitable for his army and officials; accordingly, in the year 870 AD:

> He laid the foundations of his new capital city, Al-Katai'. This name means the quarters and the city was divided into separate sections, each inhabited by a certain class or ethnic group. This was the first time a definite planning system was used by Arabs in Egypt. Touluns' administration followed the system of straight streets intersecting at right angles, forming a crude gradation plan ... In 969 A.D. General Gawher El-Sickilly of the Fatimids of North Africa started to lay out the foundations of "Al-Kahira" which means "the conqueror". Al-Kahira included a Kalipha's palace, barracks for the army, stables for the cavalry, government buildings ... etc. The site of this city was about 2–1/2 miles north of Al-Fustat.
>
> Hussein, 1965: 12

Hence the centrality of what is known today as Misr al-Qadima has been well in evidence since the outset of the Cairene urban conglomerate. In practice, Cairo's development took the shape and form of the medieval Muslim city outlined in Chapter 2: 'Each quarter of the city was assigned to a tribe or racial group that had joined the Fatimid invasion. Among these groups were Greeks, Turks, Berbers and Africans' (Hussein, 1965: 13).

Throughout the centuries that followed, Cairo expanded into a world capital; it was the most populated city in the world outside China at the time:

> The medieval cycle of Cairo's growth and subsequent decline began essentially with the accession of Saladin to the leadership of Sunni Islam. It rose sharply within the next 175 years, reaching an apogee during the long reigns of the Mamluk sultan al-Nasir ibn Qalawun before the middle of the fourteenth century.
>
> Abu-Lughod, 2004: 24

Figures 3.1 and 3.2 show the urban expansion that Cairo has gone through since the Arab conquest.

The shift to Mamluk rule was more than a mere change in dynasties. Instead, it symbolized a social revolution of grave importance. The elevation of the Mamluks into power saw the flowering of Cairo as a medieval city, yet this elevation contained within it the kernel of its own (and Cairo's) inevitable decline. Although Egypt has rarely been ruled by purely indigenous elements since the demise of the ancient Egyptian kingdoms, earlier conquerors had always eventually assimilated with the population they ruled:

> The Mamluks, on the other hand, remained a 'foreign' military caste, each generation recruited anew from abroad ... As internal strife and external

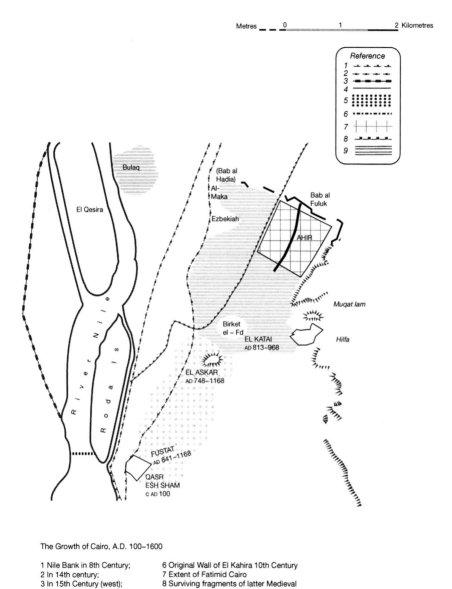

Metres 0   1   2 Kilometres

Reference
1
2
3
4
5
6
7
8
9

Bulaq

El Qesira

(Bab al Hadia)
Al-Maka
Ezbekiah

Bab al Fuluk

AHIR

Muqat lam

Birket el – Fd
EL KATAI
AD 813–968

Hilfa

EL ASKAR
AD 748–1168

River Nile
Rodais
Rodais

FUSTAT
AD 841–1168

QASR ESH SHAM
C AD 100

The Growth of Cairo, A.D. 100–1600

1 Nile Bank in 8th Century;
2 In 14th century;
3 In 15th Century (west);
4 In 1930
5 Extent of Fustat and El Askar

6 Original Wall of El Kahira 10th Century
7 Extent of Fatimid Cairo
8 Surviving fragments of latter Medieval North and East Walls
9 Built-up area in 1800

Figure 3.1 Urban expansion of Cairo since the Arab conquest.

Source: Lebon, J.H.G. (1970) 'The Islamic city in the Near East: A comparative study of Cairo, Alexandria and Istanbul', *Town Planning Review*, Vol. 41, No. 2, p. 183.

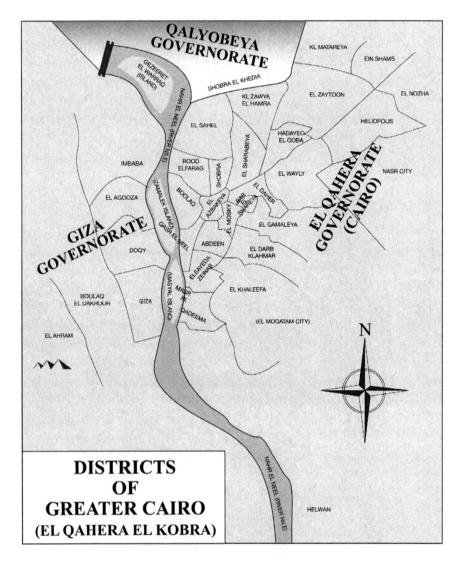

Figure 3.2 Districts of Greater Cairo.

Note: This is a detailed map of modern Cairo and its different neighbourhoods and districts. The Misr al-Qadima district, which lies on the south-eastern banks of the Nile, also includes Manial Island.

Source: Cairo City Key: *Maps & Street Index of Greater Cairo*, Cairo: Elias Modern Press, 2001.

threats multiplied, the expansion of the city came to a temporary halt. The mirror image of the rise of Islam on the Anatolian plateau, signaled by the conquest of Constantinople in 1453 by the Ottoman Turks, represented a decline in Egypt's imperial wealth and autonomy. After the Ottoman conquest of Egypt in 1517, Cairo was reduced from its former status as centre of a vast empire to a mere provincial capital. Its talented cadre of architects and artisans were removed to Istanbul where they contributed to the transformation of that Byzantine Christian city into a magnificent Islamic capital.

Abu-Lughod, 2004: 25–6

The essentiality of Misr al-Qadima as an integral segment of medieval Cairo was shown by the travellers who passed by the city at the time. Leos Africanus, who arrived in Cairo at the wake of the Ottoman invasion in 1517, describes Misr al-Qadima 'as being "endowed with a fair number of artisans and merchants". He cites that the island of … Rawdah [now Manial], across from old Cairo, as "densely settled" and "[containing] approximately 1500 hearths' (Raymond, 2000: 187).

Throughout the reigns of the Mamluks and Ottomans, and regardless of the ups and downs the city passed through, the essentiality of Old Cairo as a vital part of Cairo remained largely intact. Up until the discovery of the Cape of Good Hope route in the sixteenth century AD, the transit trade route connecting Europe and Asia via North Africa in the medieval and premodern phases flourished, gradually enhancing the importance of Al Fustat even further owing to its central location as the main port on the banks on the Nile.

Old Cairo: the habitat of *ibn al-balad*

Tracing Old Cairo's politicoeconomic history not only sheds light on the constructional development of this section of the city, but also helps in understanding the typologies of the residents who have dwelled within it. For instance, looking at the figure of the *ibn al-balad* (a term usually used to describe a person belonging to the city and enjoying a certain stature of moral goodness, literally meaning 'son of the country'; El Messiri, 1978: 2–4),[2] one notes that places like Old Cairo and other popular and traditional quarters of the city have actually served as the natural habitat for such figures:

> Historically it was the Cairenes who were identified as *awlad al balad*. From the mid-thirteenth century Egypt was dominated in succession by Mamluks and Ottomans, for a brief interval by the French, then by Muhammad Ali's regime … It was in the face of these alien Cairo-based elements that the indigenous inhabitant sought to preserve and assert his particular identity.
>
> El Messiri, 1978: 4

Traditionally, the locale of *ibn al-balad* has been the popular quarter. Today, when Egyptians refer to *awlad al-balad*, it is usually in mention of those authentic and original inhabitants of *al ahiyya' al Sha'abeya* (the folk/popular quarters). Being an original inhabitant is noteworthy as it distinguishes the *awlad al-balad* from the *Sa'idis* who originated from Upper Egypt or the Fellahin, and whose roots can be traced back to Lower Egypt. Thus, a regional or geographical element is largely influential in the features of *ibn al-balad* and is often linked to the Cairene popular quarter. Of course, Misr al-Qadima (Old Cairo) is one of the chief popular quarters of Cairo and is predominantly characterized as being a hub of *awlad al-balad*:

> These quarters are old and traditional ... *awlad al balad* are found in these quarters, whereas one would not find *ibn al balad* in newer sections such as Zamalek or Garden City, because these quarters are inhabited largely by foreigners and westernized Egyptians, who are characterized by a different set of values and life-styles.
>
> El Messiri, 1978: 38

Indeed, what is referred to today as Misr al-Qadima is an amalgamation of some relatively modern neighbourhoods (including 'Ain al-Sirra), which were all constructed at various times during the nineteenth and twentieth centuries, and a traditional popular neighbourhood whose constructional and structural features have remained more or less the same since the medieval era. The appearance of a number of these quarters 'has not changed for centuries; some of the street plans are the original ones of Cairo. The streets in these quarters are divided into *harat* [small alleys], *darb utaf* [narrow streets], and *zuqaq* [bigger streets], which probably follow the original divisions' (El Messiri, 1978: 46). By and large, the heart of Cairo's traditional urbanism lies in these districts, which have been in existence the longest, that is, the quarters of medieval Cairo.

> However, not all of today's residents of these communities descend from inhabitants in the middle ages or even a century ago. The communities are changing constantly. While a sizable number of rural migrants come to settle, at the same time many of the older residents leave their quarters for more modern ones. But despite this mobility we find that whatever traditional activities still survive in Cairo are found chiefly in these old quarters.
>
> El Messiri, 1978: 57

Today the term '*ibn al-balad*' is still used in reference to a person with the aforementioned traits and geographical or historical ties to the popular quarters. Overall, the parallels between this popular figure and those of the *futuwwa* and the *beiytakabarlu* figures, introduced in Chapters 1 and 2, are quite compelling, which reinforces the assumption that the lesser notabilities of today are indeed even more closely linked to such typologies of folk figures.

The curse of the dual city

At the beginning of the modern period of Egyptian history, usually associated with the Napoleonic French Expedition of 1798, Misr al-Qadima still constituted an integral part of the Cairene conglomerate. 'After the French invasion of

Egypt, the city was accurately described as composed of three distinct parts separated by agricultural land, Cairo the City and two suburbs, Boulack and Misr El-Kadima' (Hussein, 1965: 15). However, the arrival of the Napoleonic Expedition in 1798 brought the cycle of growth and expansion of old Cairo to a virtual halt, with the intrusion outlining the divide between a medieval Cairo that had aged and decayed and a modern Cairo that was yet to be. In essence, 'the *savants* who accompanied the brief occupation mapped the city, estimating its population at less than three hundred thousand. Although the French did not remain as colonizers, the processes of "modernization" and "reform" had begun' (Abu-Lughod, 2004: 27).

In the aftermath of the French expedition and the subsequent ascent of the Mohammed Ali dynasty to power, the importance of the older quarters of Cairo, Misr al-Qadima included, gradually started to fade. Mohammed Ali and his successors initiated a massive construction project that aimed to build a modern city adjacent to the older quarters of Cairo, shifting the chief socioeconomic, political and administrative functions that had been historically fulfilled by the older city to this new urban conglomerate. Parallel to what has taken place elsewhere in other colonized cities in the Third World, the dual-city pattern eventually stripped the older quarters of wealthy inhabitants who flocked to mimic the new consumption patterns set out by the colonizers:

> In the process, the older quarters became neglected and degraded, as new migrants from the countryside joined the poorer population left behind, subdividing the large homes of the departed rich into cubicles, unable to maintain them, and eventually spilling out to the cemeteries east and southeast of the city. All resources were devoted to paving the streets in the new quarters, to providing them with gaslights, piped water and even sewers. While the old quarters did not lose their important economic functions – handicrafts and the processing and distribution of foods – these products were increasingly purveyed to people of similar social standing.
>
> Abu-Lughod, 2004: 28

Hence, the degradation of Misr al-Qadima and other districts in the area of old Cairo was inevitable throughout the nineteenth century and up until the outset of the twentieth century.

Nineteenth-century Cairo: the tale of two cities

With the rise of Mohammed Ali's grandson, Khedive Ismail, to power, the foundations of modern Cairo were being thoroughly planned. Ismail had a deep fascination with European culture in general, and it is in this milieu that he spearheaded the establishment of a modern Cairo on the outskirts of the old one, with the goal of turning it into a London or a Paris of the East. Modern (Western) architectural plans were put forward by pioneering European architects, and a lavish budget was secured by the Khedive to ensure the successful completion of his venture. Indeed, this came at the expense of the older quarters, accentuating the theme of divisions and the dual-city pattern cited above. It was roughly at this point that Old Cairo lost its practical meaningfulness as a vital part of the city. 'Limited in space, relatively overcrowded, and structured according to a different principle of urban life, the old city offered neither a suitable ground for the new urbanism nor accommodations for a fresh influx of residents' (Raymond, 2000: 309). The inevitable constructional divisions that took place and were pursued thereafter made the importance of the older quarters of Cairo only symbolic – a mere arena where the desire to restore and preserve the heritage of the city could take place, rather than an area that had a pragmatic role to play in the course of the new phase that was in the making at the time (Sanders, 2008).

In reality, these older quarters, Misr al-Qadima included, were in dire need of proper revamping and improvement rather than negligence. The features of this deterioration could be described as follows:

> Its streets were neglected, cleaning was haphazard, water supply was only partial, and the sewers were poor or insufficient. The deterioration of these quarters was exacerbated by the rapid increase in population whose density weighed heavily on the crumbling infrastructure and inadequate public services. Between 1882 and 1927, the population of the four districts that constituted the old city ... grew from 122,411 to 259,535 an increase of 112 percent ... Old Cairo [grew] from 22,518 to 49,495 ... This population was particularly poor ... The old quarters were tending to become a refuge for the most downtrodden and recently arrived segments of the population.
>
> Raymond, 2000: 333

Therefore, with this apparent segregation, the fortunes of the traditional quarters of Cairo appeared to be inversely proportional to the expansion and modernization of the newer sections of the city. The more attention and care the modern part received, the more neglected and abandoned the older part became.

Modes of production and informal networks in nineteenth-century Cairo

There is indeed a particular importance to the modes of production of the guild members and craft-workers, who constituted the bulk of the labour force in Cairo's old (popular) quarters at the time of the inception of modern Cairo and have continued to formulate the prime section of the working population of these quarters perhaps even until today. A distinctive case here is the demise of the guild system in 1911, which occurred as the result of an ongoing tension between the state and the craftsmen and artisans, who considered the guilds to be a tool in the hands of the state that aimed to co-opt those segments of the community, rather than represent them:

> Where attempts to engage the state officially through formal and collective claim making failed, guild members and crafts workers often resorted to more illicit "weapons of the weak", dodging taxes, subverting regulations,

creating unofficial networks, and bribing officials. Crafts workers' mobilization played a significant role in bringing down their guilds.

Chalcraft, 2005: 67

Interestingly, the collapse of the guild system in the late nineteenth/early twentieth century was accompanied by a sort of confrontation between the state and a category of popular figures of authority that were somehow similar to the lesser notables, the typology of sociopolitical agents that this study is attempting to scrutinize. At that particular juncture, the official discourse of the state had stopped recognizing and approving the local autonomies of sheikh-like activities in the trades, which were then considered to 'backward', 'tyrannical' and 'malignant'. As a result, these local figures had to evade the various forms of state control that started appearing at the time. For the state, the prevalence of these sheikh-like figures of authority at the popular level acted against the scheme of modernity that was being adopted by the state apparatus:

> Indeed such local figures were not sanctioned by state regulations, which they often sought to undermine or transform in one way or another. In addition, the crafts and services trade were undergoing rapid sociological change. The speedy growth of completely new trades such as cab driving and the attrition of others, the drift to countryside of textiles on the one hand, and significant rural-urban migration on the other, and the increased participation of women meant that many in the trades in the early 1900's had no established links to a prior tradition of shaikhly authority in a trade.
>
> Chalcraft, 2005: 157

Thus, with the induction of the modern (arguably authoritarian) state and the subsequent resilient 'informalism' that was developed by guild activists in order to offset state attempts to overtake their guilds, a relatively novel scope of socioeconomic and political relations was in the making between the state and those lesser notabilities.

Cairo in the post-war period

By the post-Second World War period (1945 onwards), a clear-cut divide had been firmly established between the modern and premodern sections of the city, with a plethora of modern industrial technologies of transportation and communication all introduced and based in the newly developed quarters, leaving the older parts lagging behind in terms of infrastructure and technology. Along with the gradual segregation of the city, a residential rift based on income level, job occupation and social class was also on the rise:

> In any city, the precise location of low-income settlement will depend on the location of jobs and also the residential preferences of the affluent, since the latter can usually preempt any location they choose. In both respects, trends in Cairo seem to be broadly exemplary.
>
> Harris and Wahba, 2002: 68

Indeed, the Misr al-Qadima district belongs to the category of the older quarters, where low-income housing is prevalent. Expanding on the already existing potential of the area as a location for craftsmen and skilled and unskilled labour, due to the historical skin tannery workshops and the other crafts that had been homegrown in Misr al-Qadima for centuries, the district grew considerably into one of the main housing locations for occupational groups undertaking manual labour. In this regard, Misr al-Qadima is no exception when compared with the rest of Cairo's districts, which have all witnessed a clear trend of residential segregation based on socioeconomic standing. Looking at the statistical data in Table 3.1, this point can in fact be confirmed. Although containing the largest enduring remnants of any medieval Middle Eastern city, Misr al-Qadima, alongside the other sections of the old city, is today actually being dwarfed by the massive urban conglomerate that now encircles it: 'The population has declined, not only because residences have crumbled from age, but also because they are being destroyed by natural events (the recent earthquake) and the works of man (new highways and tunnels [and] new colonies of informal settlements' (Abu-Lughod, 2004: 27).

Misr al-Qadima today: socioeconomic and political indicators

The neighbourhood of Misr al-Qadima: Misr al-Qadima proper and 'Ain al-Sirra

This section aims to dissect the demographic profile of contemporary Misr al-Qadima area. In doing so, it can be noted that the neighbourhood suffers from social disparities that render it on the lower echelons of Cairo's various districts in terms of income distribution and education. Furthermore, a plethora of other

Table 3.1 Residential segregation of occupation groups in the Cairo urban region, 1960–1986 (age 15 years and above)

Occupation groups	1960	1986	1960–86 (change)
Skilled & Unskilled Labor	0.258	0.262	0.004
Administrative & Managerial	0.401	0.444	0.043

Note: The index of segregation is 'the most commonly used statistic. This has the useful property of varying between zero and unity so that it can be interpreted as a percentage ... In class terms; Cairo is a highly segregated city.' Here, the closer the value to 1, the more residential segregation there is, 1 indicating a complete segregation of residence and 0 indicating no segregation whatsoever. When we say that the index of segregation of Administrative and Managerial Professionals is 0.444, this implies that 44.4 per cent of this occupational group would have to move from their places of residence in order for there to be no segregation.

Source: Harris, R. and Wahba, M. (2002) 'The urban geography of low-income housing: Cairo (1947–96) exemplifies a model', *International Journal of Urban and Regional Research*, Vol. 26, No. 1, pp. 58–79.

socioeconomic and political features stand out, making this area a fertile ground for the flourishing of the sort of the socioeconomic and political agency that is typically filled by what is referred to as the 'lesser notables'.

Today, the area referred to as Misr al-Qadima (Figure 3.3) is mainly an aggregation of two chief sections between which the 400,000 inhabitants of Misr al-Qadima are almost equally distributed. First, there is the older part of this district (Misr al-Qadima proper), which consists of the old popular quarter that has been there for hundreds of years. Most of the buildings in this neighbourhood are either ancient constructional establishments, some of which were actually consolidated by the state as monumental buildings, forcing the inhabitants to relocate their residence, or relatively newer buildings made of red brick and other basic materials, which were built on the remnants of the older or historical constructional sites over various periods in the timeline of the popular quarter. Overall, scarcely any constructional activity has taken place in the old quarter since the onset of the twentieth century. Many of the streets are quite narrow and somehow irregular in design, making the movement of modern vehicles impractical in various parts of the quarter (Abdallah and Siam, 1996).

We do not have at hand any empirical information relating to the historical origin of the old quarter's inhabitants. However, on aggregate and depending on interviews with a multitude of locals residing within that quarter, it could be argued that the residents of this part of Misr al-Qadima are comparatively homogenous, what Cairenes refer to as '*awlad al-balad*', or those people that trace their origin to the same neighbourhood within which they reside, considering themselves to be the original inhabitants of Cairo. This first-hand observation is indeed re-emphasized as one notes that the wave of rural–urban migration that swept into a wide variety of popular quarters in Cairo was not actually that apparent in Misr al-Qadima proper. Some of the chief professions that still flourish in the area, such as skin tannery, have been there for hundreds of years, and a sizeable portion of the population is in one way or another involved in this industry or the commercial activities relating to it.[3]

On the other hand, 'Ain al-Sirra (Figures 3.4a and b), the second main constituent of Misr al-Qadima, which is now home to more than 150,000 inhabitants, tells a somewhat different tale. This neighbourhood was established in the late 1950s in the course of the Nasserite socialist project at the time, which targetted an enhancement of the living conditions of low- and middle-income groups, in order to provide such segments with state-subsidized housing. There were initially 200 blocks of residential units, with an average of 60 apartment buildings in each block. In the late 1960s, additional blocks were constructed to supply housing for the growing population of the area (Abdallah and Siam, 1996).

Accordingly, since its inception, 'Ain al-Sirra has been characterized by a relatively heterogeneous population, in terms of geographical, social and professional background. Along with the sizeable proportion of rural migrants who settled in the area from various provinces, especially from Upper Egypt, this area was also home to a variety of socioeconomic segments, including working-class residents, petty bourgeoisie segments of small to medium-sized merchants, and middle-class professionals such as school teachers and government employees.

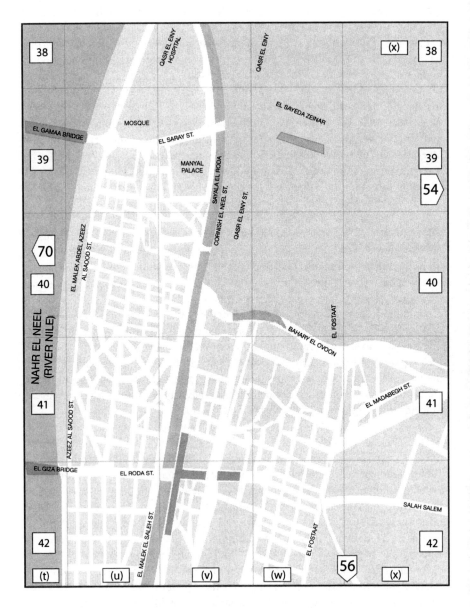

Figure 3.3 Misr al-Qadima today in detail with its streets and various sub-neighbour-hoods illustrated.

Source: *Cairo City Key: Maps & Street Index of Greater Cairo*, Cairo: Elias Modern Press, 2001.

Figure 3.4a and b
The streets of 'Ain al-Sirra.

The 1960s witnessed the neighbourhood's heyday due to the relative social mobility granted to various segments of the society at the time with the widespread subsidization of education and the tendency of the state to guarantee employment to young university graduates, whether within the ranks of the government or in the public sector. Furthermore, the Nasserite welfare state also provided popular neighbourhoods with cooperative outlets along with a set of other government agencies, which supplied the neighbourhood with the basic goods and services at subsidized rates (Abdallah and Siam, 1996).

However, with the adoption of *Infitah* policies from 1974 onwards, the entire neighbourhood experienced dire conditions, in line with most of Cairo's popular quarters at that period. State subsidies were gradually withdrawn and, in short, the preferential treatment that had been given to 'Ain al-Sirra was virtually abolished. One of the immediate consequences of this relative withdrawal of the state from the polity of the neighbourhood was the attempts made by many of the residents to redesign and expand their own houses, in order to meet the increasing growth in population that was being accompanied by a relative shrinking of income and a massive surge in the price of new housing in the late 1970s. From the late 1970s onwards, the manifestations of state withdrawal from the affairs of 'Ain al-Sirra widened to include ongoing deteriorations in the infrastructure of the neighbourhood (basic utilities, sanitation, roads, etc.), an increasing number of irregularities exercised by the residents in the absence of state regulation, and a general sentiment of distrust and rejection of the state among the area's inhabitants. In practical terms, the state had let them down (Abdallah and Siam, 1996; Misr al-Qadima locals). On aggregate, a wide array of alterations in the socioeconomic and political features of the neighbourhood came about as byproducts of the 1970s Open Door policy and then the 1990s liberalization policies, which will be discussed in more detail in the next section.

Socioeconomic and political indicators

A recent study involving the residents of Misr al-Qadima revealed that roughly two-thirds of its population were living below the poverty line. Almost 60 per cent of the total population were surviving on less than $1 a day . Approximately 30 per cent of the inhabitants of Misr al-Qadima were living on $1–2 a day, leaving only 10 per cent of inhabitants with an average income that exceeded $2 a day (Abdelfattah, 2007). Looking at the rates of education and illiteracy (Tables 3.2 and 3.3), we can see that, on aggregate, the rate of illiteracy is almost 29 per cent among those aged 10 years and above, which is significantly higher than the overall average for the Governorate of Cairo, which stood at 19.3 per cent for the same sector of the population. The unemployment rate also reached 19.7 per cent of the total population (aged 15 years and above), which is again higher than the average unemployment rate within the same age group for the entirety of Cairo, which was 10.78 per cent (Table 3.4).

In terms of the distribution of labour over the various sectors of economic activity, the figures for a relatively sizeable informal sector more or less coincided with the average rates for the Governorate of Cairo as a whole (Tables 3.5 and 3.6). In Misr al-Qadima, 40 per cent of the total labour force belonged to the informal sector. Although 97,569 of those aged 15 years and above were labelled as 'unattached', or not belonging to a formal categorization of economic sectors or job typologies, only 34,778 were considered to be unemployed, which leaves us with more than 60,000 people employed in the category of the informal sector (Tables 3.7 and 3.8). In the course of this research, informal employment will be defined, basically, as any employment that is not covered by either a legal contract or social insurance (Assaad, 2007). Indeed the aforementioned figure does not vary a great deal from the overall average for informal sector labourers within Cairo, who constituted approximately 50 per cent of the overall population of employed labour (Attia, 2009: 1–30).[4]

In a 2007 study carried out by the Economic Research Forum, entitled the Egypt Labor Market Panel Survey (ELMPS 06), it was noted that the size of the informal economy in Egypt was on the rise relative to its formal counterpart:

> Concurrent with the decline of employment opportunities in the public sector, the trend toward informalisation of the labor market, which begun in the 1990s, is continuing unabated. By 2006, 61 percent of all employment was informal, up from 57 percent in 1998. Moreover, 75 percent of new entrants who entered the labor market in the first five years of this decade were entering into informal work.
>
> Assaad, 2007: 2

With regard to the economic activities and the typologies of jobs that flourish within Misr al-Qadima, one observes that sectors C (Middle & Complementary Industries), G (Wholesale & Retail Trading) and F (Building & Construction) were the prime economic sectors, absorbing more than 32,000 workers combined (approximately 44 per cent of the labour force within the formal sector)

Table 3.2 Literacy and education in the Misr al-Qadima area (age 10 years and above)

Illiterate		Literate but no qualification		Graduate of elementary or middle school		High School Certificate		University Degree		Graduate Degree		Total	
No.	%	No.	%	No.	%	No.	%	No.	%	No.	%	No.	%
52,411	28.97	17,540	9.7	33,500	18.5	43,300	24	32,706	18.1	1,315	0.73	180,903	100

Source: Table 4, 'Distribution of population according to gender and educational status', 2006 National Census of Egypt, Central Agency for Public Mobilization and Statistics (CAPMAS), Cairo, 2007.

Table 3.3 Literacy and education in all of Cairo (age 10 years and above)

Illiterate		Literate but no qualification		Graduate of elementary or middle school		High School Certificate		University Degree		Graduate Degree		Total	
No.	%	No.	%	No.	%	No.	%	No.	%	No.	%	No.	%
1,085.745	19.31	501,437	8.92	1,128250	20.01	1,738100	30.9	1,126187	20.03	41,091	0.73	5,623654	100

Source: Table 4, 'Distribution of population according to gender and educational status', 2006 National Census of Egypt, Central Agency for Public Mobilization and Statistics (CAPMAS), Cairo, 2007.

Table 3.4 Unemployment in Misr al-Qadima and all of Cairo (age 15 years and above: working-age population)

Location	Population	Formal Labor Force	Employed	Unemployed	Unemployment rate
Misr Al Qadima	162,697	70,523	60,745	34.778	19.7%
Cairo	5,034481	2,223992	1,984,231	504,061	10.78%

Source: Table 7, 'Labor force in the Cairo governorate', 2006 National Census of Egypt, Central Agency for Public Mobilization and Statistics (CAPMAS), Cairo, 2007.

(see Table 3.5). Exactly the same sectors also occupy the first three slots in terms of labour population in the Governorate of Cairo as a whole, with approximately 45 per cent of aggregate labour belonging to the formal sector (see Table 3.6). This reflects the relative growth of these sectors of economic activity nation-wide as a result of the Open Door and then liberalization policies of the 1970s and 1990s, which meant that an expansion in intermediary economic activities (construction contracting, wholesale and retail trading, etc.) was well in place to accompany the overriding macroeconomic features of that phase.[5]

For example, with the rise of *Infitah* and after the October 1973 war, a firm expansion in the building and construction sector was inevitable, with a surge in construction activities in almost all of Egypt (Assaad, 2007).[6] With that came a sizeable shortage in the supply of workers and contractors within that sector due to the increase in skilled labour migration to the Gulf states and the increasing demand for this type of labour in the post-*Infitah* era. The issue was quite grave, to the extent that the Egyptian government had to sponsor the establishment of the Training Organization of Ministry of Housing and Construction in 1975 to train and supply entrants to the construction sector (Assaad, 1993).

Fouad Soltan, Egypt's Minister of Tourism at the time the Economic Reform and Structural Adjustment Program (ERSAP) was established, and one of the key advocates of liberalization policies, clearly stated that the Open Door policy had contributed greatly to the 'rise in commercial activities at the expense of produc-tive ones. It is not the private sector that is responsible for this tendency, but the

Table 3.5 Employment in economic activity by sector in Misr al-Qadima

Economic Activity by sector	Population Employed	Economic Activity by sector	Population Employed	Economic Activity by sector	Population Employed	Economic Activity by sector	Population Employed
A	197	G	11,261	M	2,049	S	4,683
B	67	H	4,519	N	702	T	745
C	11,569	I	1,895	O	5,222	U	34
D	388	J	1,354	P	3,802	V	1,245
E	263	K	1,542	Q	2,431	W	1,358
F	9,416	L	53	R	333	X	65,128

Total
Unattached 97,569
Grand Total 162,697

Note: The key for economic activity by sector is: A, Agriculture; B, Mining; C, Middle & Complementary Industries; D, Electricity & Gas; E, Water Supplies, Sanitation, & Recycling; F, Building & Construction; G, Wholesale & Retail Trading; H, Storage & Transportation; I, Food & Beverage Catering; J, Information & Communication; K, Insurance & Financial Intermediaries; L, Real Estate; M, Specialist Scientific & Technical Services; N, Administrative Services; O, Civil Defense & Public Services; P, Education; Q, Health; R, Arts & Entertainment; S, Other services; T, Private housekeeping services; U, International Agencies & Organizations, Embassies ... etc; V, Economic activities that are formal yet not fully categorized; W, Unspecified; X, Total.

Source: Table 7, 'Labor force in the Cairo governorate', 2006 National Census of Egypt, Central Agency for Public Mobilization and Statistics (CAPMAS), Cairo, 2007.

Table 3.6 Employment in economic activity by sector in all of Cairo

Economic Activity by sector	Population Employed	Economic Activity by sector	Population Employed	Economic Activity by sector	Population Employed	Economic Activity by sector	Population Employed
A	8,212	G	419,759	M	83,571	S	70,979
B	2,484	H	153,309	N	26,965	T	29,512
C	306,232	I	52,083	O	189,807	U	1,384
D	22,157	J	46,221	P	164,602	V	78,867
E	12,829	K	41,373	Q	65,778	W	49,208
F	191,899	L	2,082	R	11,705	X	2,031,018
Total Unattached	3,003463						
Grand Total	5,034481						

Note: The key for economic activity by sector is outlined in Table 3.5. Note that despite the fact that the recorded rate of unemployment in Misr al-Qadima was around 20 per cent, more than 60 per cent of the total labour force was labelled as 'unattached' or unsuitable for placing into any formal classification of job occupancy. This reflects the considerable size of the informal sector, which absorbs an estimate of 35–40 per cent of the total labour force.

Source: Table 7, 'Labor force in the Cairo governorate', 2006 National Census of Egypt, Central Agency for Public Mobilization and Statistics (CAPMAS), Cairo, 2007.

Table 3.7 Population by desegregation of jobs in Misr al-Qadima

I	II	III	IV	V	VI	Total
VII	VIII	IX	Unspecified	Total	Unattached	
3,817	12,119	5,178	2,850	9,557	102	
18,105	5,826	6,127	1,447	65,128	97,569	162,697

Note: The key for is typology of jobs is: I, Legislators & Senior Administrators; II, Specialists of certain scientific skills; III, Technicians & Specialist Aides; IV, Writers; V, Employees in services, shops, and supermarkets; VI, Skilled labor in agriculture and hunting; VII, Artisans; VIII, Skilled labor in factories and medium and small industries; IX, Ordinary (unskilled) & Wage labor.

Source: Table 9, 'Distribution of population according to gender & typology of jobs', 2006 National Census of Egypt, Central Agency for Public Mobilization and Statistics (CAPMAS), Cairo, 2007.

Table 3.8 Population by desegregation of jobs in all of Cairo

I	II	III	IV	V	VI	Total
VII	VIII	IX	Unspecified	Total	Unattached	
154,627	483,906	225,218	127,685	324,461	5,611	
360,358	178,646	160,085	55,421	2,031018	3,003463	5,034481

Source: Table 9, 'Distribution of population according to gender & typology of jobs', 2006 National Census of Egypt, Central Agency for Public Mobilization and Statistics (CAPMAS), Cairo, 2007.

government that failed to follow a correct and clear economic policy able of encouraging productive activity' (Soliman 1998: 12–13). On aggregate, the post-*Infitah* years were characterized by an increase in financial and commercial activities, especially importation, at the expense of industrial activities. 'Starting from 1974, the structural change in the Egyptian economy enhanced the growth of the non-traded goods and services sector of the economy at the expense of the traded commodity sector' (Soliman, 1998: 12–13). Within the milieu of job typologies, artisans and employees in services, shops and supermarkets roughly accounted for 25 per cent of the total labour force within the formal sector in Misr al-Qadima, again signifying the importance of these typologies in this municipality.

Apart from the previously estimated 40–45 per cent of the labour force within the informal sector, obtaining an accurate indication of the size and influence of this sector remains a vastly dubious process. Yet, in spite of the lack of accurate data pertaining to the informal sector and henceforth the difficulty in analysing it as an economic sector, the estimate of its sheer size in Misr al-Qadima reflects its immense role in its polity, as will be displayed later in the course of analysing the socioeconomic characteristics of the lesser notabilities. Indeed, the considerable scope of the informal sector carries noteworthy implications for the popular quarters of Cairo, Misr al-Qadima included:

> By its nature the informal sector is characterized by ease of entry and low productivity. The first feature explains why this sector has accounted for the bulk of job creation in the recent past. On the other hand, the low productivity implies relatively lower wages; compared to the formal sector … The recently observed phenomenon of increasing urban poverty can be explained in terms of such structure.
>
> Ali and Elbadawi, 2002: 183

Therefore, despite the fact that the continuously growing informal sector is in reality absorbing a sizeable segment of the labour force, the meaningfulness of its role in alleviating poverty remains quite questionable. More often than not, the informal sector seems like the easy way out for unskilled and the uneducated labour force, and, apparently, the state does not often bother with the sort of training received or skills acquired by those entering the informal sector as they are seemingly employed and generate income, however minimal.

Misr al-Qadima is no exception to the this, and despite the shortage of verifiable data on the growth of the informal sector in this area over the past years, the incremental expansion of this sector can be observed in practice. With the adoption of ERSAP in the 1990s and the ongoing privatization and subsequent contraction of government and public sector employment (Assaad and Arntz, 2005), a sizeable portion of the labour force in the area was actually forced to either retire completely or join the informal sector:

> Employment growth in the civil service has slowed dramatically and much of the burden of employment creation has shifted to the private sector … The public sector['s share of total employment] has contracted significantly

in relative terms, from 39 percent in 1998 to 30 percent in 2006. In fact, the public enterprise has continued a trend of absolute decline; at a rate of 0.2 percent per annum ... Private sector employment has been growing in excess of 7 percent per annum, with the most dynamic growth being observed in informal regular wage employment and employment in household enterprise.

Assaad, 2007: 2

Indeed, in Misr al-Qadima, the accounts of the inhabitants tell dozens of stories about a wide variety of candy and cigarette kiosks, street vendors and sometimes house maintenance boutiques, all operating without license or government approval and all of which have been increasingly observable only since the mid-1990s.

When looking at the internal migration rates, one also finds that Misr al-Qadima has a relatively high rate of internal migration to other districts in Cairo and across Egypt compared with other districts within Cairo. In 2006, the average rate of labour force relocation from within Misr al-Qadima was 20 per cent of the total labour force, a figure that is considerably higher than that for other districts within Cairo (the overall rate of internal labour force relocation within the entire governorate standing at 15 per cent of the total labour force) (Central Agency for Public Mobilization and Statistics [CAPMAS], 2007). A logical justification for that relatively higher rate of internal migration would of course relate to the scarcity of employment opportunities within the area and the resultant tendency of the labour force to move to other localities looking for jobs.

The above-mentioned figures of internal migration are in fact applicable to those aged 15 years and above. Looking at the previous data for this portion of the population in Misr al-Qadima district, compared with the average of the Cairo Governorate as a whole, we can see that the rate of internal migration in Misr al-Qadima stands roughly at 11.1 per cent, which is lower than an approximately 16 per cent figure for the whole of Cairo. However, those who left Misr al-Qadima owing to permanent labour migration constitute approximately 30 per cent of all those who migrated beyond the boundaries of the district for various reasons (study, marriage/divorce, etc.) which is a higher rate than the average for Cairo for the same segment, which stood at almost only 23 per cent of the total number of those migrating out of Cairo (CAPMAS, 2007).

Although there is a lack of accurate data, it is noteworthy to mention here that Misr al-Qadima has also witnessed a sizeable rate of immigration to the area throughout various phases in its modern history. The main bulk of immigrants to the area have settled in 'Ain al-Sirra, the newer section of Misr al-Qadima, at the height of the wave of rural–urban migration that targetted Cairo in the 1950s and 1960s. For the most part, immigrants to the area came from the Sa'id (Upper Egypt) and ended up establishing strong ties of clanship and solidarity among the members of their respective families (as reported in the interviews). The impact of this scope of solidarity will be further portrayed in Chapters 4 and 5 in the course of scrutinizing the sociopolitical agency of the lesser notabilities of Misr al-Qadima.

The political map: contextualizing the polity of Misr al-Qadima

As one attempts to delve into the intricate details of the Misr al-Qadima polity, an overview of the political map of the area is indeed vital. The area that is known today as Misr al-Qadima is in fact an amalgamation of two main sections, the first being the old (historical) quarter of Old Cairo that has been standing for hundreds of years, as mentioned earlier. The second and relatively more recent part ('Ain al-Sirra) was constructed during the reign of Nasser in the late 1950s in line with the trend of building *al-masaken al-sha'biyya* or the popular neighbourhoods, which aimed at the time to provide affordable state-subsidized housing for the lower and lower-middle classes. With the gradual withering away of the social welfare system initially introduced by the Nasser regime with the advent of Sadat and the *Infitah* policies of the 1974, the neighbourhood in its entirety started to deteriorate considerably in terms of services and infrastructure. Furthermore, the subsidies that were granted by the state to the residents, in order to waive the rent and other utility bills paid by the inhabitants, had been cancelled by the mid-1970s.

Consequently, two main features coloured the socioeconomic structure of Misr al-Qadima as well as many other popular quarters in Cairo at the time. First, a sizeable wave of youth migration to the states of the Cooperation Council for the Arab States of the Gulf (GCC) was underway, coinciding with the oil boom of the 1970s, which led to an apparent drain in all kinds of skilled labour in the area. The surge in this trend was so high that, for example, in one of the blocks (small apartment buildings), seven out of the 10 young men living in the building all eventually travelled to the GCC (Abdallah and Siam, 1996).

Second, and despite the nominal stature that the educated (university graduates) of the area upheld as the 'intellectual' grouping, the scarcity of skilled labour in the aftermath of the wave of GCC migration actually made this category of the labour force, which comprised electricians, plumbers, construction workers, etc, the *de facto* elite (notables) of the community. And, gradually, it seemed that some alteration in the value system of a large portion of the area's inhabitants took place with regard to the importance of profit-making as a main indicator in judging a person's credibility and stature. The status of a '*kasseeb*' (a person who is talented in making profit quickly) became almost equivalent to that of a doctor or professor (Abdallah and Siam, 1996).

These features influenced the scheme of political participation in the area. In the 1980s, the state had already initiated a façade of democracy by allowing three parties to operate, the most powerful of which was the state-sponsored National Democratic Party (NDP). By and large, the people of the area, who have been historically politicized since the times of Nasser, the popular political leader who practically housed those people in Misr al-Qadima, were naturally sympathetic towards the left-leaning *Tagamou'* party, the political entity that somehow championed the socialist and populist policies that the people of a district such as Misr al-Qadima would support. Another viable venue for activism and participation was the *Gam'eyat Tanmeyat al-mogtama'* (Community Development Society), a multifaceted service centre run by volunteer activists from diverse political backgrounds. This society provided the neighbourhood with a wide variety of health and educational services. However, from the 1980s onwards, the influence of the secular and leftist political forces started giving way to that of the various Islamist groups that have since then been clearly on the rise (Abdallah and Siam, 1996; Misr al-Qadima locals, 2008).

Despite the humble efforts that the leftist and secular activists are still attempting to make through the Community Development Society and other similar service centres, the playground for political action has been massively controlled by the Islamists, with some competition from the NDP until its demise in 2011. The amount of resources and networks channelled and orchestrated by the figures and institutions affiliated to these two factions, and the considerable power and influence that they have subsequently possessed, make it practically impossible for any other party or group of activists to stand in their face. Even after the outbreak of the January 25 revolution, the sheer size of the resources and networks orchestrated by these mid-level figures and the fact that most of them have not been exposed to any legal measures, as opposed for instance to some of the bigger NDP leaders who were imprisoned, suggest that there is not going to be a great deal of change with regard to the power and influence that such figures possess on the popular level. In the chapters that follow, more focus will be placed on the socioeconomic and political roles of such figures.

Misr al-Qadima today

A study carried out on a random sample of approximately 1,500 Misr al-Qadima inhabitants from varying age groups and socioeconomic classes sheds some light on the political realities of the area. Although this study was conducted prior to the January 25 revolution, which means that some of its indicators could be considered to be obsolete, especially regarding the inhabitants who turned out to vote and their perception of or affiliation to the dissolved NDP, the array of findings portrayed by the study helps to sketch a rough understanding of the political scene within the neighbourhood prior to January 25.

According to the study, 55 per cent of those surveyed perceived themselves as being politically uninterested, while only 13.3 per cent had what was described by the study as a 'relatively high level of political awareness', compared with 32.1 per cent in the middle range of political awareness and 39.3 per cent with a relatively low level of political awareness. Roughly 15 per cent of those surveyed had very little or no political awareness at all (Abdelfattah, 2007: 10–40).[7] Concerning formal political participation, 35 per cent did not participate politically whatsoever, and 64.2 per cent had only some sort of minimal political participation. Only 17 per cent of the sample held a valid voting card and had participated in the 2005 parliamentary elections, while 2 per cent had some sort of association with or membership of a political party or organization (Table 3.9). The main motivation driving the majority of the respondents to join political entities was, primarily, having friends and relatives in the political party; this was the rationale cited by 20.5 per cent of those who were members of parties. Among the other reasons cited for joining political parties and organizations, there was the

Table 3.9 Participation in civil society organizations in Misr al-Qadima

Activity	Percentage
Membership in NGOs	0.9
Membership in unions and syndicates	5.7
Membership in political parties	2

Source: Reproduced from Abdelfattah (2007).

expected benefit and services that were likely to be provided to the prospective member. Here, it is also noteworthy that over 25 per cent of all those enrolled in parties belonged to the then-ruling NDP, with the rest of the responding members scattered among other political parties (Abdelfattah, 2007: 10–40).

Political bribery was described by a sizeable portion of the respondents as a reality in the Misr al-Qadima district. A total of 45 per cent of those who were surveyed reckoned that voters usually went for the candidate who paid more for their votes, and 44.4 per cent considered the candidate's ability to provide services to the area's inhabitants as the main rationale for voters selecting their prospective representatives in the municipal and judicial councils. Overall, there seems to be a correlation between the demography of Misr al-Qadima, in terms of housing, income level, degree of education, etc., and the level of political awareness and participation of its people. At the time the study was conducted, it appears that political participation and awareness in Misr al-Qadima was less among the female population (Table 3.10), those who were uneducated and low-income earners (Abdelfattah, 2007: 22).

In fact, the first indicator concerning voter turnout after January 25 was the constitutional referendum, which showed a considerable surge in the percentage of voters in comparison to the elections and referendums held under the Mubarak regime. The turnout in Misr al-Qadima was around 50 per cent of the total number of eligible voters, a rate that was slightly higher than the national average, which was 45 per cent ('Referendum Results', 2011).[8] When it comes to active participation in political parties, however, not a lot has changed. Noting of course that it might still be quite premature to make a judgement of the actual change in this indicator over the few months that followed the demise of the regime, the fact still remains that Misr al-Qadima's inhabitants, and indeed most Egyptians, remain unaffiliated to particular political parties in terms of ideologies, political platforms and policies, etc.[9] This is likely to continue until there is an awareness of the various political parties and familiarity with choosing political allegiances based on policy and practice, rather than the persona or the character of one figure or another. The people's disenchantment with political parties is also likely to remain until the political parties are capable of developing into active political entities with clear-cut programmes and policy options.

When compared with the dissolved NDP and the political cadres associated with it, and as will be shown in the following chapters, the Muslim Brotherhood and other Islamists seem to have a comparatively sound presence in the poorer

Table 3.10 Political participation by gender

Level of Political Participation	Percentage among the Male population	Percentage among the Female population	Total Percentage
Negligible or non-existent	29.4	44.4	35.3
Weak	70	55.1	64.2
Average	0.6	0.5	0.55

Source: Reproduced from Abdelfattah (2007).

areas. Essentially, the political Islamists, in particular the Muslim Brotherhood, are more active and efficient in the areas where the mosques of al-Jamm'eyya al-Shar'eyya (JS) operate. As will be shown in Chapter 4, there is a close association between the Muslim Brotherhood and the JS. Although, officially, the JS is supposed to be an apolitical, service-oriented non-governmental organization, in reality this is not the case. On the level of the official discourse, the non-governmental organization ensures that it does not publicize the moral and material support that it actually provides to the cadres of the Muslim Brotherhood (Abdallah and Siam, 1996). Within Misr al-Qadima, and in the Dar Essalam district, known to be one of the low-income communities in the area, Islamists are considerably popular, as opposed, for instance, to Misr al-Qadima proper, which is relatively more urbanized and better off economically. With the increasing deterioration of services provided by the state, there was a fertile ground for such sociopolitical forces to intervene and play the role that the state is normally expected to fulfil, as will be shown in Chapters 4 and 5.

Conclusions: the polity of lesser notables

The findings mentioned above indicate that, throughout the Mubarak regime, with a state that was increasingly absent from the everyday affairs of the inhabitants and moreover often perceived with distrust and disappointment by the populace of Misr al-Qadima, political participation on the terms of the state was highly unlikely. Instead, understanding political participation in the wider scope of resisting or rejecting the status quo imposed by the state and working towards changing everyday realities, as portrayed in Chapter 1, one might in fact find that the residents of Misr al-Qadima were politically engaged. As displayed earlier in the context of the first chapter, patron–client networks of support are therefore one other form of disseminating resources, and the residents of Misr al-Qadima were quite aware of that and tended to seek the relevant intermediaries who were capable of best delivering the necessary resources. This scope of patron–client networks has been arguably re-emphasized with the state withdrawal displayed by *Infitah* and then with the neoliberal policies of ERSAP in the 1990s.

The logical intermediaries of this patron–client stratagem in Misr al-Qadima, along with a multitude of other popular quarters in Cairo, are the lesser notables. This intermediary role carries with it also a sort of sociopolitical agency that cannot go unnoticed. If the state is not willing to or capable of reaching the populace directly, the intermediaries are the logical solution to establish such a linkage , which makes them the fulfillers of highly important sociopolitical and economic roles. In this arena of political patronage, Islamists, represented by the Muslim Brotherhood, have had a considerably successful track record of patron–client networking; this will be dealt with in the course of Chapter 4.

Overall, this evidence also shows that, in Misr al-Qadima, there is fertile ground for sociopolitical intermediaries to flourish. This is a key factor in consolidating the sort of political agency that is maintained by the lesser notabilities. The rise in the political role of the lesser notabilities in Cairo's popular quarters is noteworthy. Those lesser notables have existed in these (popular) areas for quite some time, and there are similarities of continuing linkage between them and the traditional figures of authority in the Egyptian *harra*, such as the *futuwwa* and *ibn al-balad*. As we now see, the state is gradually withdrawing, and such figures are reappearing on the political scene to fill some political vacuum. In the aftermath of the state's withdrawal from the arena of administering the affairs of the popular polity, it is indeed logical that such figures would emerge to represent their communities politically, even if this would be done informally and via customary practices.

This chapter aimed to dissect some of the socioeconomic and political features of the Misr al-Qadima polity. The socioeconomic indicators reflect the fact that the role of the state as the main guarantor of services, employment and subsidies is increasingly shrinking. This means that the state has been virtually absent from the daily affairs of the populace and, as a result, it has been only logical for various non-state individual and organizational actors to claim the socioeconomic and political roles that the state has abandoned, as will be discussed in Chapters 4 and 5.

The next chapter tackles the role of the Islamic social institutions in fulfilling some of the functionalities that had been previously maintained by the state, and will explore the linkages these Islamic social institutions have with the Muslim Brotherhood in Misr al-Qadima. By and large, the allegiances that have been formulated between the lesser notabilities and political organizations, such as the Muslim Brotherhood, show only that the political agency of those lesser intermediaries is indeed a determining factor that plays an important role in drawing the political map of the popular polities of Cairo in the contemporary era.

4 The Muslim Brotherhood, al-Jamm'eyya al-Shar'eyya and networks of support in Misr al-Qadima

The role of the lesser notables

Overview of the Muslim Brotherhood in Cairo's popular polities

The Muslim Brotherhood (MB) has been a key player and had various degrees of influence and success within the Egyptian polity ever since its foundation in the 1920s. Throughout its comparatively vast history, the MB has maintained a fluctuating relationship with the different political regimes that have governed the country throughout these eight decades or so. Out of this multiplicity of regimes, the Mubarak regime, particularly in the post-9/11 phase, adopted a relatively pragmatic approach in dealing with the MB, an approach that mainly depended on targeting the financial and administrative networks of the group and imprisoning the leading cadres that facilitated the operation of these networks (*Al-Ahram*, 15 January 2007). The Mubarak regime realized that the threat posed by the interlinked web of patron–client bonds that was efficiently maintained by the MB was quite grave, to the extent that it required the enforced expulsion of the MB from within the Egyptian polity. This tactic was not fruitful in offsetting the elevating prowess of the MB, and eventually the regime was not successful in its attempt to trace and block the bulk of financial and administrative resources of the MB. After the demise of the Mubarak regime, the legal ban that had been imposed on the MB for decades was finally removed, and the movement established its own political party, the Freedom and Justice Party.

This chapter aims to portray the mechanisms and structural foundations underlying the scheme of political patronage employed by the MB in the pre-January 25 phase, particularly during the rule of the Mubarak regime. In doing so, it focuses on the manifestations of this patron–client stratagem at the level of state–society relations and the role played by the lesser notabilities in such a structure, with a special focus on the case of Misr al-Qadima.

The MB: an overview

In 1929, Hassan Al Banna, an Islamic scholar who was at the time working as a school teacher, founded the MB in the town of Ismailia, on the banks of the Suez Canal. From its onset, the MB was in essence a grassroots movement that aimed to address the masses or, put differently, the disenfranchised classes that represented the majority of the Egyptian population at the time. Throughout the 1930s:

> The [MB] Society began to put into practice, an Islamic ideology that was unusual in several respects. It was, first of all, an ideology of disenfranchised classes. In a country where most political movements (including liberal and modernist ones) were products of the landed aristocracy and the urban elite, the Brotherhood became the voice of the educated middle and lower middle classes (and to a lesser extent of workers and peasants) and the means by which they demanded political participation. Throughout the decade, the Society placed increasing emphasis on social justice; closing the gap between the classes (and thus restoring the egalitarianism of the early Muslims) became one of its main objectives.
>
> History of the Muslim Brotherhood in Egypt, 2008

In fact, Hassan Al Banna echoed an ongoing dissatisfaction of the upper class and the class system in its entirety. In his own words, 'According to Islam everyone is equal ... Thus, we see that Islam does not approve of the class system' (History of the Muslim Brotherhood in Egypt, 2008).

The MB was predominantly a reformist grassroots movement, with the main objective of infiltrating Egyptian society from within by establishing an expansive set of networks among the various echelons of the community. For Al Banna and the chief founders of the group, only when this infiltration expanded and became properly consolidated within society would the establishment of the Islamic state be fully actualized (Naguib, 2005). Historically, the structure of the MB reflected a somewhat egalitarian system that was more in favour with the middle and lower classes, as opposed to the mainly elitist political parties that had mostly been dominant in the pre-1952 era. In practice, the structure of the MB that was set at the time has remained more or less the same until today. The chief governing body of the group, the 12-member Guidance Bureau, was, and still is, the de facto Executive Board of the MB, with the General Guide at its apex. The Shura (consultation) council was also set, comprising 90 members and mandated with the task of electing the 12 members of the Guidance Bureau and voting on the prime policies and decisions upheld by the MB. All over the country, the reservoir of cadres that feed into the Shura Council and the Guidance Bureau have come from the 'local branches [which] were organized into districts [and] whose administration had a large measure of autonomy ... The Society's structure remained decentralized, so that branches could continue to operate if the police arrested leading members' (History of the Muslim Brotherhood in Egypt, 2008).

During the post-Second World War era, the MB grew massively. The society continued to expand the scope and magnitude of its social welfare activities to the Egyptian community, 'setting up hospitals, clinics and pharmacies, schools offering technical and academic courses for boys, girls and adults; and small factories to help remedy post-war unemployment' (History of the Muslim Brotherhood in Egypt, 2008).

The MB after 1952

In the period following 1952, the relationship between the MB and the new regime was a fluctuating one. In the first few years, there was a loose alliance in the making between the military regime and the MB as it was quite obvious that the regime needed some foundational basis of grassroots popularity to consolidate its rule. And of course the MB was the best candidate for the role, especially in the aftermath of the demise of the popularity and appeal that the liberal and modernist parties had previously at street level. This demise followed the failure of the secular/liberal project, led by Al Wafd Party, in the face of colonial hegemony, namely the British occupation and the newly established Zionist state in 1948 (Aly, 2004).

However, the honeymoon between the regime and the MB did not last for more than a few years, after which Nasser realized that the MB posed an existential threat to his rule that had to be eradicated. In 1955, the Nasser regime launched a brutal wave of attacks on the MB that targetted not only the main cadres of the movement by massive arrests, trials and executions, but also the foundational infrastructure of the MB via the nationalization of the bulk of Islamic social institutions (ISIs) that the group had developed over nearly three decades of intensive mobilization. In fact, the Nasser regime adopted an array of policies that aimed to tighten the grip of the state over the activities of ISIs, ranging from issuing specific laws that put the funding of these Islamic institutions under firm state monitoring and supervision, to banning entire organizations from upholding their activities, as was the case of al-Jamm'eyya al-Shar'eyya (JS) in 1966[1] (Shiha, 2003).

For instance, in 1964, the state issued non-governmental organization (NGO) law 32, which mandated all civil society organizations to obtain the approval of the state regarding their sources of funding prior to carrying out any fundraising activities. The law was interpreted as an attempt to stifle the ISIs in particular, given the growing concern that had developed in the regime pertaining to their growing budgets at that juncture. Ultimately, the policy was indeed effective, and many bureaucratic obstacles were put in the path of most ISIs, which halted the ability of organizations such as the JS to maintain the same level of services they had provided prior to issuance of the law. With the JS in particular, the Nasser regime went as far as to dissolve the board of the entire organization, banning it from pursuing its activities for a few months in 1966 before allowing it back with a newly appointed chairman, General Abdelrahim Amin, a regime appointee and, in effect, a watchdog for the Nasser regime over the activities of the organization (Shiha, 2003; JS members, July and August 2008).

Moreover, with the introduction of agricultural reform policies and the expansion of the welfare state system of the Nasser regime, the state had met considerable successes in co-opting a plethora of social segments within the middle and the lower-middle classes, eventually offsetting the gap that had previously been filled by MB activities (Naguib, 2005). Nonetheless, the relative success of the state in counteracting the MB proved to be temporary as, with the advent of the

Sadat regime and the Open Door policies of 1974, the MB yet again came to the forefront of the Egyptian polity as the prime sociopolitical movement.

Sadat and the revival of the MB

Indeed, there was a multitude of factors that nurtured the resurgence of the MB as a viable sociopolitical force in the 1970s. First off, there was the failure of Nasser's Arab Socialist project, which was embodied in the 1967 defeat. Also, in pragmatic and politicoeconomic terms, the Egyptian state had met with only minimal success in attaining its developmental goals with the demise of Nasser (Naguib, 2005).[2] In the aftermath of the massive bloating experienced by the state during the Nasser years, the co-optation by and social contract of the welfare state with the middle/lower-middle classes was no longer in place. With that came the advent of Sadat's *Infitah* (Open Door) policies in 1974 and his accompanying determination to empower Islamist sociopolitical forces within the Egyptian polity in order to offset the threat that the leftist student movement and the socialist Nasserites posed to his rule. The result was a wide resurgence in the scope and magnitude of MB activities, but this time under the sponsorship of the Sadat regime (Aly, 2004).[3]

The resurgence of the MB's networks of resources: the patron–client stratagem

There were primarily three chief sectors that formulated the backbone of the MB's resurgence in 1970s: the communal mosques (which lie outside state jurisdiction);[4] the ISIs, which operated in the services, cultural, educational and health realms; and the capitalist Islamist institutions (corporations, print shops, etc.). By the mid-1990s, thousands of mosques were operating under the direct sponsorship of the MB and other Islamist groups. The wide scope of these mosques and their geographical distribution over mostly all of Egypt enabled the MB to vitalize its welfare system and extensively widen its social base. In addition, by the year 2000, there were over 5,000 ISIs operating under the umbrella of the MB. A few of these social institutions provided the basic seemingly apolitical services of teaching the Koran and organizing *hajj* trips, yet the majority of them were focusing their activities within the services sectors, establishing clinics, educational facilities and vocational training centres, with a particular emphasis on concentrating these activities in Cairo's popular quarters (Naguib, 2005). Often:

> the criteria for enjoying the opportunities and benefits in Islamic social welfare institutions is adherence to Islam (including the codes of social and family morality) also [operating within] networks of patronage and client-ship, communal membership and loyalty, and possibly political allegiance.
>
> Clark, 2004: 946

Some of these ISIs, such as JS, functioned on a nationwide scale with an overall membership that surpassed 2 million members in 2005 (Negm, 1996).

The sustainability of the funding and the overarching web of patron–client networks maintained by the MB play an important role in consolidating the power of the movement, especially within the poorer/popular quarters of Cairo. This was ensured by the utilization of the *zakat* funds that were channelled through mosques, and extensive endowments deriving from Islamic banks and corporations, mainly owned by businessmen who are MB affiliates and sympathizers. This cycle of funding is further enhanced by the reinvestment of the profits of these Islamic ventures in low-cost services in the arena of education and health and other fundraising activities in the realm of religious books and audiovisual products.[5] Logically speaking, 'the social dimension of these acts of charity allows for the development of bonds and ties between givers and recipients, in some cases taking the form of relations of patronage and clientelism' (S. Ismail, 2006: 81).

A vivid example of one of the most prominent Islamist ventures utilized by the MB here is that of the small and medium-sized Islamist publishing houses, which played an immense role in the revival of Islamic rhetoric. Those houses also operated a recruitment facility that guaranteed a continuous breed of cadres benefitting from, and helping to publicize, the ideological spectrum of the MB (MB cadres, June 2009). Overall, the Islamist spectrum of patron–client networks was predominantly decentralized and entrenched within the societal structure of the community which made most of the regime's attempts to uproot or even contain it virtually impractical.

The 1974 Infitah: the socioeconomic context of MB resurgence

The *Infitah* (Open Door) policy was an economic liberalization programme that began with optimism in the early 1970s. Bromley and Bush (1994: 202) state:

> Sadat's strategy was to harness Arab capital, western technology and Egyptian resources by removing Nasser's statist shackles which were seen to have restricted growth and initiative. Yet during this initiative, fees from the Suez Canal, oil sales and remittances accounted for more than three-quarters of current account receipts and more than 40 cent of GDP by the mid-1980s, compared with just 6 per cent in 1974. Per capita income doubled during the oil boom years between 1974–1985 from US$334 in 1974 to US$700 in 1984. The economy was therefore acutely vulnerable to external shocks, and in order to sustain high growth rates after the mid-1980s, Egypt accumulated massive balance of payments deficits and a huge foreign debt. The balance of payments deficit reached US$5.3bn in 1986, equal to 15 per cent of GDP, and the budget deficit reached US$8.8bn, some 23 per cent of GDP.

As a result, by the end of the 1970s, the Egyptian state was in a dire economic situation that was reflected in its inability to pay off the services of an accumulating foreign debt. Tables 4.1 and 4.2 show aspects of the financial crisis that the state was going through in the early 1980s.

Table 4.1 Egypt's external debt ($ millions)

Year	1971	1973	1975	1976	1977	1978	1979	1980
Total Outstanding	2,319.4	2,912.9	7,254	8,780.9	12,607	14,311.6	16,037.2	17,385.7

Source: Aulas, M.C. (1982) *Sadat's Egypt: A Balance Sheet*, MERIP Reports No. 107, Egypt in the New Middle East, July–August.

Table 4.2 Balance of trade, 1974–1979 ($ millions)

Merchandise	Year					
	1974	1975	1976	1977	1978	1979
Export	1671	1566	1609	1992	1984	2512
Import	3467	4321	4288	4513	5283	6675
Net	(1796)	(2755)	(2679)	(2521)	(3299)	(4163)

Source: Aulas, M.C. (1982) *Sadat's Egypt: A Balance Sheet*, MERIP Reports No. 107, Egypt in the New Middle East, July–August.

On aggregate, this socioeconomic context of the state after 1974, characterized by an incremental erosion of its ability to allocate resources and provide services to society, provided a very favourable environment for the establishment and further growth and consolidation of the MB's co-optation strategies, especially among the lower-middle and lower socioeconomic classes. Empirical evidence displays that, for instance, whereas the labour force witnessed an aggregate increase of 2.2 per cent between 1976 and 1986, the increase in number of university graduates was approximately 7.5 per cent in the same period. Yet those fresh graduates could no longer be contained within the public and governmental sector, as was the case during the Nasser era. The logical outcome was a massive upsurge in the rate of unemployment from 2.1 per cent in 1969 to 7.7 per cent in 1976, and ultimately 12.2 per cent and 14.4 per cent in 1985 and 1996 respectively. In 1996, university graduates constituted more than 25 per cent of the total unemployed population. Of course this virtual army of unemployed university graduates was a potential reservoir for co-optation by the MB. Table 4.3 shows the exponential increase in the number of university graduates between 1964 and 1984 (Naguib, 2005: 91).

The rise of the lesser notable cadres in the popular polities of Cairo

In the milieu of the low-income communities, *Infitah* policies also facilitated the ascent of a socioeconomic class described by Alan Richards as 'nouveaux riche comprador elements', a class that 'has both benefited from the (partial) economic liberalization and encouraged the regime to continue to liberalize' (Richards,

Table 4.3 Increase in university graduates

Year	Total Number of University Graduates Nationwide	Percentage of Growth
1964/65	16,268	100% (base year)
1974/5	41,916	257.6%
1984/5	115,744	711%

Source: Naguib, S. (2005) *Al Ikhwan Al Moslemoun: Ro'eya Ishtirakeyya*, Cairo: Center for Socialist Studies, p.88.

1984: 325). As mentioned earlier, the ascent of this class in the Egyptian society was virtually completely associated with the adoption of *Infitah* owing to the sorts of economic opportunity that it made available, primarily the speculative and commercial activities on which such nouveau riche elements thrived. This nouveau riche typology indeed constitutes the pool from which the lesser sociopolitical notabilities rose to prominence in the popular communities. In actuality, scrutinizing the MB's tactics in Cairo's popular quarters, where the ground is quite fertile for the sort of co-optation nurtured by the MB to take place, sheds some light on the success of the movement in consolidating its power base within the Cairene polity, primarily via co-opting relatively large segments of this socioeconomic class.

As reviewed before in the case of Misr al-Qadima, the social fabric is fairly heterogeneous in a variety of Cairo's popular quarters, with sizeable segments of petty bourgeoisie, professional lower and lower-middle classes as well as rural–urban migrants. Most of these segments share the suffering from burdensome economic conditions, where unemployment prevails and adequate health and educational services are considered a rare commodity. In such a context, the conditions for the proliferation of *da'wa* (connoting the publicity of the MB's value system and the parallel recruitment of cadres who are capable of disseminating the relevant networks) and the consolidation of the social welfare system (establishing an alternative scheme of social institutions *vis-à-vis* the modern/secular state) become quite favourable indeed. Clark (2004: 948) states:

> The Islamist project, therefore, is an attempt to create a seemingly seamless web of religion, politics, charity, and all forms of activism. All of these realms should reinforce one another and promote public virtue and personal piety. In this invention of tradition, the concept of *da'wa* becomes central. Beyond simply proselytizing or preaching (as traditionally defined), *da'wa* becomes the very act of "activating" Islam through deed in all spheres of life ... ISIs form just one part of a larger network of Islamist institutions; the intention of which is to activate or apply Islam to all spheres of life. Working or volunteering for or donating to an ISI as a form of activist *da'wa* is an important component of Islamist identity.

Henceforth, the role of the *do'at* (the cadres responsible for undertaking the proliferation of *da'wa*) is somewhat central as it fulfils the essential function of creating viable networks of members and sympathizers.

In order for such cadres to actualize their role proper, they often have to have certain qualities that enable them to disseminate *da'wa* among the communities within which they dwell. The profile of a sizeable proportion of these cadres fits the typology of the lesser notable that was introduced earlier in Chapters 1 and 2; their educational background is largely irrelevant, as long as they are well versed in the foundations of the Koran and Hadith, which enables them to portray an image of piety and moral goodness that typically endows them the title of Hajj. In addition, their possession of material resources and networks within the community, primarily depending on the infiltration of familial ties and the kinds of commercial activity they are involved in, is also pivotal as it facilitates the consolidation of the socioeconomic status maintained by these lesser notables within various echelons of the popular polity (JS, June and July 2008; MB Cadres, June–July 2008).

The machinations by which *da'wa* operates also tell a lot about the extent of its entrenchment within the Egyptian polity, especially in the popular quarters. By and large, there are three main interrelated categories of *da'wa*. First, there is the individual scheme of action. The *do'at* are regularly present in the mosques before and after prayers, usually leading the prayers by virtue of being well versed in the Koran and Hadith. They are also active at centres offering social welfare and services, which grants such cadres a natural opportunity to communicate with a variety of segments from the population on a personal level. After these cadres have identified potential recruits, they work on winning them over by empowering them and advising them to start playing a role in the observation of Islamic codes of morality first at the level of the nuclear family and in the workplace, and then on the level of the neighbourhood as a whole.

The second main hub of *da'wa* is the public domain, which involves a greater level of participation and utilization of public venues, such as mosques and awareness centres, to call for and popularize the values, principles and objectives of the Islamist project.[6] Then there is also the published domain of printed material, which makes good use of the plethora of publishing houses and print shops associated with MB figures and also plays a crucial role in spreading the values and ideas of the Islamist project in a simplified manner, predominantly through small booklets that are easy to print and read (Naguib, 2005: 92–3; MB cadres, June 2009).

Thus, the Islamist project of the MB is, in essence, an attempt to reshape the boundaries of state–society relations:

> An essential aspect of Islamist identity therefore is the creation of alternative institutions to those of the state. ISIs are not only alternative institutions to state institutions but represent the foundations of an alternative society. They stand in direct contrast to secular states that appear to have lost their concern for the poor. By offering successful social welfare services in the name of

Islam to their fellow citizens that their respective states seem unwilling or unable to do, ISIs represent an ideological and practical alternative to the present system. As institutions, ISIs are more than just representative of a populist ideology; they are that ideology put into practice and central to the Islamist vision of a new society and Islamist identity.

Clark, 2004: 949

Indeed, the Islamist project of the MB has been quite successful in cultivating an amalgam of networks that has, in many cases, filled the vacuum left by the secular state. Later in this chapter, more light will be shed on the role of ISIs and the linkages they maintain with the MB.

Socioeconomic background of MB cadres: the professional middle class and the syndicates

Since its outset, the MB has been a social movement that has aimed to attain change within the society via a bottom-up approach, infiltrating the popular echelons of the Egyptian community and mobilizing the masses at the grassroots level. However, when looking at the operative cadres of the MB, one finds that, almost predominantly, the key players have always been, one way or another, associated with the professional and technocratic middle class. The founding father himself, Al Banna, was a school teacher, and most of the members of the Guidance Bureau in the pre-1952 era also came from various technocratic backgrounds. In the Nasser era, most of the active cadres of the MB came from similar professional middle-class backgrounds, being engineers, physicians, teachers, etc.

Today, the strong societal and political footholds of the MB rest within the professional middle class. The paramount dominance and mobilization that the MB has at this level can be portrayed, for instance, at the level of the professional syndicates and associations. The boards of the doctors' syndicate, the engineers' syndicate and the lawyers' syndicate, among other professional syndicates, have all been run and administered by MB cadres who have won their seats in considerably free elections since 1991. This does not necessarily imply that the majority of Egypt's professional middle class are MB adherents and supporters, but rather that the MB has been fairly savvy and successful in mobilizing support among these circles, quite prudently organizing their activities and pivoting their candidates in the electoral venues of the syndicates (Doctors' syndicate members, July 2009).

Also, from the viewpoint of the ruling authority, the realm of the syndicates could be relatively less confrontational and challenging to the political regime than, say, the realm of parliamentary elections. Therefore allowing the MB to operate in the syndicates seemed like an affordable cost that could be tolerated by the regime and used at times as a bargaining tool with the MB, in return for the MB's reduction of its outright political mobilization in the public domain (Doctors' syndicate members, July 2009). Subsequently, the predominance of the MB in the context of the professional syndicates peaked in the early 1990s.

In 1992, out of the 61 board members who had been elected to the engineers' syndicate; 45 belonged to the MB. Table 4.4 shows the gradual progression of the MB candidates in the doctors' syndicates elections in the period between 1985 and 1992.

Overall, and despite the increasing limitations and restrictions placed by the Mubarak regime on the cadres of the MB in the ranks of the professional syndicates, such cadres have still constituted the most viable and well-organized blocs in most all of the professional syndicates to date.

As a result of the incremental domination of the MB and affiliated Islamist cadres over the professional syndicates, the state eventually placed the country's two biggest professional syndicates, the doctors' and the engineers' syndicates, under judicial guardianship with the pretext that the two syndicates were advocating the political causes of the banned MB. Subsequently, the resilient MB presence again re-emerged within the branch syndicates, those subsidiary syndicates operating on the level of governorates and which are still considered as strong footholds for the MB (Charbel, 2009).[7]

In addition to focusing its efforts on dominating the professional associations, as shown in the case of the syndicates, the MB was also adamant that it would infiltrate the popular polities of Cairo and the other cities, as these areas were important constituents according to the mission and vision of the group, as stated earlier. So the intermediary agents, represented by various categories of lesser notables and other sociopolitical forces, played an instrumental role in reaching out to the popular polities. Whereas educated and professional individuals have predominantly constituted the reservoir of policy and decision-making circles in the MB, the grassroots basis has also been crucial in spreading the *da'wa* and services of the MB at the popular level. This dichotomy is displayed, for example, when one compares some of the MB's most influential operative cadres, such as the 88 MB MPs elected in 2005 on the one hand, and other notable cadres such as the merchants/businessmen who belong to the category of the 'lesser notables', on the other.

Whereas the first group mostly belongs to the professional middle class, the second shares the characteristics of the popular lesser notables, with a humble educational background, a strong network of familial/clan ties within their

Table 4.4 The Muslim Brotherhood's electoral votes in the doctors' syndicate (1985–1992)

Year	Total number of members registered in Doctors' Syndicate	Total number of members that voted in elections	Total number of members that voted for the MB candidates
1985	60,000	12,600	5000 (40% of total votes)
1992	90,000	21,000	15,000 (71% of total votes)

Source: Naguib, S. (2005) *Al Ikhwan Al Moslemoun: Ro'eya Ishtirakeyya*, Cairo: Center for Socialist Studies, p. 96.

popular polities, and, quite often, a set of commercial activities and a scope of accumulated wealth that enables them to dispense various resources and services among respective subordinates. Sometimes also the boundaries between these two categories become somewhat blurred, and indeed a few prominent cadres in the ranks of the MB possess some features of this lesser notability persona despite their professional middle-class backgrounds.[8]

The MPs of the MB

Most of the MB parliamentarians have a middle-class background, yet the majority of them could also be considered to be active and influential cadres at the popular level in their constituencies. In fact, looking at the organizational affiliation that the (2005–10) 88 MB parliamentarians have with the MB, one finds that these MPs come from two main sectors: first, the *da'wa* (religious awareness), and second the social services sector. These two prime affiliations make the MB cadres involved with them deeply tied to the communities within which they operate. The first sector, *da'wa*, includes the social religious leader-ships that spread religious awareness to the populace in the alleys of the popular neighbourhoods and villages. By doing this, the key figures in this sector are the popular leaderships who, for example, lead the people in prayers, present the Friday sermons and provide the needy with monthly allowances from the local mosques.[9] The second sector, the social services division, is composed of the cadres affiliated to the *ber* (charity) committee of the MB. Those members are the operative cadres who work with and facilitate a wide variety of social organizations and networks that provide an array of services to the low-income communities (Tammam, August 2008).[10]

In parliament, the diverse professional backgrounds of the MPs give the MB a profound edge as a political bloc:

> The Brotherhood has historically drawn many of its members from the professions. [This] gives the bloc in-house specialists to rely upon when Parliament takes up technical issues. Brotherhood MPs include, among others, doctors, dentists, engineers, lawyers, scientists, academics and legal experts.
>
> Tammam, August 2008

According to one MB parliamentarian, 'As 88, we have specialists from all fields and we are better able to support one another and facilitate cooperation' (Shehata and Stacher, 2006). Yet having such a professional middle-class background, this group of MB parliamentarians still also possesses attrib-utes of popular leadership and sound connectedness with their grassroots basis. As mentioned above, those MPs come from two main backgrounds – *da'wa* and the social services sector – and in both cases they live and work in their constituencies, which only reinforces their role as popular leaders. Table 4.5 displays the occupational backgrounds of the (2005–2010) MB parliamentarians.

Table 4.5 Professional occupations of the 88 MPs of the Muslim Brotherhood in the 2005 parliament

Profession	Number of MPs	Percentage out of the MB bloc
Workers	9	10
Preachers and Imams	8	9
Doctors and Pharmacists	8	9
Agricultural Engineers	2	2
Lawyers	6	7
Engineers	12	14
Accountants	6	7
Businessmen	2	2
Teachers	7	8
University Professors	11	13
State Employees	17	19
Total	88	100

Source: *Political Participation in the 2005 Parliamentary Elections* (2006), Cairo: Egyptian Association for Community Participation Enhancement, p. 285.

Socioeconomic class stratification and ideologies within the MB: pragmatists versus conservatives

Hence, the socioeconomic background of MB members shapes, to a great extent, the kind of role that they are to play in the ranks of the organization. But other factors too, such as the generation and regional origin from which the member comes, help to define the sort of mandate and sometimes even the line of thought by which the MB members are classified. By and large, two main political orientations do exist within the MB:

> The pragmatists are more willing to negotiate with the Egyptian state, so as to be ready to take advantage of cracks in the authoritarian order. It is this group of activists who engineered the takeover of most of the professional syndicates and served in parliamentary coalitions with the Wafd and Labor Parties during the 1980s ... They are ideologically flexible and open to compromise [and] frame their positions on the basis of political and civil rights; notions of rule of law, rather than moral or religious rectitude, drive their thinking and strategy. The other leading trend—more ideologically rigid—also has membership in the various departments, and on the Shura Council and Guidance Office. They tend to view politics as a byproduct of the outreach mission, which one performs by being a consummate Muslim to convert citizens to an Islamic lifestyle.
>
> Stacher, 2009

Several observers suggest that the conservative group is in fact the driving force behind the bulk of tactics and policies adopted by the MB, and that this was confirmed by the attacks of the Mubarak regime that were intensified in the few years before its downfall. The two main factors that help to shape the political orientation of MB members are primarily the geographical (rural/urban) origin and the generation (age group) of the cadre.

Generally, the older generations of the MB seem to be more conservative than the younger ones. Nonetheless, even within the younger generations, those who originate from the countryside seem to align themselves more to the conservative line in terms of their sociopolitical views and policies. Essam El Erian, the prominent MB cadre and head of the Political Bureau of the group, notes:

> Most newcomers to the Guidance Office in the past decade have come from the provinces rather than the cities. They have brought with them the stereotypical villager's "traditional" values: suspicion of the new, unquestioning loyalty to leadership and lack of critical thinking skills ... The countryside is affecting the Muslim Brotherhood more than the Muslim Brotherhood is affecting it.
>
> Stacher, 2009

Another factor that contributes to the increasing power of rural as opposed to urban MB cadres is of course the fact that the urban centres of Cairo and Giza were the target of most of the policing campaigns and repressive tactics exercised by the previous regime, in contrast to the rural areas, which gave the MB cadres in these relatively remote areas the opportunity to organize more freely and operate under less pressure.

Thus, with this ongoing struggle for the soul of the MB, it seems that the conservatives are advancing further than the reformists in the milieu of the MB's prime policy-making bodies: the 12-member Guidance Bureau and the 90-member Shura Council. The rural–urban divide appears to be a decisive factor in this process, with the influence of provincial, mostly conservative, cadres on the rise in the face of the urbanized and seemingly more liberal and pragmatic MB cadres.

The financial arm of the MB's lesser notables

The consolidation of patron–client networks of services and resources has been a prime factor in the success of the MB as a political organization, particularly at the popular level. These networks are indeed fairly infiltrative within several businesses and commercial activities in addition to a plethora of ISIs, which has made the task of the state quite complicated as it has targetted and attempted to terminate such networks. According to the patron–client model presented in Chapter 1, political patronage is mainly carried out via a pyramidal relationship that rests on the dissemination of resources from the top cadres to subordinate incumbents until they reach the grassroots level of the community. As will be shown in this chapter, such patronage networks are, in the case of the MB, predominantly orchestrated via individual cadres that also utilize the ISIs operational at the popular level in order to extend this distributional process to the popular communities. By and large, the previous regime found it plausible to try to halt the activities of the individual cadres themselves rather than the ISIs within which they were operating.

In the early days of 2007, the Egyptian state launched a sizeable campaign against the 'financial arm' of the MB all over Egypt, arresting hundreds of MB cadres who were allegedly linked to a variety of commercial ventures that were funding the wide scope of activities of the MB (*Al-Ahram*, 15 January 2007). The state's clampdown on the MB was mostly an attempt to secure consolidation of the power of the National Democratic Party (NDP) in the face of the MB. The list of the arrested cadres included chief MB figures such as Khairat al-Shater and Hassan Malek:[11]

> They were eventually charged with money laundering, financing banned political activity and trying to revive the Brotherhood's paramilitary wing. A month after the arrests, on January 28, Egypt's prosecutor-general froze al-Shatir's assets, along with those of 29 others. Businesses owned by Brothers, including several publishing houses and import/export firms, a pharmaceuticals manufacturer and a construction company were closed, the merchandise confiscated. The frozen assets have been valued at tens of millions of dollars ... Seizing the assets of major financiers such as Khairat al-Shatir might discourage others from funding the organization. The measures could also have been intended to drain the Brotherhood's campaign coffers before the June [municipal] elections.
>
> Shehata and Stacher, 2007

By then, it was quite obvious for the ruling regime that the Islamist forces operating on various levels within the Egyptian polity had succeeded in posing themselves within the already existing structure of the state system, building interconnected alliances and networks with state authorities and personnel along the way.

The case of El Swerky, the famous merchant and owner of Al Tawhid Wal Noor[12] and also a prominent MB affiliate, was yet another episode in the clampdown on the MB's lesser notables in the course of what the state media came to describe as the 'financial arm' of the MB. El Swerky in fact belonged to the category of those whom the MB could depend upon for endowing resources and services among its adherents and supporters. However, the state exercised a type of malevolent patronage upon him – letting him fall from grace. When it was felt that El Swerky was increasingly threatening the popularity of other competing NDP figures with his growing influence in the popular district of Shobra, and amassing a sizeable amount of wealth that was supporting the activities of the MB along the way, a law suit was virtually fabricated for him by the state and he was imprisoned (MB affiliates, 2008). Perhaps this is a significant difference between the two typologies of social base enjoyed by the NDP and the MB: whereas similar NDP-affiliated figures possessed a great deal of state patronage and protection, the MB suffered from a lack of this state protection, and this was sometimes used against them to offset their influence, as we have seen in the case of Al Tawhid Wal Noor.

Resourcing MB and ISI activities

The sources of funding for the MB and the affiliated ISIs, such as the JS, which will be elaborated upon in the coming section, are quite diverse, surpassing the stratum of benevolent individual contributions. Islamic businesses (owned and operated by MB members and affiliates) operate as investment depositories as well as legitimization façades for the resources of the MB. These businesses, which are usually operative as sizeable firms of the wholesale-retail trade, furniture and home appliances stores, clothes and garment factories, etc., are mostly utilized by the MB in order to hire and expand the network of individual incumbents and financial resources in a legitimate fashion that is active under the legal codes that govern the market. In the course of the aforementioned 2007 state clampdown on the MB, some state apparatuses, such as the police and the General Prosecutor, have considered this to be an act of 'money laundry' due to the MB's illegal nature as a banned political organization at the time, as well as the direct links that the capital invested in most of these ventures had with the financial resources and contributions of key MB figures and personnel. And the cycle continues: the MB pumps more money into these firms, this is subsequently invested, and the revenues generated are then used to fund MB activities and so forth. According to state officials, the profit made by such firms is utilized to fund the MB's various activities. The clampdown launched by state authorities against the so-called 'financial arm' of the MB allegedly aimed to dry up the resources that were circulating within such ventures (*Al-Ahram*, 7 February 2008).[13]

Here, an important query comes to mind: does the financing of MB and ISI activities take place at the local (district) level or do the poorer areas receive support from elsewhere within the organization? In fact, the MB and ISIs such as the JS enjoy a certain degree of decentralization. Whereas the JS has a hierarchical structure that allows for the presence of a quasi-board of directors at the level of the district or neighbourhood, in the MB the decision-making process regarding the financial allocation and distribution of resources among the various regions and districts of Egypt rests mainly within the Guidance Bureau and the MB Shura Council. Such decisions are usually implemented by the Financial Committee, which is mainly composed of a group of businessmen and merchants responsible for ensuring the proper allocation of such resources. The leading figures within the Financial Committee include MB figures such as Khairat Al-Shater and Hassan Malek (*Al-Ahram*, 15 January 2007; MB affiliates, 2008). By virtue of its mandate, and also due to the aforementioned observation on the relative absence of the then-ruling NDP and its affiliates from low-income communities in the urban popular and rural areas, the MB tends to focus a sizeable portion of its financial and administrative resources on such poorer or popular areas.

Another question then arises concerning the sources of funding for the MB and the ISIs and whether or not they are all domestic, as claimed by the majority of cadres and policy-makers in these organizations. For example, the official books of the JS say that the society's sources of income are all domestic, stemming from the endowments of benevolent and wealthy sympathizers and membership fees from all over Egypt. However, there are claims that some sizeable funding for the JS and other ISIs comes also from wealthy contributors in the Gulf countries, particularly Saudi Arabia.[14] This is more observed in the case of the MB, which, in particular in the heyday of its resurgence within the Egyptian polity in the 1970s, depended to a great deal on the financial support of the cadres that lived, worked and had considerable investments in the states of the Cooperation Council for the Arab States of the Gulf, especially in Saudi Arabia (Naguib, 2005; MB, 2009).

The friendly relations that existed between the Mubarak regime and its counterpart in Saudi Arabia might lead one to discard the possibility of this financial support happening at the level of Saudi state institutions for instance. However, close relationships between the ISIs in the two countries have often been reported. A case in point here is the Islamic Solidarity Committee, an offshoot of the Egyptian doctors' syndicate that had a mandate to organize nationwide campaigns to gather donations in the 1990s for the major Muslim crisis areas, mainly Bosnia, Afghanistan and of course Palestine. The Committee had sound ties with a multiplicity of donors from Saudi Arabia and other Gulf states and was eventually dissolved by the Egyptian state in 2000 due to the nature of its activities, which were perceived as a direct non-state threat to the sovereignty of the Egyptian state (Syndicate doctors, 2009).

Overall, in its attempts to curb the MB, the Mubarak regime selected the path of targetting the individual cadres of the MB as this was easier to justify and publicize on the grounds of criminal or security/political threats. Yet the tale is quite different when it comes to the ISIs, those service-oriented NGOs that provide a very wide range of services to the common people in the popular quarters of Cairo and elsewhere. This will be dissected further in the next section as we delve into an exemplar case of what could be described as Egypt's most powerful ISI – the JS.

JS: background and history

The JS is arguably Egypt's largest and most powerful ISI. The array of activities sponsored by the JS includes a wide variety of services that range from building and renovating mosques and religious institutes to the sponsorship of orphans and aid and pension programmes for the needy. The scale of JS's activities is so great that more than 261,000 children had been enrolled in its orphan sponsorship programme by the end of 2000. The sources of funding for the JS are predominantly local and, according to its own balance sheets, the society does not receive funding from abroad. Its sources include, first, the annual membership fee of the members, which is around 100 LE per member (with the total number of JS members in 2000 surpassing 1.5 million across Egypt). Furthermore, other sources of funding also include the endowments, donations and various types of *waqf* granted to the society from the wealthy, in addition to the support it receives from the government as a recognized charitable organization (Shiha, 2003).

On aggregate, the JS has an extensive network of funding and a budget that is bigger than the budgets of several government ministries. The society has over 120 items for expenditure on welfare; under item 12, for example, which is dedicated to orphanage sponsorship, the society had specified a budget surpassing that of the entire Ministry of Social Affairs. These organizations work under the label of Islam, of which *zakat* is a main pillar. Noting that the majority of the revenue of the society depends on *zakat*, which is, by and large, paid by every Muslim regardless of his or her social or economic background, one finds that it is only sensible for such organizations to control such massive budgets (Bahi, 2008; JS members, 2008).

Organizational structure

As illustrated in Figure 4.1, the hierarchical structure of the JS is quite elaborate and is characterized by a great degree of systemic institutionalization. The General Assembly is the inclusive entity on which all branches of the JS across Egypt are represented by three members, with one vote for each branch. The assembly meets on an annual basis and is typically mandated with tasks relating to the approval of the annual budget, the appointment of the General Treasurer and the election of the Executive Board. This Executive Board, on the other hand, is the *de facto* governing body of the JS. It comprises 15 members, who are usually nominated by the Senior Ulama Committee, and in fact the CEO of the Board has to be from the Senior Ulama Committee itself. The Executive Board is responsible for selecting the General Secretary from its members and monitoring and approving the bulk of the financial activities of the Society.

The chief committees shown in Figure 4.1 are self-explanatory, but it is worth noting here that exactly the same structure of committees is also present at the provincial level. For the purpose of the study at hand, one of the most important committees is the *da'wa* committee, mandated with the task of gathering and channelling funds. This committee is also considered as the hub where the *do'at* of the Society operate (Shiha, 2003).

The socioeconomic background of JS members varies in accordance with their occupation within the hierarchy and the role they are supposed to play in the context of the JS. For instance, looking at the Executive Board that was operational in the mid-1990s, one finds that the 15 members of the board were mainly an amalgamation of Azharites (religious scholars from Azhar University) and small or medium-sized merchants. Whereas the presence of the Azharites was indeed crucial in order to provide the board with expertise in the realm of religious guidance, the merchants and the businessmen were mainly responsible for supervising the financial affairs and allocation of resources relating to the society's social welfare activities (Negm, 1996).

In spite of the massive scale upon which the JS operates, the degree of dedication of its members and their connectedness with the society are relatively high. In a cross-sectional analysis carried out on a random sample of JS members, it was shown that, despite the relatively mediocre educational background of those members (almost 35 per cent barely having a high-school certificate), the majority had a clear vision of the goals and objectives of the society and were capable of identifying the aspired targets that they were expected to achieve in terms of accomplishing tasks and the recruitment of new cadres. On aggregate,

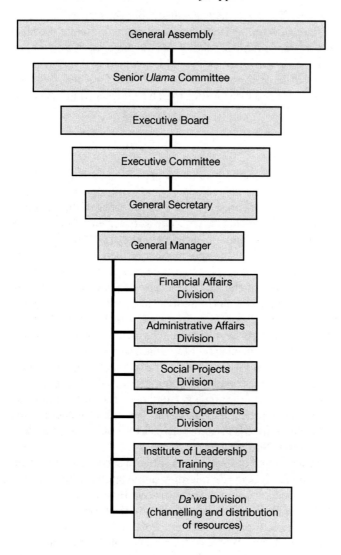

Figure 4.1 The hierarchical structure of al-Jammʻeyya al-Sharʻeyya.

Source: Nagwan F. Shiha (2003) *The Accountability of NGOs Applied to Egypt: The Case of Al Jammʻeya Al Sharʻeyya and Al Saʻid Cooperative for Education & Development.* Cairo: Faculty of Economics & Political Science, Cairo University.

the degree of accountability of the society as a whole, in terms of the consistency of the General Assembly and Executive Board meetings, and meeting the government's deadlines for the submission of monitoring and evaluation reports and financial audits, was quite high compared with that of other local organizations working in the field of social services. In addition, the fact that the JS depends mainly on local sources of funding, as opposed to the majority of the civil society organizations that primarily depend on foreign donations in undertaking their activities, makes the JS one of the most autonomous civil society organizations in Egypt (Shiha, 2003).

The political role of the JS and its relationship to the MB

Since its establishment, the JS has been, according to its own charter, an apolitical civic organization that aims to spread Islamic awareness and provide social and economic services to the needy and deprived segments of the society. However, in practical terms, the picture is somewhat different. Looking at the typology of activities undertaken by the JS, particularly in the realm of social welfare, as pointed out earlier, one notes that the scope of services provided by the JS substitutes a plethora of roles that are supposed to be fulfilled by the state. And with the resurgence of the MB in the 1970s, there has been a growing relationship of cooperation and synchronization between the JS and the activities of the MB. In addition to the pragmatic affiliation that exists between the MB and the JS, the ideological spectrum of the society also overlapped with the goals and objectives of the MB (Negm, 1996).

For example, in the period between 1975 and 1978, *Al-E'tessam*, the monthly periodical and mouthpiece of the society, repeatedly called for the right of the MB to be allowed back into the political arena as a recognized political force. The same periodical also led a vigorous attack on the regime in 1985, adopting the discourse of Mamoun Al-Hodaiby, the General Guide of the MB at the time, by describing the government as a minority-rule entity that captured rule by terrorism and forgery. *Al E'tessam* similarly also nominated the MB as the best alternative to the ruling party, in light of the regime's irregularities against MB candidates in the municipal elections of the same year (Ashour, 1985). Eventually, in 1990, the Mubarak regime dissolved the board of the JS due to its close ties with the MB. At that juncture, most of the members of the board were either fully fledged MB members or sympathizers. This confrontation forced the JS to play down its affiliation with the MB, making it less pronounced, but in practice the linkages between the JS and the MB have continued to prevail up to the present (Negm, 1996).

The affiliation between the JS and the MB takes place on two main levels, the first being the ideological realm, where one notes that the discourse of the society on macro-socioeconomic and political issues, as well as the micro-level daily affairs spectrum, corresponds largely with that of the MB. Here the example of *Al E'tessam* stands out, as the publication voiced the discourse of not only the JS, but also the MB. More importantly, however, at a pragmatic level, the interrelated scope of activities goes far beyond a mere resemblance of projects. For the most part, congruent membership of the two organizations is a recurrent case, and it takes place on all echelons of the JS, as we have previously seen with the case of the JS board. In the lower echelons of the JS, many cadres hold dual membership of the MB and the JS. For example, some of the health-care and educational centres run by the society employ almost completely MB members and affiliates. In addition, the Orphanage Sponsorship Program, the JS's biggest social project to date, is funded by MB members and affiliates (Negm, 1996).[15] The following section sheds more light on the political role of the JS in Misr al-Qadima.

Political Islam in Misr al-Qadima: the MB and the JS

The case of the JS in Misr al-Qadima highlights some relevant findings concerning the political role of the society in Cairo's popular quarters. As mentioned earlier, the growth of the JS in Misr al-Qadima coincided with the expansion of its activities in a variety of Cairo's popular quarters. The Misr al-Qadima JS branch was established in the early 1970s, in line with the resurgence of the ISIs in low-income communities since the Nasser era. The JS gradually grew in terms of the scope and magnitude of the services it provided, which coincided with the incremental withdrawal of the state from the arena of social welfare. Initially, the JS branch focused its efforts on building new small mosques and renovating old ones. In addition to regular prayers, these mosques were also utilized in social welfare activities such as providing aid to poorer families and organizing private tuition for students outside prayer time. The society eventually also succeeded in constructing a new kindergarten for the area's families. Then, in 1979, the presence of the JS in the area was boosted tremendously when the MB candidate, Hajj Hassan Al Gamal, became the Misr al-Qadima MP in parliament. Al Gamal's role in enhancing the profile of the JS branch was instrumental. Backed by the MB, he supplied the mosques and the youth who belong to the JS with copious financial and moral support. For the MB, this constituency was immensely important as it represented a strong electoral and political foothold for the MB, which was, after all, still considered as the political melting pot supported by the majority of the Islamist forces in the area (Abdallah and Siam, 1996).

The spectrum of services and activities provided by the JS in Misr al-Qadima progressed at a steady pace, coinciding with the consolidation and continuous growth of political Islamism across Egypt, and by the mid-1990s the society was, by and large, the biggest, richest and most resourceful social welfare institution in the entire quarter. In addition to the aforementioned basic services with which it initiated its activities in the area, the JS now sponsors a vocational training centre for the youth of the area and organizes on regular basis a variety of small markets and conventions for selling products manufactured by the JS members and affiliates. The association between the cadres working in the JS and the MB is known now in the area and at times of elections, most recently during the 2005 parliamentary elections, the resources, networks and personnel of the society, are usually mobilized to support MB candidates. Primarily due to the state-imposed ban on the involvement of the JS in political activities, the mobilization of most of these JS cadres and the usage of the resources in their acquisition for the benefit of the MB is often portrayed by the JS as a voluntary scheme of support based on the personal initiative of its individual members. JS members extend their support to the MB during elections via a variety of activities that include utilizing JS offices to organize campaigning activities for MB candidates, distributing and hanging campaign material and posters, and publicizing MB candidates among networks of families, friends and personal contacts in the area (Abdallah and Siam, 1996; Misr al-Qadima residents, 2009).

The JS in Misr al-Qadima – Hajj Mohamed: the lesser notable in action?

A field visit to the JS headquarters in Misr al-Qadima was crucial in order to gain a closer look at the society and understand the scope of its operational activities in the area. In fact, the JS building in Misr al-Qadima is very hard to miss; on the main road connecting between 'Ain al-Sirra and Manial, the signposts of the JS stand out, signifying the paramount location of its headquarters (Figure 4.2). At first, it is somewhat unclear whether the entry to the office of the society is the same as that of the mosque but then, as the housekeeper of the mosque ensures that visitors should take their shoes off upon entering the premises, it can be seen that the JS office is located literally inside the mosque.[16]

Hajj Mohamed was the person in charge of the JS office is Misr al-Qadima. From our first meeting, one could note some resemblance between Hajj Mohamed's profile and that of the lesser notable. He introduced himself as a

Figure 4.2 Headquarters of the al-Jamm'eyya al-Shar'eyya in Misr al-Qadima.

leather merchant and a son of the area, in which he had spent all his life. Later on in the discussion, Hajj Mohamed clarified that he thought the educational background of the person is irrelevant if he wanted to join the ranks of the JS, as long as he held a good reputation in the area and possessed piety and moral goodness. In essence, Hajj Mohamed was probably referring to people like himself, as he holds only a high-school diploma, yet by piety and charitable activities he had been able to reach this position at the apex of the JS in Misr al-Qadima (Hajj Mohamed, 2008).[17]

From the onset, Hajj Mohamed assured me that the society is mainly a charitable organization. He said that there is no other entity that provides such a scope of services to the people of the area, and asserted that the JS is entirely self-funded, which reinforces its autonomy.[18] The society's programme of action is divided into three main sectors: the awareness (*da'wa*) sector, the aid sector and the activities sector.

Awareness

The *da'wa* component lies at the heart of the society's goals and objectives, according to Hajj Mohamed. Raising the religious awareness of the people of the area is of paramount importance, and this is achieved via regular lectures by key Islamic figures, lessons on the Koran all year round, discount trips for the *'umra* and *hajj*, a comprehensive library that is open to the public and a periodical journal by the society, *Al Tibyan*, which is apparently the successor of the *Al E'tessam* periodical cited earlier (Hajj Mohamed, 2008).

Aid

The aid programme orchestrated by the society is probably the strongest and most viable means by which the JS can extend its services to the populace. Under this programme, The *kafala* (sponsorship) projects that aim to support orphans, widows, female divorcees and patients in need are quite extensive and usually provide those segments of society with financial help in the form of grants. In most cases, a monthly stipend is also maintained in order to assist those groups with meeting their financial commitments, and, in case of senior citizens, a pension programme is also available. The orphanage project is probably the society's biggest venture, both according to Hajj Mohamed and as was previously stated in the course of this study. The contribution of local people to fundraising for this project is viewed as an incentive in itself; it is a service provided to them by giving them a window of opportunity to take part in a charitable activity that will

> bring them closer to God. There is a certain system by which this project operates and it depends on extended networking. Every new member joining the program, i.e. supplying the Society with donations, will be expected to bring in five new donors and so on.
>
> Hajj Mohamed, 2008[19]

Indeed, the society follows a fairly modern scheme of organizational management, as stated by other interviewees, predominantly depending on mapping, networking, etc:

> The Society [JS] is very well organized, and it is indeed successful in infiltrating popular neighborhoods, often via modern methods of social work that are usually followed in social service NGOs ... They begin by mapping the area, detecting the social and economic background of its population and the heads of the households within the neighborhood, then start networking with the families, knowing their needs and the kind of services they require. For instance, when the head of the household on their payroll passes away, they immediately allocate the necessary funds for the funeral and provide the family with a monthly income. They also sponsor the children, and supply the family with the basic clothing and school expenses in accordance with the number of their children enrolled in schools.
>
> Bahi, 2008[20]

This outlook on JS activities in the community is also in line with the narratives of the local people, who assured me that the social services provided by the JS and its personnel in times of dire need have often surpassed similar support services that the state might sometimes provide.

Many Misr al-Qadima residents recall the aftermath of the 1992 earthquake when many houses in the neighbourhood either collapsed or were severely damaged, with thousands of people subsequently left homeless. The JS, along with other ISIs, was actually much quicker to react than the state authorities, and from the first day they initiated a massive campaign to supply the people with blankets and food supplies. After a few days, the police intervened and banned the ISIs from pursuing their campaign, claiming that it was illegal as it had not been authorized by the relevant state authorities, primarily the Ministry of Social Affairs. But it was not until a few days later that the Ministry started to react and supplied those people with food and temporary shelters (Misr al-Qadima locals, 2008).[21] Here, it is safe to conclude that this personalized scheme of services provided by the JS is unmatched by the government or the NDP and that it undoubtedly plays a immense role in increasing the popularity of the MB on the ground, especially in the popular quarters, where economic and social hardships prevail.

Under the aid programme of the JS, direct donations are additionally granted to the people of the area, supplying them with their basic needs: covers and sheets in the winter, food supplies, etc. There is also a marriage services section, which provides matchmaking services to young Muslim men and women who prefer a guaranteed and well-monitored process for selecting of their future partners. The medical sector is crucial too as it supplies the needy with a variety of medical services that are free of charge. One of the most important service units under the aid programme is the emergency fund, which is allocated for individuals' immediate needs (such as the demolition of their home, exposure to an accident, etc.) (Hajj Mohamed, 2008).

Activities

In addition to the aid and awareness programmes, the activities sector is mainly concerned with needs that require more specialized expertise and involves a sizeable amount of outsourcing of human resources that might not be available within the ranks of the society:

> Most importantly, there is the specialized daycare center for the children and the daily medical clinic which employs skilled physicians and nurses who are capable of dealing with the more severe medical conditions that require a high level of specialized medical attention.
>
> Hajj Mohamed, 2008

In fact, the comparatively wide scope of services provided by the JS in Misr al-Qadima means that some of these services will have to be relatively limited compared with others. Setting the priorities of expenditure takes place at the local (branch) level according to the amount of funding allocated from the central JS authority, and here a degree of decentralization is somewhat granted to the local branches, allowing them to set their own priorities in accordance with the socio-economic and political particularities of the area in which the branch operates. Overall, Hajj Mohamed reckons that the most important thing that the JS has done for the community of Misr al-Qadima is to help its people with some needs that had not been addressed by the state (Figure 4.3):

> Look outside … you will find this bread outlet across the road. This booth was funded and supervised by the Society. It is such mundane services that assist the simple people here the most … In the midst of the recent bread/ food crisis, people were in dire need for these basic necessities and the government was too busy to help them. This is when we come in!
>
> Hajj Mohamed, 2008

On the other hand, Hajj Mohamed assured me that the activities of the JS have no political connotations:

> We have no political agenda … we help the people of the area become better Muslims and provide them with some of the means by which they can over-come their daily hardships, and if you want to call this political action then be it, but, on the official level of the JS, we have nothing to do with elections or party politics.

Nevertheless, despite Hajj Mohamed's reluctance to admit the linkage with the MB or other Islamist activists, it is obvious to see, right outside, posters displaying the MB candidates for parliament and the Municipal Council hanging over the walls of the JS headquarters. Here, sympathy with the MB is rather explicit in terms of the rhetoric and political views adopted by JS members and affiliates, and this is reflected in the sizeable degree of coordination present at

Figure 4.3 Bread outlet run by al-Jamm'eyya al-Shar'eyya.

the operative level, as highlighted earlier. When asked about their political view-points and allegiances, those JS members who were willing to voice their opinion stated that, unlike the current state politicians and regime personnel, who are tarnished with corruption and have ignored the demands of the people for years, the MB actually deserves the support of the people in the community as it has, to the contrary, served the area and provided it with some basic services (JS cadres, 2008).

The JS and the state in Misr al-Qadima: a note on the priorities and limitations of the JS

By and large, the influential role played by the JS in Cairo's popular quarters is defined and further consolidated by the sociopolitical vacuum created as a result of the ongoing state withdrawal from the arena of welfare services. The bulk of services provided by the JS can be classified into two prime categories: first, a set of services that aim to fill the gaps in areas that have been almost totally aban-doned by the state at certain points, such as the above-mentioned example of the 1992 earthquake catastrophe; and, second, an array of services that compete with services that are supposedly provided by the state but, for a multitude of reasons, have deteriorated in terms of quality and/or quantity. The example of the JS bread outlets belongs to the latter category.

Hence, it could be argued that the JS has been quite savvy in prioritizing its set of activities in Misr al-Qadima and similar popular quarters of Cairo. After all, and despite its considerably massive scope of activities, the JS is a social organization that has a specific budget with limitations, and it has to prioritize its activities according to the budget available. The JS has more than 120 items of activity on its agenda, but if we are to interpret the prioritization of these activities according to the budget allocated, we will find that, according to its annual plan and budget ,and as testified by members of the society, the *kafala* programmes lie at the core of the JS service sectors, with a budget that exceeded 150 million LE ($US 28 million) in 2000 (Naguib, 2005). These programmes typically aim to provide low-income earners and needy segments of society such as orphans, widowers, etc., with constant financial and material support in the form of stipends and regular personalized social counselling. For example, it is reported that more than 250,000 children all over the country are enrolled in the Orphanage Program, making it the biggest and perhaps most viable orphanage service programme in all Egypt (JS members, 2009). In doing so, the JS has firmly established its standing within the Cairene popular quarters as an advocate of the poor and the disenfranchised classes. Unsurprisingly, when asked where they would go in case of extreme financial need or if there was a sudden catastrophe or a crisis in the area, even those who did not consider themselves sympathetic towards the Islamist tendencies of the JS responded that the JS was a much more reliable and helpful social service organization than the NDP office and most of its affiliated NGOs in Misr al-Qadima. In fact, most of the respondents said that they would be more likely to seek assistance from the JS in such cases (JS members and Misr al-Qadima residents, 2009).

ISIs and the MB in Misr al-Qadima: 'Ain al-Sirra versus Misr al-Qadima proper

As illustrated in Chapter 3, Misr al-Qadima is divided into two main districts: Misr al-Qadima proper (the old quarter) and 'Ain al-Sirra, the relatively newer quarter that was constructed in the 1950s. The two areas share some commonalities owing to their geographical proximity, particularly in terms of their socioeconomic features, i.e. the prime economic problems they suffer from, the predominant issues of state withdrawal from the services sector, the deteriorating status of their infrastructural utilities, etc. Yet the two also have some clear differences, for example with regard to the professional and socioeconomic backgrounds of their inhabitants and the geographical origin of their current residents. A higher number of rural–urban immigrants reside in 'Ain al-Sirra than in Misr al-Qadima proper for example, and this in turn considerably affects the types of political affiliation and activity within the two areas.[22]

The socioeconomic differences between the two quarters help to shape the kinds of ISI and MB policies and activities in each of them. On aggregate, it could be argued that, although they are actively operational in the two areas, the MB and the ISIs are more present and influential in 'Ain al-Sirra than they are in Misr al-Qadima proper. Hajj Ahmed Najar, the then-secretary of the *shiyakha* (district) of the NDP in Misr al-Qadima, echoed this observation when he stated that the overall socioeconomic profile of the various constituencies of Misr al-Qadima plays a paramount role in determining the prowess of the MB and the affiliated ISIs within these areas (Hajj Ahmed Najar, 2008).

Hajj Najar runs a car accessories shop in the area as well as a small travel agency, and his family has resided there for several generations. He also operated the People's Services Office of the NDP. By and large, Najar could be considered as a lesser notable with a respectable social and economic profile, based on his profitable business and sound reputation as a family man who has strong ties with the members of his community. Najar had a sizeable political role to fulfil as an NDP member and a close aide and advisor to the MPs and the Municipal Council members of the area at that time. When asked whether he thought there was a greater presence of the MB than the NDP at the popular level in Misr al-Qadima, he stated that it varied according to the socioeconomic status of the area. The Sunni mosque had been used by some MB figures, but by that time there was a tight security-hold on such venues and they were not operational. 'A few years ago these venues were operational but there seems to be a security revival nowadays that was largely successful in halting the activities of their cadres.' In other areas, however, the MB cadres might be more active due to the prevalent socioeconomic context. In some areas of 'Ain al-Sirra, for instance, and due to the harsh conditions in which people were living, it was easier for the MB to gain more popularity. People there are mainly manual labourers and suffer from extremely rough living conditions, so it is easier for them to be polarized in the direction of the Islamists or in the direction of drugs and crime (Hajj Ahmed Najar, 2008).

Whereas the prime beneficiaries of the social welfare activities of the ISIs and the MB mostly reside within the poorer areas of Misr al-Qadima, the cadres that in return ensure the delivery of these services, i.e. the doctors and the social workers who organize such activities, are not necessarily from these areas. A sizeable number of those cadres

> have to be trained or educated in certain fields in order to be able to deliver these services ... The expertise is not always available in the poorer areas of 'Ain al-Sirra itself and, subsequently, such cadres have to be recruited from other places; such as Misr al-Qadima proper or Manial for instance.
>
> Hajj Ahmed Najar, 2008

The politicization of Misr al-Qadima: mechanisms of political co-optation of the MB and NDP

As stated in Chapter 3, in the pre-January 25 phase, the level of participation of the people of Misr al-Qadima in the voting process in municipal and parliamentary elections was directly linked to the harsh economic conditions from which the majority of the locals of the area suffered. In order to shed more light on some of the features of this process, a meeting with Hajj Sayyed Abdelaal was put in place. Hajj Abdelaal was described by the people of the locale as a Misr al-Qadima veteran and a 'vote expert'. He had been a prominent leather craftsman and merchant but was now retired due to the lack of commercial opportunities for profiteering from small-sized skin tannery and manufacturing workshops, thanks to the oligopoly of the major leather tycoons of the area, which will be elaborated upon in further detail in Chapter 5 in the testimonies of NDP cadre, Hannan Al-Saidi and others. Hajj Abdelaal was suffering from very harsh economic conditions and had to feed an entire family. He considered himself a politicized person who had experienced the ins and outs of the Misr al-Qadima polity and had a few things to say about the political affairs of his district.

Hajj Abdelaal said that he had stopped working primarily because of the market recession and instability caused by the quasi-monopoly exercised by a few big names in the field of skin processing and tannery. In practical terms, it became too costly for people like him to maintain their businesses in the face of those unequally titanic competitors. 'Now I have friends who help me with the daily costs of living ... I have the responsibility of feeding a big family that is composed of five sons and four grandchildren' (Hajj Abdelaal, 2008). Many other people are exposed to the conditions from which Hajj Abdelaal suffered. A multitude of people had profitable professions that now lay idle owing to the new economic realities that had forced them out of business.[23] Hajj Abdelaal insisted that these new realities had to be fully considered in order to comprehend the so-called process of 'political participation' in the area of Misr al-Qadima:

> Political participation is existent but it is entirely influenced by money and people who participate get direct financial benefit. There is no secrecy in this matter and candidates compete to pay more for the voters ... All of my sons are registered in the electoral schedules and get direct material benefit for their participation. The benefits vary from hard cash to bags of basic supplies (oil, sugar, bread, etc.) that are usually distributed among voters prior to and during the electoral season.
>
> Hajj Abdelaal, 2008

Having been a resident of the area for 50 years or so, Hajj Abdelaal affirmed that this mode of voter bribery and state absence had been on the rise since the 1995 and the 2000 parliamentary elections and had reached a peak during the 2005 elections. These recent years had witnessed an immense surge in the role played by businessmen and an increasing disappearance of the state. People in this district and other similar popular quarters had been suffering from an apparent lack of the basic services that were supposed to be provided by the state. Hajj Abdelaal said that, for example, if a person looked just around the corner here, he or she would find that the main bread outlet in the neighbourhood had been idle for 10 years or so. This might seem like a simple service, yet it is crucial for the lives of the thousands of citizens residing in the area, for whom the scarcity of the state-subsidized bread produced by such outlets has been a major problem:

> Now the reopening of this outlet has become the item on the top of the list of all the local council candidates in our area. Will the elected ones succeed in doing that? Well, thus far it is not clear, but if they do then the credit will go for them and not for the state. The state has turned a blind eye on us and millions of others that are like us all over the country.
>
> Hajj Abdelaal, 2008

The mechanisms of voter bribery were not only exercised by NDP candidates: other political forces did the same as well. In fact, most of the viable candidates in the 2005 and the supplementary 2007 parliamentary elections were either NDP or independent candidates not belonging to an official political grouping. Practically speaking, there were no other political forces (parties) that played any meaningful role in the area, except for the MB of course, whose candidates usually run as independents. This has in part been caused by the official ban imposed on the MB, which forced all of their candidates to run as independent candidates. On the other hand, throughout those elections, the NDP depended on its well-known policy of co-opting the winning independent candidates into its ranks after the elections.[24] And this change did not seem to bother the voters at all as it did not really matter to them which party the candidate would adhere to after winning. In addition, being independents, those candidates usually had a greater flexibility in manoeuvring around in terms of political allegiances, provided that they did not have to stick to a certain ideology or party platform. However, on aggregate, the same line was followed by most electoral candidates, be it for parliament or for the local council. Having access to networks of familial and community support and acquiring copious financial resources were the essential prerequisites that had to be secured in order for these candidates to compete in the elections. The formula is quite simple and straightforward: some candidates grant 100 LE per vote,[25] while others give 50 LE in addition to a bag of supplies (Hajj Abdelaal, 2008; Misr al-Qadima, 2008).

The MB in Misr al-Qadima's old quarter versus 'Ain al-Sirra

As stated earlier, in general the MB has a stronger standing in 'Ain al-Sirra than in the old quarter of Misr al-Qadima owing to the relative abundance there of potential beneficiaries of the services of the MB and the JS. This observation was emphasized by the people of the district, who noted that the MB and the JS were more present and active in 'Ain al-Sirra. The accounts of the people of 'Ain al-Sirra suggest that, with the overwhelming resentment towards the state that is shared by the majority of the people, the appeal of an organization like the JS must be quite resonant in such an area. In addition, the MB cadres seem to be considerably savvy when it comes to their political performance in the legislative or municipal councils. In fact, over the years, the MB has worked very hard to profit from the tarnished image of the regime and the NDP as corrupt and inefficient entities, aiming to provide a counterexample, primarily by keeping alive the sound ties with the grassroots social base in these popular quarters. In 2008, one of the four MPs of Misr al-Qadima was an MB cadre, and he was, according to the testimonies of various locals, far much more organized, down to earth and in touch with the constituency than the three other MPs. This also coincides with what Shehata and Stacher (2007) have suggested with regard to the successful approach that the MB has been following in their electoral constituencies, unlike the NDP, which lagged behind in this realm, especially in the popular urban and rural quarters (Misr al-Qadima locals, 2008).

Nonetheless, several people from the area noted a significant phenomenon characterizing the 2005 parliamentary elections to have been the rising role of the NGOs. Initially, in the 1980s and 1990s, it had been mostly the Islamist foundations (the ISIs) that were proactive in this realm. More recently, however, similar NGOs affiliated to NDP figures had started to enter the sphere of social services. As previously stated, the role of an organization such as the JS has often been pivotal in the electoral process. The headquarters of the JS in Misr al-Qadima has usually been in the service of the MB candidates, acting as the base for their electoral campaigns. During the elections, the social services provided by the JS and the activities of the MB candidates usually come under close scrutiny from local inhabitants. For example, when the MB candidate associates himself with the wide array of services provided by the JS, it is likely that the voter will consider the benefits he or she will receive if this MB candidate makes it to office. Starting with the 2005 parliamentary elections, and then the 2007 municipal elections, similar NDP-affiliated NGOs entered the arena of politically driven social services (Hajj Abdelaal, 2008; Misr al-Qadima locals, 2008).

When asked about the lesser notabilities of the area and whether respondents thought they played a role in the polity of Misr al-Qadima, a considerable number of respondents made references to the *biytkabarluh* figures, those traditional figures of authority in the popular quarters of Cairo who were introduced in Chapters 1 and 2. Respondents stated that such figures are largely pivotal, if not as candidates then as the main reservoirs of votes for the candidates, who are most likely to be lesser notable figures as well. There are different categories of what we would describe as lesser notabilities, the most powerful being the ones that are capable of playing a viable political role, which is mainly achieved via controlling votes, i.e. by being able to mobilize a certain number of votes in favour of a certain electoral candidate during the time of elections (Hajj Abdelaal, 2008; Misr al-Qadima, 2008).

This scheme of vote allocation is possible only when the *biytkabarluh* figure makes a reputable name for himself within the community, and that depends on two things: first, the financial capacity that enables the notable to endow benefits on supporters and members of the family, clan or community, and second, a strong social standing within his clan or community as a man-of-good and a moral leader:

> This social/moral role is also quite important as it establishes a good reputation for the person as a pious notable and, you know, in our community this persona of giving, helpfulness, and piety is essential if a certain figure is to gain credibility and popularity. I think that most of them don't have a political line (agenda) of any sort ... some of them end up allying with the NDP as this guarantees state support and good ties with the police, while others belong to the MB as it provides them with more popularity ... In areas like ours, simply going against the NDP, the party of the government, could make one very popular due to the distaste that the inhabitants have developed towards the party and the consequences of the policies that they

see that it stands for; mainly corruption, biases against the poor and the marginalized, economic stagnation, etc.

Abdelmajid, 2008

Yet this was not always the case in the pre-January 25 era. Associating a candidate with the NDP could be positive owing to the sound linkage with the state authorities and the anticipated benefits this could reap for the people of the neighbourhood. Of course, this changed after January 25 and, after the dissolution of the party, the association with the NDP was indeed a disgrace that most political figures would want to avoid.

The lesser notables of Misr al-Qadima: exemplar roles in mediation and conflict

Just like the majority of popular areas, the *kbir* (notable) plays a paramount role in the community of Misr al-Qadima. Madiha Ahmed, a social worker who had worked closely with the electoral campaigns in Misr al-Qadima, said:

> If a problem erupts between me and a certain person and remains unresolved, it is very likely for me to target the notable of the area/community/ extended family or clan that this person belongs to and he (the *kbir*) will be able to resolve the dispute. The power and influence of these notables are usually determined according to their position within the family or clan, in addition to the size of resources they possess.

Madiha Ahmed, 2008

An example that could be mentioned here in the area of Misr al-Qadima is someone like Hajj Gad Megahed. He is an affluent merchant with very little or no education who enjoys a very prestigious standing within the Megahed family, which originates from Upper Egypt:

> A few days ago he was visited by another merchant and a quarrel erupted between the two, which ended up with the visiting merchant beaten severely by Megahed and his people. The beaten merchant reported the case to the police, who, in turn, contacted Megahed. This conversation took place while my husband was there ... The police asked Megahed whether he wanted this merchant released from the police station or not and Megahed responded that this man (the beaten merchant) is a hazard to the community and that he should not be released until he is straightened. So, ironically, the man who got beaten ended up in prison for a few days, simply because he antagonized the wrong person.

Madiha Ahmed, 2008

Prior to January 25, such occurrences used to happen on daily basis, and they regularly reflected a high degree of coordination between those *kbir* figures and the police stations of the areas within which they operated. Of course, this involved a multitude of services and resources allocated to those police stations and personnel. As will be described in the following chapters, in their desperate attempts to prevent the demise of the Mubarak regime after January 25, NDP cadres and several members of the police apparatus utilized the lesser notabilities as middlemen in order to mobilize *baltagiya* (thugs) with the aim of instigating incidents of violence and disorder, especially during the 18-day sit-in that took place in Tahrir Square.

Hajj Megahed was therefore capable of resolving disputes between people because of these sound ties with the police authorities and also by virtue of his standing as one of the head figures of the Megahed family. Yet getting him to act as the problem-solver also meant that he would benefit from certain resources or services that could be given to him in return for the problem-solving service that he provided. Logically, the bigger the service provided, the higher the price. Figures like Hajj Megahed are quite influential, and a few of them are well known in the area, for example Tawfiq Diab, Ramadan Abu Lebda, Waheed Hemdan, then a local council member and originally an *ahwagy* (café waiter) who later opened his own café, and Fathy Gelid (an ex-MP with Islamist tendencies and ties with the MB) (Madiha Ahmed, 2008). In fact, all of the aforementioned figures seemingly share the features of the lesser notables, and their political affiliation seems to be irrelevant as some of them have actually swung back and forth between the NDP and the MB. This tendency to switch allegiances will be shown in the next chapter as we scrutinize the typology of the lesser notabilities that were associated with the dissolved NDP.

The notables and the household in Misr al-Qadima: job creation

Given their stature within the popular quarters of a district like Misr al-Qadima, the lesser notabilities are often given the role of the 'natural leaders' who are typically approached by the locals to facilitate their everyday mundane affairs. In addition to the generic services that are provided to the general public in the name of a particular notable or his or her affiliated NGO, usually in the form of health and education facilities or food and other basic supplies, there is also a more personalized scheme of services and favours that is offered by the notables. In addition to their conciliatory role in mediation and conflict, some Misr al-Qadima notables, especially those of the MB, are well noted for their ability to provide jobs where applicable to the people of the area, mainly due to the interconnected nature of the financial and administrative networks operated by the Islamist political activists, as described earlier. In Misr al-Qadima, certain notables are capable of finding the people jobs, better than any public company or Labor Ministry. Some of them, such as Ramadan Elewa and Fathy Gelid, require only the name of the person seeking employment and sometimes his or her resumé, and, regardless of how well qualified the person is, he or she will get a job. Of course, the employment favours asked by those who are more pious and religiously committed are very unlikely to be turned down (Misr al-Qadima locals, 2008, 2009).

These notables often grant employment either in their own commercial ventures or within the vast interconnected network of commercial activities that is maintained by MB affiliates and cadres in Misr al-Qadima and elsewhere in Cairo. Indeed, the MB-affiliated notables could be considered as an efficient employment agency in the popular quarter. This augments their sociopolitical profile with an economic dimension that complements their role as key figures of authority and influence.

Lesser notable figures in relation to the MB and the state in Misr al-Qadima

In Misr al-Qadima, the lesser notables who are affiliated to the MB have a significant role to play in the local polity, serving a multitude of functions, as shown above in the cases of the JS and the MB, where the intermediary members who are concerned with building and enhancing ties with the social base mostly belong to this category of notability. Despite the fact that the MB almost boycotted the municipal elections that took place in 2008,[26] the standing of the notables associated with it is still quite sound in the area (Saidi, 2008).

The case of Hajj Bakr Omar, who comes from a traditionally MB-affiliated family, represents an example of the interaction of such figures with the state authorities. Hajj Omar is a wholesale/-retail trader in Misr al-Qadima and has been a *beitkabarlu* figure in the area owing to his good repute and extensive familial ties and connections. He ran for parliamentary election in 1995 and 2000, and in both cases was allegedly banned from proceeding in the electoral process by the state security, despite the fact that he had won more votes than any other candidate. So in the 2005 elections he actually joined the NDP, and subsequently succeeded in becoming an MP. Nonetheless, after state security reports that linked him to the prominent MB MP Yousry Bayoumy (Figure 4.4), another lesser notability and an MB cadre who reportedly supported Omar with votes and resources, the state security started considering Omar as a threat in spite of his official affiliation to the NDP. As a result, Hajj Omar was exposed to continuous police surveillance, and sometimes arrest, owing to his suspected ties with the MB (Saidi, 2008).

So, as has been mentioned in several previous examples, especially in the pre-January 25 phase, the lesser notables associated with the MB depended to a great extent on their personal, familial and commercial networks and on the interconnected web of networks orchestrated by the MB and its affiliated ISIs as their main sources of power and influence in the popular polity. Some of them were unlikely to have strong ties with the police apparatus or gain access to state resources; however, that did not seem to be an obstacle preventing them from maintaining their stature within the community.

Conclusions

As portrayed throughout this chapter, it is safe to say that the MB has succeeded in consolidating its power base in Cairo's popular communities over decades. By and large, the MB has been tactically savvy in dealing with the populace for most of its history. In many aspects, it has utilized and helped to enhance the state of

Figure 4.4 Posters of Muslim Brotherhood candidate Yousry Bayoumy.

Islamization that has been prevailing in the Egyptian society, and has benefited from it to increase its popularity at the street level:

> Look at slogans like 'Islam is the Solution!' Quite generic, yet effective and wholesome in a comparatively religious society like ours. Such simple and general themes and mottos are powerful tools in the hands of the MB as well as other Islamists, yet it is important to assure that these slogans by themselves are not the only tactics used by the MB. They are used in conjunction with pragmatic and street-level operative schemes that aim to provide services to ordinary citizens. In a sense, the MB represents the only alternative available to the state-sponsored NDP, associated with a tarnished image of corruption and inefficiency.
>
> Tammam, 2008

As stated earlier in the course of this writing as we delved through the socio-economic backgrounds of the MB parliamentary bloc, it is rather apparent that the popular appeal that MB MPs have at the street level is attributed to their close connectedness with their constituencies and their ability to voice the needs and demands of the people of their respective districts.

The relationship between certain services or charity organizations, such as the JS, and the MB is evident. The main association is shown by the example of the operative cadres within organizations such as the JS, where many of the key players are in fact MB members and affiliates. In the mid-1990s, the Mubarak regime realized this functional relationship and aimed to clamp down on the JS, shutting down some of its branches, imprisoning some of its cadres and accusing them of assisting in funding the banned MB. Despite this repression, which affected the scheme of socioeconomic networking implemented by the MB, the group was still capable of extending its web of services through the multitude of networks in synchrony with it. Overall, the attempts of the Mubarak regime to contain and suppress the informal networks and the amalgam of financial and human capital orchestrated by the MB were met with minimal success.

The JS is one of the biggest and most influential ISIs in Egypt. It comprises over 10,000 mosques operational across the country. In 1995, the state came close to terminating the activities of the JS due to its considerable influence and apparent relationship with the MB; however, that did not take place owing to the sizeable apparatus possessed by the JS and the extremely negative impact that would have occurred at the street level had it been shut down. For the state, the JS was a ticking bomb awaiting detonation by the MB and other Islamists. Instead, severe attempts were made by the police apparatus to suppress the cadres who were involved with both entities, the MB and the JS, the end result being an implicit agreement with the leadership of the JS that there should be a separation between its activities and those of the MB (Tammam 2008; JS members, 2008). But in reality, and as shown in this chapter, that separation was never achieved. To date, the wide scope of services presented to the populace via those 10,000 or more mosques is synonymously provided to the people in the name of the Islamist forces and figures associated with this NGO.

At the core of the web of networks that is maintained by the MB, one finds the lesser notables, this category of sociopolitical actors who thrived in the popular communities in the aftermath of the 1974 *Infitah* policies. Those notables are characterized by being the societal actors who are successful in infiltrating the communities in which they dwell, thanks to the resources and networks in their possession, which makes them the best candidates for the sort of social work and *da'wa* on which the JS and other ISIs depend for establishing and further consolidating their social base. Due to their sound interconnectedness with the popular communities and the fact that they have access to these embedded socioeconomic networks, those notables have a plethora of roles to fulfil in the contexts of formal/informal politics, state–society relations, mediation and conflict, the generation and direction of resources and awareness and the reproduction of culture.

In some respects, the state is colonized by local notability and operates within the framework designed by the notables and their aides and associates. More often than not, the state is brought down to the stratum of the people, where it becomes a locale of everyday quarrels and disputes (S. Ismail, 2006). As shown in several examples throughout this chapter, via their sound networks with public institutions and their positioning within the community, those lesser notables are often sought out by their clients to resolve disputes and provide them with a wide variety of the services that the formal institutions of the state have failed to deliver. As seen in the case of Misr al-Qadima, lesser notabilities appear to be the winning card of political agency, and there is an ongoing competition between the political forces over co-opting them. In Cairo's popular communities, the socioeconomic and political role of the lesser notability as influential societal actors is becoming increasingly noticeable. With the gradual withdrawal of the state from the everyday affairs of such populaces, lesser notabilities, in conjunction with other entities such as the ISIs, sometimes act as intermediaries and viable alternatives to the official state apparatuses. Thus, in the milieu of the popular quarters, the 'lesser' nature of these notabilities, who stand in opposition to the classical landowning notabilities and the rather modern mega-business notabilities, is in fact changing due to their increasingly elevated standing within the popular polity. It could be argued that the lesser notability of Cairo's popular communities is gradually moving out of its 'lesser' status, and further to the forefront of the popular polity.

Unsurprisingly, in 2007, a considerable number of those MB cadres who were arrested and accused of being the 'financial arm' of the MB belonged to this category of lesser notability. By then, it was clear that the state security apparatus of the regime had predominantly failed to contain the sizeable influence of these sociopolitical agents and that it consequently had to resort to oppressive mechanisms in order to limit their increasingly influential role within the Egyptian polity. Since the January 25 revolution and the demise of the Mubarak regime, the power and influence of the MB in the popular communities is expected to continue and perhaps develop after the removal of the state-imposed ban on its activities. The dissolution of the NDP and the termination of the state security apparatus that targetted the MB cadres throughout the reign of Mubarak also mean that the limitations under which the MB was operating will be considerably reduced. However, it may still be too early to outline the prospects of the MB as a sociopolitical institution in the post-Mubarak phase. Analysing the impact of the January 25 revolution on the socioeconomic and political networks orchestrated by the MB in the milieu of Cairo's popular communities is an endeavour that is worthy of further research.

5 The dissolved National Democratic Party-affiliated lesser notability in Misr al-Qadima

Introduction

The National Democratic Party (NDP), established by Former President Anwar Al Sadat as the majority party, succeeded the Arab Socialist Union (ASU) that had been set up by the Nasser regime in the 1960s in order to fulfil the role of the sole political forum of the state. But with the increasing emphasis upon the supposed theme of economic reform as the main national policy of the state throughout Hosni Mubarak's rule, more particularly strengthened by Egypt's adoption of the Economic Reform and Structural Adjustment Program (ERSAP) in 1991, the party seemed to be facing an existential threat that was challenging the very grounds upon which it had been constituted. Some argued that the existence of the NDP, an inheritor of the Nasserite mobilization instrument, the ASU, 'contradicts regime rhetoric of open markets and political pluralization ... The NDP's sole remaining important function is to hold together a loyal and massive majority in parliament through the distribution of patronage' (Abdul Aziz and Hussein, 2002: 83). Yet the scheme of patronage channelled through the ranks of the NDP was not only limited to the echelons of the parliamentary elections. Regime cronies who had formulated the backbone of Hosni Mubarak's ruling clique since 1981 were also linked to a wide scope of irregularities that included financial corruption and the exploitation of official posts to serve personal, familial and other clientelism-related purposes, and to consolidate their positions within the NDP and the Egyptian polity at large.

In the aftermath of the January 25 revolution, Egypt's Higher Administrative Court ordered the dissolution of the NDP and the confiscation of its assets. The ruling put a practical end to the existence of the party as a political entity. Furthermore, most of the leading cadres of the party, including Gamal Mubarak himself, were imprisoned on charges of corruption. However, the bulk of the active cadres associated with the former ruling party, especially the operative cadres within the middle and lower echelons of the NDP, were not really affected. This meant that, in spite of the demise of the party, the amalgam of the alliances and networks that constituted the interconnected web of political patronage embedded in the socioeconomic and political setting of the society was still there. This chapter first aims to dissect the chief features of the political profile of the dissolved NDP in Misr al-Qadima and then ventures into scrutinizing the role that the lesser notabilities played in liaison with the NDP in this popular district. In doing so, some light will be shed on the sociopolitical agency of the lesser notabilities and the prospects of their political role in the post-Mubarak phase.[1]

The Neo-NDP (2002–2011)

With the ascent of Mubarak's son Gamal to the apex of the NDP in 2000, there seemed to be a tendency among Mubarak Jr. and his aides to reformulate the foundations of the NDP in order to make the party more suitable for the neoliberal policies of their reformist faction.[2] Entering the higher stratum of the Egyptian polity, Gamal Mubarak had to comply with the rules of the game and acquire his own power base within such a polity. In this case, best fitting with Gamal's persona and affiliations, the suggested power base was the newly flourishing business community of Egypt. Mainly comprising prominent businessmen who were on the rise with Egypt's adoption of a more liberal economy, this new class of business-owners started controlling the policy-making circles of the NDP. Furthermore, a sizeable structural modification took place with the rise of Mubarak Jr., via which a newly established set of secretariats orchestrating the work of the NDP were created; most important of these was of course the Policies Committee, spearheaded by Gamal himself. This committee was responsible for setting the framework of the main macro-level politicoeconomic policies that were adopted by the NDP from 2002 onwards (Abdul Aziz and Hussein, 2002). By then, it was rather obvious that the president's son was on his way to consolidating control over the party, and the Policies Committee eventually became the most influential entity within the NDP.

As described by the *Economist* (2003), Egypt's neo-NDP was in a nutshell a patronage machine:

> A party that has governed for a quarter of a century would seem an unlikely instrument for change. But the ... NDP, the lumbering patronage machine that holds all but a few seats in Egypt's rubber-stamp parliament, has just embraced a platform of sweeping economic, political and social reform.

This platform of reform was, however, clearly questionable as the foundational basis of the party remained unaltered. Patronage politics exemplified in the favouritism and the co-option policies undertaken by the NDP prevailed as the ruling party's main strategy in acquiring new alliances in order to constitute its prowess within the Egyptian polity.

In practice, the NDP was not a party with a clear platform and a unified strategy. When we refer to the 'NDP', we have to understand that this so-called party was in fact a fragmented entity comprising a diverse set of ideas, beliefs and personnel that did not manifest a unified vision. Since its establishment in 1978 as the party of the state, the NDP was, in essence, an extension of the single-party state system that had been in place since 1952. There was no unified ideology that characterized the party; within its ranks, one could find the secularists and the religious, the leftists and the right-wingers, the pro-American neoliberals and the antiglobalization socialists. All these coexisted and operated within the ranks of the NDP on the various echelons of the party, which shows that the party had no clear-cut political platform. This is of course reflected in the typology of social basis on which it depended for popular support and the kind of relationship established between the party and this social base (NDP members, 2009).[3] Logically, this relationship would not be based on the people's conviction related to the party platform or their support of the ideas and beliefs that the NDP was championing. Conversely, such a relationship, which existed between the NDP and various types of individuals and communities, was based upon material benefit and co-optation (Tammam, 2008).

Hence, the services and resources provided by the party to its beneficiaries were in fact a mechanism to co-opt some societal forces into the state structure. This co-optation was rather noticeable in Cairo's low-income and popular quarters, where young men and women used to join the NDP because they sought upward socioeconomic mobility, an elevation into the higher echelons of the society, which was more likely to be attained if one were in the ranks of the NDP. Employment, health care and a wide scope of state services were likely to be guaranteed for NDP members and affiliates (Tammam, 2008; Misr al-Qadima NDP members, 2009).[4]

Despite the fact that the chairman was at the apex of the hierarchical structure of the NDP, most of the policy-making processes took place within the milieus of the Political Bureau, the General Secretariat and the Policies Secretariat:

> The organizational structure of the party consists of the following levels from bottom to top: 1-Party Unit level, 2-District Unit, 3-Central level and this consists of the General Secretariat and the Political Bureau. The Party Unit Committee is in charge of the affairs of the various units. Each of the committees at the various governorates and districts is responsible for party affairs in its realm of mandate. The General Secretariat and the Political Bureau are responsible for the central level.
>
> 'About Us', Official Portal of the NDP, 2009

Within the central, district and party-unit levels, the role of Gamal Mubarak was quite influential, particularly at the central and to a lesser extent at the district level, by virtue of being the chairman of the Policies Secretariat, the entity responsible for outlining the main political and economic policies of the party and the central government. Arguably, one of the main features that characterized the organizational structure of the party was the power balance that existed between Gamal Mubarak and Safwat Sharif, a member of the old guard of the Mubarak regime and the last Secretary General of the party, whose influence was, on aggregate, more dominant at the district and party-unit levels. This was primarily attributed to the sizeable scope of networks of political patronage that Sharif and other old-guard-affiliated figures, such as the late Kamal Al Shazly and Zakaria Azmy, had established and consolidated over the years (Misr al-Qadima NDP members, 2009).[5]

As will be shown in the course of this chapter, there appeared to be a conviction among Gamal and the new-guard NDP cadres that one of the chief remedies for this lack of presence at the popular level could be consolidating the grip of the party over the local Municipal Councils (MCs). Again, as will be displayed despite the willingness of the new guard to spread the influence of the NDP to the municipalities, it was the wide array of patron–client networks orchestrated by the old guard that would largely enable the NDP to actualize this objective.

The rising importance of the MCs on the NDP's agenda[6]

The NDP was involved with a set of contradictory trends and policies concerning the decentralization of local governance and the subsequent role played by local MCs in this process. A realization of the importance of the role that could be played by the municipalities in counteracting the popular appeal of and services provided by the Islamic social institutions (ISIs) arguably led the NDP to invest further in these institutions of local governance. Yet the main objective was not to empower these local municipalities and turn them into meaningful actors at the community level, but rather to co-opt them and ensure their loyalty to the central authority, so that they could be utilized as a community-level power base in the face of the rising ISIs (Abdalla, 2007).

In fact, local administrative units in Egypt were, in practice, extensions of the executive authority. The central government made the decisions and policies, and imposed them. In addition to this, it directed the activities of the administrative system, which implemented the policy (Abo Talib, 2007). Overall, local governance was characterized by a weak participation of citizens due to the dilemma of the single-party system, which entailed a hegemonic role for the NDP and a virtual absence of the already weak opposition parties, along with an electoral system that was tainted with a considerable degree of irregularity and governing-regime manipulation. This of course almost terminated any sort of popular participation in municipal elections owing to a decreasing trust in the fairness of elections and the widespread phenomenon of family and tribal voting. Logically, without participation from the bottom up, local governments are incapable of accurately structuring or administering public services. Popular participation is indeed necessary if accountability within local institutions and responsiveness to the community's needs are to be created.

Local financial and fiscal decentralization is also quite limited. By and large, the local MCs suffer from a scarcity of self-funding, and a weak role in managing their budgets, as the majority of their financial resources come from central government in the form of subsidies. Therefore, the subnational government bodies in Egypt have relatively little fiscal autonomy. All governorate, district and municipal budgets form part of the central budget approved by the legislature. The transfer of funds from central government accounts for almost 90 per cent of local revenues. Local governments raise funds through urban real-estate, agricultural land, motor vehicle registration and licensing. Most regional and local funds are allocated to existing expenditures, such as salaries and debt management. The absence of capital at the local level undermines the ability of these governments to initiate developmental projects of any kind in their own localities. Overall, without control over their own revenues and budgets, local governments cannot operate autonomously (Abdalla, 2007).

Nevertheless, and despite the aforementioned features of local governance in Egypt, the political discourse of the dissolved NDP had stressed decentralization since November 2003 (Ministry of Planning, 2006). This in fact seemed to be well in synchronization with the objectives of the neoliberal reform schemes adopted by the World Bank and the International Monetary Fund, under which the decentralization of local governance plays a paramount role in loosening the grip of the state over the localities, reducing its size and budget in the process. But what the Mubarak regime did in practice, spearheaded by the NDP, was no more than pay lip service to this discourse of decentralization. Instead, the NDP, backed up by the security apparatus, ensured that these MCs were filled with NDP loyalists who were keen on enhancing the stature of the ruling party in their own localities at the expense of other contesting political forces, such as the MB and its affiliated ISIs.

In the period from 2003 to 2007, the municipal elections were frozen by presidential decree, and throughout this period the government instead appointed *ad hoc* committees, composed mainly of NDP members and affiliates, in order to run the affairs of the municipalities. The result was a range of stagnant and predominantly inefficient MCs that, by and large, failed to fulfil their commitments as executive branches of local governance (Abdalla, 2007). As will be described below for the case of Misr al-Qadima, the 2008 municipalities' elections consequently witnessed a considerable degree of state intervention that was aimed at securing the bulk of MC seats for NDP loyalists. In short, it is safe to argue that, with the ascent of Egypt's neoliberal phase, the Mubarak regime was adamant on manipulating the municipalities in a manner that ensured these entities of local governance were to serve the interests of the regime and its subordinate party.[7] Eventually, after the fall of the Mubarak regime in 2011, the Administrative Court ordered the dissolution of the MCs owing to their role in corruption during the time of Mubarak.

Relationship between the NDP/state institutions and non-governmental organizations in the popular polity

Another facet that has also shaped the socioeconomic/political policies adopted by the NDP and its government regarding the popular communities has been the incrementally growing role of non-governmental organizations (NGOs) in the popular polity, which coincided with the NDP's discourse of neoliberalism, championed by the new-guard-orientated Policies Committee. This discourse stressed a bigger role for the private sector and civil society, and a reduction in the role of the state in managing and administering society's socioeconomic affairs. In the NDP's last party platform drafted by the Policies Committee in 2005, there was a clear emphasis on the important role of the civil society in substituting for the state when confronting the community's socioeconomic hardships: 'It is crystal clear that governments alone can not satisfy all the needs of their citizens. Neither can the governments solve all the problems society faces alone' ('About us', Official Portal of the NDP, 2009).

However, this recent rise in the scope and magnitude of NGO activities in the milieu of the popular communities was also associated with attempts to utilize this phenomenon to serve the interests of the NDP cadres in the popular polity. As will be shown in this chapter, different categories of sociopolitical actors, including some lesser notabilities associated with the NDP as well as NDP patrons and elitist notabilities operating within the popular echelons of the community, have all attempted to establish and consolidate their control over various NGOs. Quite often, the aim of the NDP patron or cadre is to channel a wide variety of resources and services to the populace in the name of the political cadre him- or herself and the party. Thus, there is a sense of competition between various NGOs in the arena of providing services to the populace, not for charitable, but rather for political purposes. As will be shown in the cases of Mamdouh Mekky, Ilham Bahi and, to a lesser extent, the female lesser notable Hannan Al-Saidi, various NDP figures were all in charge of a set of NGOs that were either self-funded or dependent upon donations and financial support from the state as well as a plethora of development donors. As attested by most of these cadres, the NGO has often been utilized by the NDP figure who controls it for personal benefit in order to raise his or her sociopolitical profile within the constituency in which he or she operates.

Misr al-Qadima and the NDP

As illustrated in the previous chapter by the case of the Muslim Brotherhood (MB), the geopolitics and history of Misr al-Qadima also played a great role in shaping the stature of the NDP in this popular quarter. In Misr al-Qadima proper (the old quarter), the NDP's arrival on the political scene coincided, more or less, with the construction of the newer quarters of 'Ain al-Sirra in the 1960s. At that time, the ASU, the NDP's predecessor, was introduced into the area as the mobilizing engine of political action, with sizeable numbers of young people subsequently joining its ranks, seeking the actualization of the ASU's proclaimed objectives: national independence, social justice and pan-Arab cooperation and development. The ASU, which was by and large synonymous with the state, represented itself as the guarantor of services and subsidies to the people, and it maintained a considerable degree of popularity in the district, especially in 'Ain al-Sirra, the part of Misr al-Qadima that had originally been constructed by the Nasser regime to provide housing to the low-income segments of the society (Abdallah and Siam, 1996).

With the advent of Sadat and his Open Door policies in the early 1970s, the stature of the state-sponsored ASU gradually declined all over the country, until it was ultimately dissolved by Sadat in 1972. Eventually, the vacuum left by the ASU was loosely filled by the NDP, established in 1976 as the political party representing the state. The party had a somewhat vague platform that was described by the regime then as a 'centrist' ideology, generically calling for national unity, economic development and political stability. The mobilization machine and relative popularity that had previously been maintained by the ASU were in no way inherited by the NDP, especially within the popular quarters where the state withdrew from its welfare services and subsidies, as shown in Chapters 3 and 4. Instead, the NDP focused most of its activities on the realm of elections, functioning as the chief vote-gatherer for the candidates representing the party in the parliamentary and municipal elections.

In the 1980s and 1990s, the role of the NDP as a vote-securer had been somewhat solidified. In Misr al-Qadima, a district (*shiyakha*) office was established, along with a plethora of smaller offices (party units) around the various sub-neighbourhoods of the area. The *shiyakha* office was the leading party organization in the area, operating as the intermediary linkage between the higher echelons of the NDP and its grassroots basis in the lower strata of the Misr al-Qadima polity. Under its auspices came the smaller party units, which acted as the venues for recruiting new party cadres who would presumably disseminate the resources and services to the populace, maintaining the allegiance of these popular bases to the party, particularly during election time. However, and as was the case with a multitude of low-income and popular quarters, the 1980s and 1990s also witnessed an enormous rise in the scope and magnitude of services provided by the ISIs of Misr al-Qadima, which in turn led to a sharp rise in the popularity of the Islamists in the area, particularly the MB. The waning popularity of the NDP in Misr al-Qadima was rather apparent with the 2000 and 2005 parliamentary elections, when the four seats in parliament were equally distributed between NDP and MB affiliates (Abdallah and Siam, 1996; Al-Khashab, 2008).

In fact, the results of the 2005 parliamentary elections were shocking for the NDP, as the MB succeeded in becoming the most sizeable opposition force in parliament, with 88 seats (out of 444) despite the harsh oppression and intimidation exercised against its candidates by the police apparatus all over the country. This was the ruling party's biggest parliamentary defeat and, with it, it seemed as if the NDP had finally realized that the immense retreat in its stature was so grave that some fundamental alterations were required to the strategies and policies implemented by the party on the ground:

> I have been in the party for over 15 years now and I can sense the change taking place ... A few NDP members are now aware of the importance of addressing the needs of the lower level/popular level constituencies ... Yet those remain to be a minority, and the majority could still be considered to be much more interested in consolidating the domination of the NDP over popular politics, perhaps, among other factors, due to the traditional vision that is widespread among these cadres regarding the unimportance of transparency or democracy, unless utilized for the best interest of the ruling party.
>
> Saidi, 2008

One of the chief cornerstones of the reformed NDP policies that were encouraged by the new guards of the party was how it viewed and attempted to utilize local municipalities in raising the sociopolitical profile of the party and its incumbents in the popular and rural quarters.

Detachment from the popular power bases and attempts of reform

An increasing degree of detachment indeed occurred between the NDP and the street-level power bases. This lack of popularity at the street level was one of the main reasons for the 2005 parliamentary elections witnessing the worst results for the NDP:

> The NDP suffers from a lack of popularity on the street level when compared to the MB. Most of the candidates nominated by the NDP in the 2005 elections lost, and if it weren't for the 'independent' candidates joining the ranks of the party after the elections, the NDP wouldn't have enjoyed a majority in the parliament today. In fact in 2005 I presented a paper to the Policies Committee arguing that the lack of a meaningful scheme of services to the people is bringing the party down to the gutter ... Now the party is realizing the importance of spreading the scheme of its social services in the popular quarters ... Ahmed Ezz, secretary [of organization] of the NDP, has specified over 100,000 LE for every MP to provide services to his constituency.
>
> Bahi, 2008

Perhaps this allocation (almost equivalent to US$ 20,000 at 2008 exchange rates) is an indicator of the increasing attention that was being given by the party's decision-making circles to the consolidation of popular power bases. Despite the fact that 100,000 LE is probably insufficient to fund the social services needed in a single popular quarter, it could still make an important contribution to this end, a sum that could be utilized to provide small to medium-sized benefits to a good number of people in a popular locale.[8]

There was thus a divide between the higher ranks of the NDP and the lower echelons that supposedly connected the party with the popular constituencies. As will be shown later in the course of this chapter, despite the emphasis that the NDP placed on the MCs and the relevant elections, the fact remains that those pivoted around the MCs and the party units depended on the alliances and networks of the old guard of the NDP. As will be described later, the old guard was more capable of dealing with the intricate details of the popular communities than the new guard.

The MC of Misr al-Qadima: notabilities within the state

The local MC of Misr al-Qadima lies on Salah Salem Road, almost at the junction between 'Ain al-Sirra and the older quarter of Misr al-Qadima (Figures 5.1 and 5.2). As shown in Figure 5.1, the moderately constructed building that hosts the council is also home to a variety of other state administrative units operating in the area. Upon arriving at the MC, which occupied an entire floor of this four-storey building, the researcher was met with a warm welcome from a person who introduced himself as the chair of the local council. This was Mahmoud Al-Khashab, a friendly man who was apparently willing to present a picture of the MC's activities. Another member of the council, Khaled Abdelfattah, joined the discussion later and revealed some insightful and in-depth details about the sociopolitical realities of Misr al-Qadima.

Figure 5.1 The complex housing the municipal council of Misr al-Qadima.

Figure 5.2 The entrance to the municipal council and the various subdivisions of its offices.

The profiles of the Misr al-Qadima MC members were in fact quite diverse. The majority came from two main categories: business-owners or merchants like Abdelfattah himself, or state employees, like Al-Khashab, the chairperson of the MC. The 22 MC members were almost distributed equally between these two categories. Abdelfattah, the MC member, seemed to be more involved in and aware of the daily affairs of the area than Al-Khashab, the actual chair of the council. These two MC members came from two considerably different backgrounds. Al-Khashab was an accountant and a state employee at the Ministry of Social Affairs, which meant he was available at the MC only on part-time basis. On the other hand, Abdelfattah was a prominent Misr al-Qadima leather merchant and a local notable. He had a primary education certificate, and his political profile included a zealous NDP membership that had lasted for over two decades and granted him a prime position in the party as the secretary of the *shiyakha*, a position that had previously been occupied by his late father (Abdelfattah, 2008; Al-Khashab, 2008).

Abdelfattah had from a very young age embarked upon a wide scope of social and political activities. In a sense, he had inherited his father's role, not only as the leading leather tannery manufacturer and merchant in the area, but also as a leading figure in the ranks of the NDP and the MC. In addition, he also pursued his line as the board member of the Commercial Chamber of Skin Tannery:

> My father had an excellent repute as someone who provided services to the people of his area and, after he passed away, there was a certain responsibility that I had to bear in order not to let down those that depended on him as the facilitating broker with the state authorities.
>
> Abdelfattah, 2008

His father's demise meant that Abdelfattah had to go through the internal elections of the party to win nomination for the MC elections, which he did. Eventually, he won a seat in the MC and also made it through in the local NDP elections that took place the same year (2006), becoming the secretary of the party's *shiyakha*.

Although some of the secretaries of the NDP districts prefer not to occupy a position in the MC, as they consider the tasks expected of a person occupying both positions to be somewhat burdensome, Abdelfattah had a certain rationale for occupying these two seats:

> I think that in order for someone like me to be able to serve the people of his area properly, he has to occupy as many posts as possible. This gives the person a versatile window of opportunity, through which he can serve the people in a multiplicity of ways. For example, being on the Board of the Commercial Chamber has enabled me to provide a lot of services for the skin-tannery labor, business owners, and merchants, who constitute a sizeable portion of the population of our area. After all, in order to be efficient and helpful to the people of such an area, I have to be in the MC. The Local Council lies at the core of any scope of services that could be

supplied. Infrastructure works, electricity, sanitation, building permits, etc., are among the mandates of the municipalities, and these are crucial services that are indispensable to the people.

Abdelfattah, 2008

With the emphasis that the party put on the municipalities and the essential nature of their role in leading the process of socioeconomic development,[9] especially in the popular areas, the importance of the municipalities arguably surpassed that of the legislative councils, i.e. the parliament and the Shura Council:

> Indeed those at the municipality are responsible for getting things done for the people on the ground. That is why when an MP is willing to provide a certain service to the people of his district; he has to go through the municipality first.

Abdalla, 2007

Thus, the administrative role that the municipalities played and their involvement in overseeing activities such as the necessary constructional and infrastructural works within the municipality were valuable assets that could be capitalized on by the NDP. It seems that because of this same administrative part that was played by the MCs, the NDP considered the MCs to be a potential foothold against other political forces owing to the fact that the municipalities were more crucial than other state institutions, such as parliament, for the purpose of consolidating the NDP's influence at the popular level.

The MCs: a strong foothold against other political forces?

At the local level, it was the municipalities that did most of the work pertaining to executing the NDP's policies, according to Jamilla Abdelmajid, the Misr al-Qadima MC member. MC members were directed by the NDP at a policy level and, accordingly, these members took care of things at the executive level. In comparison with political forces other than the MB, the NDP was considered to be the one that was capable of achieving some actual changes on the ground in the popular communities:

> Health and educational services are primarily provided by the NDP and its members. Now with the new wave of NDP reform and the increasing financial and authoritative empowerment of the MCs, other political entities, including the MB, will be incapable of keeping up with us.

Abdelmajid, 2008

Perhaps the main realm in which the NDP easily overcame any competition was the construction of new facilities. Owing to the need to obtain permits from relevant state authorities and ministries, mandatory for any new buildings to be erected, the NDP and its affiliated members could proceed in this arena with relative ease compared with other political forces, especially the Islamist ones. Over the past few years, in 'Ain al-Sirra, and to a lesser extent also in the old Misr al-Qadima quarter, the local party unit, under the guidance of several NDP notabilities in the area, actually constructed new cooperatives, medical daycare centres and two new schools (Abdelmajid, 2008). For NDP members and affiliates like Abdelmajid, these activities reflected the NDP's responsiveness to the needs of the area's inhabitants. However, for most locals in Misr al-Qadima, these relatively recent NDP-sponsored services dealt with only a small portion of the people's needs, and, the gap that was left with regard to their actual needs remained huge (Misr al-Qadima locals, 2008).[10]

This also reveals that the MCs indeed constituted potential powerhouses for exploitation of the executive and administrative powers that lay in the hands of MC members. As they monopolized the issuance of construction and other permits, MC members and other local NDP officials and politicians were often engaged in rent-seeking activities that aimed to gain personal benefit – usually a certain sum of money – in return for the permit or the authorization granted by the MC with the help of the MC member or NDP official. It was not uncommon to find that, in Misr al-Qadima and in most other urban locales in Cairo, there was a certain price for such permits, and that these prices varied according to the socio-economic status of the neighbourhood and the nature of the permit needed. For example, permits in the more affluent areas of Cairo were likely to cost more than they did in the popular areas. In addition, the building permit for constructing an entirely new building would typically cost more than the one needed for adding an extra floor to an already existing building.

Of course, the NDP cadres associated with the MC would refuse to acknowledge that such irregularities existed, but a multitude of these cases were reported in Misr al-Qadima and in other districts all over Cairo. The MCs have undoubtedly been tainted with cases of corruption that mainly involved an MC member facilitating the authorization of a building permit or a commercial license for a certain price: 'These prices are well-known to the locals of an area like Misr al-Qadima. For example, it would cost almost 10,000 LE to issue a permit for a new building' (Misr al-Qadima locals, 2008; *Al Masry Al Yom*, 20 December 2009).[11]

This also suggests that it was virtually impossible to draw the line between the jurisdiction of the party and that of the state or central government. Hence, it was quite difficult to make a distinction between the two , especially for the majority of the people on the street:

> This expansion in social services on the popular level is in the electoral program [of the party]. These priorities are set on the budget of the local councils and the relevant ministries, such as the Ministry of Education and Ministry of Construction for example. Local council members are responsible for ensuring the allocation of land designated for building new schools, for instance, and some lobbying is needed within these ministries also to facilitate and speed up the bureaucratic and procedural processes within

such government entities in order to obtain building permits, secure approvals for financial allocations, and so forth.

Abdelmajid, 2008

This overlap between the dissolved NDP and the state apparatuses benefitted the NDP affiliates as it reinforced the conviction that, in order for the people to benefit from the resources and services provided by the state, they had to ally themselves with the NDP.

Abdelfattah reckoned that he had helped to provide the people of the area with a multitude of services , utilizing his position(s) in these entities, primarily the party and the MC. He was adamant that he would provide anything he could to serve the people of the constituency. In addition to the basic services typically provided by the MC, other services were also created to help mitigate some of the socioeconomic predicaments faced by the people of the area. For instance, Abdelfattah initiated an employment campaign whereby young people with relatively limited skills and education could apply for work and then, acting as a facilitator, he would utilize his networks within the party and the chamber to find them opportunities for trainings and apprenticeships and then fixed-term jobs, mostly as workers in leather and other factories. His work in conjunction with other NGOs during the crisis of the skin tannery workshops' relocation (see note) was also of great benefit to the area's people, he believed. Abdelfattah reported that the MC of Misr al-Qadima did its best in order to assist the locals of the area during this relocation crisis (Abdelfattah, 2008; Al-Khashab, 2008).

First, the municipality succeeded in voicing many concerns to the government, as there was much hype and social unrest associated with the decision to relocate the workshops:

> A variety of NGOs and other social organizations fought to resist the decree or, at least, get the best terms possible for such a move and I think these forces combined succeeded in halting the transfer, and, to date, the interests of the skin tannery community have not been negatively affected by the decree.

Abdelfattah, 2008[12]

As stated earlier, the state froze the municipalities across the country for over four years before deciding to bring them back to life and re-emphasize their role in 2007. The initial freeze and the subsequent decision to reactivate the municipalities at that point was justified by Abdelfattah in the light of a set of new policies that the NDP had started to adopt in the realm of, as he put it, 'popular participation':

> When the time of the MC elections came in 2007, the NDP was aware that the best way to reach the popular communities was via the municipalities, especially with the rise of the various Islamist forces that succeeded in providing a wide array of services in the popular areas in particular.

Abdelfattah, 2008

So, for the NDP, there were no alternative outlets that could offset or even compete with the social networks of the Islamists, other than the municipalities. The reactivation of the municipalities was also accompanied by a variety of 'capacity-building' training sessions and workshops that targetted the representatives of the NDP in the MCs (Abdelfattah, 2008).

The 2008 MC elections

What was probably viewed by some NDP members and cadres as an attempt to empower the MCs could be very well also perceived by others as an attempt to consolidate the hegemony of the party over these local governing councils. A good case for the NDP's intention to consolidate its grip over the MCs was shown in the 2007/2008 municipal elections. For Hannan Al-Saidi,[13] a prominent Misr al-Qadima NDP cadre, the 2008 MC elections were a big failure for the NDP:

> I resigned from the Women's Committee, protesting the atrocities of these elections. The irregularities started from the time of registration of the candidates for the elections. Potential candidates wanting to register for the elections were faced by harsh interrogations from State Security and were consequently deterred from running for the elections.
>
> Al Saidi, 2008

Although it was initially said that such a move was aimed against the MB candidates, the truth is that it deterred many other candidates who had nothing to do with the MB from participating.

Al Saidi argues that the policies of reform that seem to be championed by the NDP are actually collapsing as a result of such irregularities:

> The selection of candidates for those elections was tainted with favoritism. In Misr al-Qadima, almost 1000 out of the total 7000 NDP members in the area resigned in protest. Even party members are now disillusioned ... At the street level, feelings of hatred and mistrust towards the NDP have increased. Empowered and working from within, there was a good case for someone like me to defend the NDP. But now, after the failures in these elections, I couldn't even defend the line of the party to the layman on the street.
>
> Al Saidi, 2008

At the time, the presidential elections were expected to be held in 2011, and the parliament and the municipalities were to play the biggest role in these elections in accordance with the 2005 constitutional amendments.[14] According to these amendments, any independent presidential candidate was required first to secure nominations from at least 250 MPs and MC members before being eligible to run in the elections. It was therefore essential for the then-ruling party to ensure that it had a very tight grip over these local councils, from which a plethora of votes could be very easily secured, in order to block the chances of an independent candidate running for presidency.

NDP notables in Misr al-Qadima

Hajj Ahmed Najar: the 'classical' lesser notable

Hajj Ahmed Najar was the secretary of the *shiyakha* of the NDP in 'Ain al-Sirra. He ran a car accessories shop in the area as well as a small travel agency, and his family had resided there for several generations. He also operated the People's Services Office of the NDP. By and large, Hajj Najar could be considered to be a lesser notability owing to the respectable socioeconomic status he preserved, based on his profitable business and good reputation as a family notable with strong ties to the members of his community. Hajj Najar did not have much of an education, yet he knew how to make money and had a sizeable political role to fulfil as an NDP member and a close aide and adviser to the MPs and the MC members of the area. Since his childhood, he had been interested in political action in the district. Actual membership of the NDP came in 1990 when he became a member of the party unit:

> In 2008, I was appointed as the secretary of the district. I did not actually look for the post but it was offered by the party. This post requires some free time throughout the year, and that is why I could not accept it earlier. When the time was suitable, I accepted it.
>
> Hajj Najar 2008

Hajj Najar is widely perceived in the area as a man-of-good and a notable to be sought out in dire situations. Some people in the neighbourhood were not even certain of his political affiliation, yet stated that they were well acquainted with him as a helpful and influential figure in 'Ain al-Sirra, and they were likely to approach him to resolve a dispute or facilitate a health or an administrative service from the state authorities ('Ain al-Sirra locals, 2008).

The services office supervised by Hajj Najar ensured the delivery of all kinds of services to the area's inhabitants. In addition to the usual health, educational and social services, the office also acted as a link between the people and the MPs, and Hajj Najar himself ensured that the people's requests were submitted to and followed up on by the parliamentarians. The social activities that the centre provided probably constituted its biggest set of services, these including frequent services to the poor, the orphans, the unemployed, etc. Students who were incapable of paying their tuition fees, patients who could not afford their treatment and unemployed youngsters were among the various echelons of locals that the office served. For example, if a patient was incapable of affording the cost of the hospital he or she was to receive the treatment in, or the price of the relevant medication, it was sometimes sufficient for such a patient to approach the office for his to her financial condition to be assessed by the social worker in the office. More often than not, the verification-of-need process was quick and simple in order to ensure the patient's swift treatment. If the case was assessed to be eligible for treatment in one of the NDP-sponsored health clinics in the area, the patient was then directed to the clinic with the required expertise. If necessary, the office would also liaise with the relevant state hospital at which the patient could receive the treatment (Hajj Najar, 2008).

Of course, such services were quite popular, given the relatively harsh economic conditions that the majority of locals were facing. However, Hajj Najar said that the office did its best not to turn down any request that it received. Yet, logically speaking, it would be virtually impossible for the few service offices of the area to meet all the demands of those in need in an area like Misr al-Qadima, and consequently the waiting lists of these offices were fairly long. Some of the locals who attempted to apply for the office's services asserted that, in order to be considered for such services in a timely fashion, one had to have some personal connection or relationship with a figure like Hajj Najar to facilitate the process. Others said that it was those who were, in one way or another, associated with the official rankings of the NDP who would be expected to get some preferential treatment from these service offices ('Ain al-Sirra locals, 2008).

The funding of these services mainly came from the donations of some 'benevolent' notables in the area, according to Hajj Najar, in addition to contributions allocated by the central party. The local MC, which was mainly composed of NDP members, played a role in this process, as it often facilitated the distribution of these donations among the families in the area. The office run by Hajj Najar was set up in the area in 2007, and there was another office also across the street, run by Shahin Fouad, the MP at the time, which orchestrated a plethora of similar services and activities (Hajj Najar, 2008).

During the parliamentary or municipal elections, the role of a figure like Hajj Najar was pivotal:

> Being the secretary of the district, I have to take care of a lot of issues relating to the NDP in the parliamentary and the municipal elections. Being educated or high classed is not sufficient here ... you have to be humble, helpful to the people, and subsequently you will be popular: loved and accepted by the locals. This helped me in actualizing the role I opt for as the secretary of the *shiyakha*, campaigning for the candidates of the NDP in the parliamentary and municipal elections. Gathering/securing votes is a tedious process that requires a lot of networks, not only resources. In other words, you could have the funds and resources needed, but lacking the information on how to channel them or who to give them to can turn these capacities to idle resources.
>
> Hajj Najar, 2008

In line with the testimonies of several other respondents, Hajj Najar thought that, throughout the few years that had preceded the termination of the party, there had been a relative improvement in the scope of services provided in the popular neighbourhoods in the name of the NDP. He stated that there was, overall, some positive change in the way the NDP dealt with the popular basis of society. On aggregate, the party was then more focused on actually ensuring that it got through to those in need with the greatest amount of services possible: 'Sometimes also the services that are being increasingly channeled to the people do not stem directly from the party itself but from businessmen and other figures that are affiliated with it' (Hajj Najar, 2008).

The examples mentioned were Dr Ahmed Shahin and Hajj Abdelhamid Sha'ban, the current MPs, who were both, according to Hajj Najar, benevolent businessmen who spent from their own pockets for the good of the people. Shahin was the chair of the Islamic Unity NGO and a board member of the charity foundation of Al Nour Mosque.[15] Yet what Hajj Najar referred to as mere benevolence is not exactly so. The social and financial services provided by these figures played a crucial part in consolidating their socioeconomic profile and popularity in the area as men-of-good. This, in turn, led to a sizeable boost in terms of their political prospects within the party and on the street, which undoubtedly increased their chances of dominating any elections that might take place in the future. And as asserted in Chapters 1 and 2, for such figures being an MP is a predominantly symbiotic process. In return for disbursing funds and resources within the patron–client network, the MP/businessman moves closer to the circles of power within state institutions.

In the 'Ain al-Sirra area, there were attempts to attract people via direct incentives: jobs, tuition fees, health services, etc. For quite some time, the activities of the NDP were concentrated in the realm of recreational trips and seminars, but that was by no means sufficient to counterbalance the wide array of services provided by the MB. The realization of the importance of popular support was also reflected in the criteria set by the leadership of the party in selecting the party candidates for the 2007 municipal elections, for example. NDP Secretary of Organization, Ahmed Ezz,[16] decided that in order for a member to be eligible for party nomination, he or she had to recruit a certain number of new members into the ranks of the party. This encouraged the cadres of the party to focus more on networking and campaigning at the popular level. In Misr al-Qadima, the lowest number that was gathered by an NDP cadre was 100 new memberships, some cadres reaching 200 or 300. This also helped to inject new blood into the forefront of the NDP, and these new faces were more adamant on popular networking than some of the old cadres who were not involved in the affairs of the polity on the ground level. A lot of the old faces fell in the elections in this district due to the lack of networking and popular appeal.

Hajj Najar also states that, at street level, the popularity of the NDP could still vary from one area to another:

> I think we have been scoring more points of popularity in the area lately. Sometimes, there is no unitary logic that determines areas of power and influence of the NDP vs. the MB. On aggregate, the socioeconomic status of the area affects to a great extent where its allegiance is. We have the Sunnia mosque nearby and it has been used by some MB affiliated figures, but now there are no such venues and they are not operational. However, in some other areas they might be more active due to the socioeconomic context. In areas like 'Ezbet Qarn, for instance, and due to the harsh conditions that people live in there, it is easier for the MB to gain more popularity. People

there are mainly manual laborers and they suffer from rough living conditions, so it is easier for them to be polarized in the direction of the MB.

Hajj Najar, 2008

Still, Hajj Najar believed that a lot more needed to be done by the NDP if it were to compete with the MB and other Islamists. More emphasis had to be put on services; people were in need, and there was still a lack of most of the basic services. The number of people who eventually benefitted from the direct services of the NDP was still limited compared with the proportion who were supported by the MB and other Islamic forces.

Exemplar cases of various categories of NDP-affiliated lesser notabilities: Hannan Al-Saidi versus Abdelhamid Shehata

In the Misr al-Qadima polity, there was a diverse set of lesser notabilities associated with the NDP. The socioeconomic, cultural and political backgrounds of these notables varied from one to another, and the variations were so sharp that they led to tension and conflict between these figures. As stated earlier, the lack of homogeneity was rather apparent within the NDP owing to the absence of a clear ideology or platform characterizing the party, which led to this largely chaotic and sometimes contradictory set of profiles for NDP leaders and members. The example below suggests, however, that within this pool of different sorts of notabilities, certain notables were by far more influential and successful than others.

Hannan Al-Saidi was one of the most active operative cadres of the NDP in 'Ain al-Sirra. Her family had originally come from Assiut in Upper Egypt, as had a multitude of other families in Misr al-Qadima, but she had been born and raised in 'Ain al-Sirra and considered herself to be a *bent balad* (daughter of the land),[17] in reference to her strong affinity with and belonging to the popular area. Al Saidi was an interesting and rather rare example of political agency in the area, and perhaps in the entirety of the popular quarters of Cairo, where political participation and leadership by females is considerably limited, especially in the milieu of official institutions: political parties, NGOs, etc. Al Saidi was the chairperson of the local Women's NDP Secretariat and director of the New Fostat NGO (Figure 5.3). In 'Ain al-Sirra, she was widely perceived as a respectable and influential figure capable of extending support to the area's people ('Ain al-Sirra locals, 2008).

The activities of New Fostat are fairly diverse and include a variety of training sessions and course offerings related to interpersonal skills, political awareness and empowerment, in addition to vocational skills programmes for local inhabitants. Misr al-Qadima suffers from a set of socioeconomic problems of which, according to Al Saidi, school drop-outs, child labour and unemployment are some of the most pressing issues facing the area (Al Saidi, 2008). One of the biggest achievements of New Fostat was in helping the area's local skin tannery workforce to lobby against the relocation of their workshops from Misr al-Qadima to Al Robiki on the outskirts of Cairo (almost 50 kilometres away from their original location). Prospectively, 22,000 workers and shop-owners

Figure 5.3 The headquarters of New Fostat.

were expected to suffer from the consequences of this relocation, authorized by the Ministry of Industry and the Industrial Chamber at the time:

> Under the auspices of New Fostat, a multifaceted campaign was organized to freeze the process or, at best, ensure the best terms possible if this relocation was to take place. The tannery workshops had their own demands that had to be fulfilled ... A media campaign was also organized to present the various dimensions of the issue to the public. The NGO organized the necessary networks with the media. A surprise visit to the designated area was also organized in the presence of the media and a meeting with the deputy minister of industry took place on the spot. Accordingly, some of the demands of the skin tannery workers were met; mainly exempting the workers from the cost of the new workshops.
>
> 'Ain al-Sirra locals, 2008

Of course, many of the demands of the skin-tannery industrial community were not met, and hence New Fostat's campaign against the relocation continued.[18]

The lack of proper commuting facilities and the inadequate design of the new workshops were among some of these still unresolved issues.[19] Five major businessmen were in control of the Industrial Chamber of Skin Tannery that stood for this inadequate relocation, and as a result they were consequently sacked from the board during its elections. There was a lobbying process within the chamber that succeeded in bringing other new faces to the chamber's board, and New Fostat also had a role to play in this scheme. The NGO worked on presentation and negotiation skills with the skin tannery professionals who were eligible to vote, and helped them to organize their campaign inside the chamber against those businessmen and board members who had supported the relocation of the workshops (Al Saidi, 2008).

Being an NDP member did not necessarily make Al Saidi's case stronger: 'I do not think it was the NDP affiliation that made things happen in that campaign. It was the NGO itself that made the difference ... The NGO is independent of the

NDP' (Al Saidi, 2008). Saidi also asserted that she would not allow her NGO to turn into an arm of the NDP, differentiating it from other deficient examples of some NGOs that were merely subservient to the whim of some political or religious order. Yet, she noted that, although by law it was banned for there to be a role for the party in channelling resources to the local population via an NGO, there were still some functional ties between the NGO and the NDP. Some networking existed between the NGO and the party members who could be helpful when it comes to obtaining permissions or services from the relevant government authorities: 'Some politicians do not respect this divide, and end up establishing NGOs to increase their popularity and attain political objectives' (Al Saidi, 2008).[20]

Contrary to the widespread conviction of the area's residents that the NDP was rather inefficient regarding the problems faced by the populace, Saidi said there was still much good that could come out of the NDP in this area. For the most part, the problems were huge and required a plethora of policy reforms:

> We worked on altering some laws. As an NGO we tried to establish conventions that witnessed the participation of parliamentarians in order to address the problems faced and the means by which they could be overcome if new legislations were to be adopted.
>
> Al Saidi, 2008

Some successes resulted, for instance in modifying the labour law to reduce child labour, a predominant social phenomenon in the area. The new law was much stricter as it severely punished business owners accused of facilitating or allowing child labour in the workplace. In the aftermath of the recent successes of the MB in the realm of direct services, the NDP had to follow suit, and similar ventures, including medical caravans that provided health services to various segments of the society throughout the year, were put forward by the NDP as well (Al Saidi, 2008).[21]

'Ain al-Sirra and Misr al-Qadima proper: sociopolitical differences and the role of immigrants

One of the main sociopolitical differences between the two constituencies of the Misr al-Qadima district is the impact of immigration from Upper Egypt. As opposed to the relatively homogenous and stable population of Misr al-Qadima proper, 'Ain al-Sirra is still characterized by a sizeable population of immigrants who have come from the Upper Egyptian governorates of Sohag, Assiut and Qena. These waves of immigration have been ongoing until relatively recently, with a plethora of second- and third-generation immigrants currently residing in the area. A big portion of those *Sa'idi* (Upper Egyptian) immigrants are engaged in economic activities such as operating small restaurants, kiosks and juice shops or opening up contractor workshops that provide semi-skilled workers (painters, builders, etc.) for constructional activities. These *Sa'idi* people indeed constitute a reservoir for the generation of lesser notabilities. In addition to the extended family or clan aspect that sometimes characterizes the biases and political decisions of this immigrant population, there is also a dimension of regional solidarity, whereby the people of Sohag are expected to unite together in the face of those who come from other provinces and so forth. In the local polity, one finds that, within the six local party units, much networking and coordination takes place between some members based on this regional solidarity, particularly in the party units of 'Ain al-Sirra (Abdelmajid, 2008).

Big families ... enter the notables

Big families and notables play an important role in the polity of Misr al-Qadima. As was the case with the areas of influence of the notables associated with the ISIs, introduced in the previous chapter, the influence of the big families and notables affiliated to the NDP was more apparent in arenas such as electoral competitions, mediation and conflict resolution between the inhabitants of the area, and in channelling resources and services to the populace. The dominance of the sociocultural values of family or clan bonding and unity among the *Sa'idi* people ensures that these families and clans constitute sizeable voting blocs in any elections:

> They [the big families] have a very important role in elections. Magdy Allam (The NDP MP), for instance, depended on the support of the big families of Fom Al Khalij area, who simply vote in groups, often according to the recommendations of the big family notables. Some of the big leaders of certain areas have a certain price in accordance with the amount of votes they can secure. For example, a certain big name could guarantee that 1000 votes (his following) would go in a certain direction if he was bought out by a certain price, say a 100,000 LE. Another could guarantee 2000 votes and would, consequently, cost more, etc. Some of the big names in the Masr Qadima area include Fathy Galid and the Abol Seoud family.
>
> Al Saidi, 2008

Regional alliances also play a role in the political decisions taken by the notables. For example, some of the powerful figures who originated from Assiut would establish their own NGOs to ensure the delivery of necessary services to the families of Assiut, other leading figures originating from Sohag would do the same, and so forth. More often that not, such regional alliances would also play an important role in determining the direction of votes (Al Saidi, 2008).

It would be expected that, if the notables of Assiut decided that their votes would go to a certain candidate, it would become an issue of regional solidarity *vis-à-vis* the people of Sohag, and vice versa. Of course these regional solidarities are consolidated and further enhanced on the basis of mutual benefit. Again, based on the patron–client model introduced in Chapters 1 and 2, the clan leaders and sub-leaders act as the patrons and sub-patrons of their communities, and the disbursement of the resources both vertically and horizontally reinforces the loyalty of the client (clan member, voter, etc.) to the respective patron.

Example of an NDP-affiliated lesser notability: Abdelhamid Shehata

Abdelhamid Shehata is yet another example of a lesser notability in Misr al-Qadima. He was a construction worker and, over the years, accumulated a considerable pool of savings that enabled him to become a real-estate contractor and construction/pebble factory owner.[22] He gradually built a good reputation for himself in the area as a benevolent societal leader, and started establishing good contacts with the police and other state authorities. He usually intervened with the local state authorities to resolve conflicts erupting between locals and often helped in getting individuals out of jail (Shehata, 2008; Misr al-Qadima locals, 2009). He was also a *semsar* (election trader); he would first register for the elections, knowing quite well that he would not win, and then other candidates would start approaching him to persuade him to withdraw while ensuring that the votes he controlled went to them. Shehata has earned a reputation among those people originating from Assiut as a problem-solver and dispenser of resources and services to the simple workers and other similar societal segments in the area. He controlled an average of 3,500 votes in Misr al-Qadima and Dar Essalam, and there was usually an announced price for this bulk of votes. According to several respondents, the price of Shehata's votes was around 250,000 LE. This sum of money was usually divided between Shehata and the voters he controlled (Misr al-Qadima locals, 2009; Misr al-Qadima NDP members, 2009).

Sometimes, however, there might be a conflict between the regional alliance and the financial agreement. Depending upon the solidarity of the Assiutis in the area, figures like Shehata would sometimes direct the votes for the benefit of a candidate from Assiut instead of another candidate who had already paid the dues for these votes. Logically, such a scam would be almost impossible to discover, as it would be practically impossible to find out exactly where those votes had gone. When it came to the 2008 municipal elections, Shehata's influence was so immense that his son was subsequently put on the lists of most candidates and eventually won a seat in the MC. In 2005, Taissir Mattar, the MP in Misr al-Qadima for the NDP at the time, depended on his collaboration with Shehata for votes (Misr al-Qadima locals, 2009; Misr al-Qadima NDP members, 2009).

The tactics used by Shehata to consolidate his power in the area varied. He could, for instance, make people spread rumours regarding his bravery and benevolence around the traditional cafés, which are quite popular in the relatively low-income communities. To reinforce this image, he could utilize his strong ties with the police and make them arrest a few suspects, and then appear as the hero of the day by walking out of the police station a few days later alongside the briefly imprisoned individual, again as a display of power and influence in the neighbourhood. Shehata later joined the NDP as a member and helped to ensure that a good number of people also joined the NDP with him (Misr al-Qadima locals, 2009; Misr al-Qadima NDP members, 2009).

Some irregularities performed by Shehata could be overlooked by the authorities as long as he ensured that the votes he controlled went to the candidate supported by the regime. For instance, the police apparatus was quite aware of the money paid to Shehata by certain candidates, but that was acceptable provided that the votes would eventually go to the NDP candidate. For figures like Shehata, the relationship with the regime was a mutually beneficial one. For the police apparatus, Shehata fulfilled a multitude of roles; sometimes as an informant on the activities of the oppositional figures in the community who might be deemed threatening or unwelcomed, and sometimes as a dispenser of resources and services presented to the populace in the name of the NDP.

The 2007/2008 MC election stand-off

Hannan Al-Saidi was initially encouraged by various leaders within the party to apply for the internal preliminary elections within the NDP. However, the preliminaries were in fact a scam, a theatrical façade staged to ensure that certain figures were pivoted forward into the elections. Apparently, some powerful figures from the NDP in Misr al-Qadima were adamant on preventing her from advancing beyond the stage of the preliminaries. Violence was used against her campaign team, and the secretary of the NDP's local office, Diab Ramadan Abo Lebda, championed the scheme to prevent Al Saidi proceeding in her electoral campaign. Al Saidi's brother was attacked and injured by *baltagiya* (thugs) who were allegedly, according to Al Saidi and members of her campaigning team, linked to Abo Lebda, and although the case was reported to the police, no action was taken against the aggressors. Ultimately, as a result of this ongoing pressure, Al Saidi withdrew her candidacy (Al Saidi, 2008).

Abo Lebda in fact had a strong relationship with Bakr Omar,[23] an MP from the Misr al-Qadima region. There seemed to be a tacit agreement between the two that figures such as Al Saidi, who had previously refused to be co-opted by their clique, which also included the previously mentioned NDP notable Abdelhamid Shehata, should not proceed in these elections. In the aftermath of the elections, Al Saidi resigned from her post as an NDP secretary. Mofid Shehab, then State Minister for Legal Affairs, contacted her to try and make her change her mind over the resignation, but she had decided. Later, the party denied the fact that it had received Al Saidi's and others' resignations, although these collective resignations were submitted to the party, but Al Saidi had kept a copy from the resignation memo she originally submitted. Given that the police apparatus was on the side of those who almost violently forced her out of the elections, and the fact that the party was incapable of supporting her case, Al Saidi could do very little to deal with the situation in which she had been placed. The only thing she could do, as the MC elections began, was to utilize New Fostat to monitor the elections and report the irregularities that were expected to take place during the process:

> We actually monitored the elections ... our group which was mostly comprised of young men and women, observed the polling stations and monitored the irregularities. In front each of the poll stations, we had an observer that monitored the operational times of the ballot boxes, the number of voters, etc. We were planning for a press conference to publicize the results of our report to the public but we had to cancel it due to immense pressure from the police. The report indicated that there was a huge amount

of irregularities that were almost directed and manipulated by the strongmen of the area and the party in order to ensure the success of certain candidates.

Al Saidi, 2008

Overall, the practices of the NDP and the relevant state authorities involved in the electoral process showed that the party supported certain figures who would maintain a mutually beneficial relationship with the regime. Such figures were mostly the strongmen and powerful leaders who had ties with the police and the big families, and these were expected to listen to and implement the orders of the party without much thinking or discussion.

In fact, over the 30 years or so that preceded its demise, the NDP was adamant on co-opting the popular figures in order to gain access to the populace in the low-income communities:

> Typically, such figures will have to either belong to, or be in close touch with, the big families and clans of the areas within which they reign supreme, be it in the rural areas or the popular quarters within the urban areas. I come from Upper Egypt and usually the party leaders would go and look for the notables of the families and clans of the village or town and co-opt them to join the ranks of the NDP, particularly prior to the elections. During the Nasser years and afterwards the modern state/party regime was more or less shaped and made to fit with the traditional society/polity of the rural and popular areas. This enabled the NDP to look for and lure the traditional leadership of the family/clan/village, etc.
>
> Tammam, 2008

Al Saidi's case brings to the forefront some interesting observations regarding the dichotomy that existed between the so-called 'new-guard' cadres and the old-guard powerhouses of the party, and the societal forces associated with the two factions.

Tensions and conflict within the NDP

Within the NDP, there was some contradiction between the discourse of the party and the actions taken on the ground. The discourse of reform and democratization promoted by the higher levels was transformed into alliances built with notable figures, regardless of the legitimacy of their activities, in order to secure votes and popularity on the street. Figures such Al Saidi and other like-minded NDP members fell out grace with some NDP and state circles after attempting to stand in the face of the popular notables and the police apparatus. As a result of the lack of power and leverage needed to stand in opposition to the state-sponsored notabilities, these figures could not provide the people of the area with the same scale of services as before. For example, prior to this electoral dilemma, it was possible for someone like Al Saidi to get through to the relevant ministers and other figures of authority in the state system, but after the clash with the powerhouses of the party it was almost impossible for her to organize a press conference, let alone reach powerful figures within the state system.

Indeed, people like Shehata, and other figures such as Bakr Omar and Yousry Bayoumy, who were both introduced in Chapter 4, constitute a particular typology with their profitable commercial activities and their sociocultural profile as family notables with sound political networks. Subsequently, the people of the area would seek such figures for conflict resolution and mediation due to their intermediary roles with the government:

> These are just a few examples and there are more of them on the lower levels. The people in these communities would be keen on helping this clique of patrons accomplish their objectives by connecting them to the people on the street and, in return, people gained protection from the thuggery orchestrated by patrons like Shehata and Abo Lebda and benefited from the array of networks that such figures maintained with the government.
>
> Ahmed, 2008

In short, financial resources and sound social and political networks within the community and with the state apparatus were the main tools for political accession. These attributes were obviously crucial for the political ascendance of figures such as Hajj Najar, Khaled Abdelfattah and Abdelhamid Shehata. For others, like Hannan Al-Saidi, and despite her NDP affiliation, the lack of the right scope of networks within the community and the state apparatus, and even within the NDP itself, apparently hindered her from actualizing her role as a notable, despite her successes in providing a multitude of services to the people of Misr al-Qadima via New Fostat. And here the role of the NDP's central authorities in promoting certain NDP cadres at the expense of others was noticeable. The case of Al Saidi reflects how a lack of necessary linkages with the interconnected network of alliances, which involved the old-guard patrons at the central level of the party, and with key figures in state apparatuses and within the lower echelons of the polity, such as the police and lesser notabilities, damaged the political prospects of someone like Al Saidi. In the next section, more light will be shed on the role played by lesser notabilities as intermediary sociopolitical agents.

Patronage and clientelism in Misr al-Qadima: intermediary sociopolitical roles of lesser notabilities

This section aims to scrutinize the role that the lesser notabilities played within the popular quarters as intermediary sociopolitical agents between the higher echelons of the NDP and the popular segments of the polity. In doing so, it also attempts to understand the advent of the lesser notabilities and their potential impact on the prospects of the popular polity after the fall of the NDP.

Ilham Bahi: a counterexample of the lesser notable? The female, well-educated figure and the collusion with lesser notability

Ilham Bahi is the founder and chairperson of an NGO that operates in Misr al-Qadima and 'Ain al-Sirra. She started her social activism in the areas of Misr al-Qadima and Manial (the more affluent middle-class or bourgeois neighbour-hood adjacent to Misr al-Qadima) in 1985, driven, as she says, by the desire to empower the women of her district. She considered running for the parliamentary elections more than once and was admitted into the NDP Policies Committee in 2005 (Bahi, 2008). In a sense, Bahi represents a certain sort of notability, but it is by no means a lesser notability. With a PhD from abroad and a strong functional relationship with people like Gamal Mubarak at the apex of the NDP, Bahi represented a sort of elitist notability. Nonetheless, for someone like Bahi, in order to get through to the lower echelons of the polity, strong alliances with lesser notabilities had to be in place in order to ensure a dissemination of resources and services to the people. Thus, the interactions between such elitist notabilities at the zenith of the political hierarchy with the lesser notabilities help to reveal how the lesser notables of a popular quarter such as Misr al-Qadima played an essential role also in consolidating the power and influence of the party and the higher echelons of notables associated with it.

Bahi said that the majority of the political figures who entered the arena of social services were aiming to gain political benefits. There were also, however, those who were already involved in social work and afterwards got involved in the political process in order to serve the people further:

> I think I belong to the latter category, which is by and large the minority. In 1984, I started my career in development by focusing on the popular quarters, which was a pioneering initiative as these areas were predominantly neglected on the level of the public discourse. Our NGO was a pioneer in many senses, being a secular, non-sectarian, development/women-oriented NGO. Most of our social services were also novel at the time. For example, we were the first NGO to introduce projects of microcredit in the popular quarters. More specifically, women were also at the core of our social services.
>
> Bahi, 2008

Bahi also claims that joining the NDP was not really a priority for her. She was mostly focused on the realm of the social rather than the political, but it seemed that the relative success of the NGO on the popular level in the areas of Manial and Misr al-Qadima drew the NDP's attention , especially with the advent of the new generation of Gamal Mubarak and his entourage. In 2004, Bahi was approached by the NDP to join the ranks of the party, to which she agreed. At the time, she was in fact convinced there was some positive change in the way the party was being operated:

> I had my own agenda and I was pretty much able to say what I wanted in the ranks of the party even if it went against the whims of the members of the Policies Committee. I am not a militant and I've always believed in the possibility of change from within the ranks of the system.
>
> Bahi, 2008

Bahi therefore considered joining the party to be an opportunity to lobby for benefits for the people of the area; skin tannery workers, street vendors and female heads of households were among the segments she worked with closely. Bahi liaised with several other NGOs and politicians with regard to issues such as the dilemma surrounding the relocation of the skin tannery workshops, mentioned above, in which there was some scrutiny by and coordination with people such as Al Saidi from New Fostat.

According to Bahi, the party's failure to deal with the problems of the poor and disenfranchised classes was exemplified in the way it dealt with street vendors. In 2005, a massive campaign was launched aiming to remove street vendors from the streets of Cairo, coinciding with the 2005 presidential elections. As if the party was aiming to reduce its popularity on the street at the time of the elections, this governmental campaign was poorly timed and even targetted those who had official licensing to practise their commercial activities in designated areas:

> We (the NGO) held regular meetings with the street vendors of the district and developed organizational charts of their tentative numbers and the scope of their activities. We also organized a media campaign that aimed at unfolding the brutality of the authorities in dealing with them.
>
> Bahi, 2008

These efforts were partially fruitful in presenting the vendors' case to the public and a prospective solution suggested was to direct some of the microcredit activities of the NGO towards these people. The NGO initiated this scheme, but then the preachers of some of the mosques became involved in order to obstruct the co-optation of those segments by Bahi's NDP-affiliated NGO. Subsequently, an alternative scheme of funding was provided by some MB-affiliated ISIs. Eventually, the funding provided by the ISIs was so massive that it simply overshadowed Bahi's efforts.

The electoral machine ... money talks

Magued Hammam was a lawyer and a professional manager of electoral campaigns who worked with various key NDP figures, including Ilham Bahi. Hammam specialized in the business of elections and had been involved in the elections within the lawyers' syndicate prior to pursuing his career in Misr al-Qadima. He was born and raised in the area and considered himself an original local of this constituency. Reflecting on the municipal and parliamentary elections in Cairo, Hammam assured me that it was all about money. Votes had certain prices, and those candidates who would pay more were likely to win (Soliman, 2006; Hammam, 2008).[24] The example of the 2005 elections was only a case in point, whereby Shahinaz Al-Naggar, the candidate who had allegedly spent more than any other parliamentary candidate in this area and perhaps in Cairo as a whole, channelling millions of pounds for this purpose, was subsequently able to secure victory in the elections. The voters, predominantly poorly educated and suffering severe economic conditions, were limited to only a short-term-sighted approach that favoured direct material benefit at the time of the elections; however, they then ended up being deprived of any long-term services from their prospective MPs, who had practically paid for their votes at the time of the elections and who, as a result, were not expected to do anything further for the constituency as MPs (Hammam, 2008).

Patronage and clientelism in electoral campaigns

The fact that political figures like Bahi were involved in social work in the areas in which they practised their politics facilitated to a great extent the work that had to be done at the popular level in order to publicize the candidate and portray him or her as a benevolent community figure. For instance, Bahi had been already involved in the local polity of the area for several years as the chairperson of an NGO that was mainly concerned with empowering the women of the district, which made her the prime candidate for winning the parliamentary elections in 2005. At first, Hammam and his campaign team tried to facilitate things for her, building on her existing good reputation in the area. Of course, this reputation by itself was insufficient, and they still had to provide resources and services to the constituency, just like the rest of the candidates. Yet having this reputation provided Hammam and his team with a very good starting point.

On the ground, several basic steps had to be taken to organize a successful electoral campaign:

> First, we look at the districts (*shiakhat*) within the constituency. In our electoral circle (#22), there are five districts: Fom Al Khalig, Abol Seoud, Manial East, Manial West and Manial Al Roda. Then, in accordance with the dominant social and economic statuses of these districts, we start designing our plan. For starters, the relatively well-off areas are less important than the ones with harsher socio-economic conditions, as they don't have those potential voters who are willing to go through the hassle of voting in order to reap the benefits of voter clientelism. Conversely, those that reside within the low-income communities are more willing to do so. In our electoral circle, therefore, more attention was given to the districts of Fom Al Khalig and Aboul Seoud as they clearly belonged to this category.
>
> Hammam, 2008

In such areas, all kinds of services had to be provided to the constituency at a certain time before the elections. Direct financial endowments sometimes had to be granted to the notables of the area in order for them to have the sufficient funds they expected in return for directing the votes they controlled for the benefit of a certain candidate. There were almost four or five notables in every district, and the amount of money they took had to be set in accordance with the number of votes they were expected to guarantee. The massive influence of those notables not only stemmed from their economic status as the influential merchants and commercial actors within the area, but was also shaped by the positions they usually occupied as the heads of families that originated from Upper Egypt (Misr Qadima NDP members and social workers, 2008).

At the lower level – that of the ordinary people (the commoners) of the neighbourhood – a wide array of supplies of goods and services had to be secured for the locals. Blankets, stoves, fridges, Ramadan food packages, etc., were usually distributed to the residents according to their respective needs. Simple verification-of-need procedures were followed in order to facilitate the transfer of such goods and services, and more often than not a simple visit to the candidate's office or NGO was sufficient for a resident to get his or her demands fulfilled. Social duties are also important. Either the candidate or his or her representatives have to be present at weddings and funerals, depending of course on the status of the deceased or the newly wed and the stature of his or her family within the community. The candidate or the representative offers congratulations or condolences, and provides the family of the deceased or the newly wed with financial aid to help with the cost of the social congregation and the relevant commitments (the funeral, wedding expenses, etc.) (ibid). In fact, in Misr al-Qadima and other popular communities, only a few NDP cadres upheld these activities in a consistent manner regardless of the elections in order to maintain an ongoing relationship with the people in their constituencies, although the majority attempted to focus and intensify such efforts at election time (Soliman, 2006; Misr al-Qadima locals, 2008; Shobra locals, 2008).

A candidate's NGO would often also play a role in facilitating the process of getting through to the key players at the popular level:

> The NGO served as the basis and the starting point of most of our activities. The 'Natural Leaderships' (the cadres of the social work in the NGO) usually have their networks of contacts within the various neighborhoods. We would gather with them and outline the main key-players in every district, and then capitalize upon that in our publicity. The cafés also played a crucial role. Note that we are now in a cafeteria (Rahraha) in Al Roda ... I must acquaint myself with the owner, the waiters, etc, and then also, through them, get to know more about those that frequent the place and their affiliations. This of course does not just happen automatically and I'd have to dispense some resources to those working at the cafeteria as well.
>
> Hammam, 2008

In fact, this very same cafeteria served as the meeting point for the chief campaigners during a multitude of campaigns with which a lot of NDP members had worked, including Bahi's campaign.

Bahi had her own experience with the parliamentary elections in Misr al-Qadima, first in 2005 and then in 2007 in the supplementary elections. In 2005, Shahinaz Al-Naggar won the elections:

> she spent more than any other candidate (more than 10 million LE). She was virtually an unknown face and, within the ranks of the party, she was not

wanted because she was an independent candidate, at the time of the elections, but she joined the party right after winning of course.

Bahi, 2008

But, importantly, the NDP was also somehow wary of Al-Naggar as she was
competing with Mamdouh Thabet Mekky, the strongman of the NDP in this
locality: 'I think she simply won because she knew how to utilize her resources
best and, above all, she was very successful in infiltrating the police and the
state security administrations, which both played a crucial role in the electoral
process' (Bahi, 2008). In fact, as long as these state authorities succeeded in
blocking the Islamist candidates from winning, the higher ranks of the government and the party did not really care that much about who won, as long as
it was not an MB candidate. The tactics typically employed by the security
apparatuses to limit the chances of a certain candidate winning in the elections
involved arresting the strongmen, usually the lesser notabilities, who were
supporting this candidate a few days before the elections. Indeed, in 2005, they
arrested the agents of Mekky and other candidates, but not those of Al-Naggar
(Bahi, 2008).

In 2007, the NDP had to pick a new candidate to compete in the supplementary
elections that were held to fill in the position vacated by Al-Naggar, who had quit
her post. With no other potential candidates in sight, it was only logical for Bahi
to run as the party's nominee. Surprisingly, however, the party nominated Magdy
Allam, who had no constituency or popular support. None of the indicators really
stood on his side, but nonetheless, because Ahmed Ezz wished it, he was chosen
to represent the NDP in these elections. As a result, Bahi subsequently decided to
run as an independent candidate.[25] Bahi had some support from the people of the
district as a result of the scope of services provided by her NGO over the years
and at the time of the elections as well: 'Thousands of school cases, educational
funds, short and long-term loans, and home appliances, etc. were distributed to
the people of the constituency by the cadres of our NGO.' Bahi admits that she
spent a lot of money in her electoral campaign, sometimes utilizing the NGO's
resources: 'you have to spend a lot if you're entering the parliamentary elections
in an environment like ours ... But it was nowhere near to what someone like
Shahinaz [Al-Naggar] spent' (Bahi, 2008).

Eventually, the will of the security apparatus, dictated by Ezz and his clique,
prevailed, and thanks to an unprecedented amount of violence and coercion
at the polling stations, which virtually prevented a lot of people from casting
their votes, Allam eventually won the seat (Misr al-Qadima locals, 2009; Misr
al-Qadima NDP members, 2009). Hence, despite Bahi's relative successes in the
Misr al-Qadima district as a societal and political leader, she was not yet capable
of confronting the state and security apparatuses that were mobilized against her
on the instructions of the regime's patron, Ahmed Ezz. Bahi was nonetheless
successful in gaining some access to the lower or grassroots levels of the Misr
al-Qadima polity, and perhaps tracing the hierarchy of networks that she utilized
can shed some light on the various strata of the Misr al-Qadima polity and the
interactions that take place within the varying socioeconomic and political levels

and classes in the area. In fact, tracing these alliances will reveal that lesser notabilities have a major role to play in the sociopolitical ascendance of figures such as Bahi.

The collusion of elitist and lesser notabilities: patron-client networks

In order to consolidate the stature of Bahi and such NDP leaders as the benevolent and philanthropic patrons of the Misr al-Qadima community, some linkage between the social services provided by their NGOs and their political role as the leaders of the community had to be established. Madiha Ahmed was one of the active social workers who worked on achieving this objective. She could be described as a prime aide and consultant to several prominent NDP figures in Misr al-Qadima as she had been involved in the arena of social work in Cairo's popular quarters for over 15 years. Ahmed worked in Bahi's NGO for almost 10 years, and for a long time she was considered to be one of Bahi closest aides. She worked with Bahi as the resident representative of the NGO in Manshiyet Nasser,[26] and then, when Bahi decided to proceed further in the elections, Ahmed was transferred to the Misr al-Qadima/Manial office. Her role was primarily to ensure the establishment of sound ties with the community and to facilitate the delivery of resources and services to the people. This also had to be actualized by recruiting cadres (leaderships) who might be beneficial in this scheme of networking: 'We started by enhancing the base of services provided to the Misr al-Qadima/Manial community via the NGO, then capitalized upon that to further advance the sociopolitical profile and repute of Bahi' (Ahmed, 2008).

Initially, working with the NGO allowed people like Ahmed to broaden their communication skills and raised their awareness of the problems faced by the community. The prime social service provided by the NGO was short- and medium-term loans and, by investigating the case studies of the people who were granted loans, Ahmed and her team worked closely with the people of the area and came to know a fair deal about their social and economic needs. Subsequently, when Bahi entered the political scene, her reputation was already well established as the benevolent notable. By entering the political arena, Bahi was also capable of serving the community further by occupying an official role in the NDP's decision-making circles: 'Our district is mostly a poor one, which meant that the scope of services provided to it by the political patron would not go unnoticed and would, to a large extent, determine the degree of his/her popularity and appeal' (Ahmed, 2008). In the course of this patronage network, a wide array of services was provided to the people of the area:

We would provide the people with pretty much anything that our budget could allow, depending on the financial resources allocated by the NGO ... If you are to establish a reputation as the patron in a popular area like Misr al-Qadima, you have to meet the expectations of the locals. For example, when I was working with the NGOs that were primarily concerned with women's affairs, we used to get requests from the women of our district to obtain all kinds of things for them, ranging from stoves and ovens and all varieties of home appliances to educational loans, employment opportunities, and works of restoration and renovation in their households.

Ahmed, 2008

In addition, another crucial factor that played an important role in consolidating the sociopolitical prowess of such patrons was their interconnectedness with the intermediaries, the lesser notabilities who were likely to broaden their patron–client networks in order to guarantee a proper dissemination of these services among the populace.

Lesser notables: networking, features of their profile and their role in elections

The notables in the area are mostly influential figures within the big families (clans). The area (Manial and Masr al-Qadima) had over the previous three decades or so witnessed a massive overflow of immigrants coming from Upper Egypt, so those whose families originally came from Misr al-Qadima or Manial are actually considered by the Upper Egyptian families to be Cairenes (*Masarwa*). This divide affected the way in which those extended families lobbied and voted in the elections. There was usually severe competition between the candidates over the votes of those big families because their votes come en masse and the Upper Egyptians are more likely to vote than their Cairene counterparts, given their dire socioeconomic status and their involvement in networks of solidarity and kinship (Hammam, 2008).

The *kbir el -'Eela* (family notable) is capable of directing the votes owing to his respectable status within the family and, accordingly, the community as a whole. The notable would often receive a certain amount of money in accordance with the number of votes he was expected to generate. These notables are generally involved with commercial activities; they are usually merchants and intermediaries of food supplies, cement, appliances, etc. The social and the economic factors combine here to determine the degree of influence and power possessed by the notables. The financial aspect helps the notabilities in elevating their status within their families and communities by dispensing the resources needed to the people and also by pulling some strings with the state authorities when needed:

It is no secret to reveal that there is an amount of corruption and bribery going on within the various state authorities, including of course the security apparatus, and having the financial capabilities helped in creating strong ties with the police.

Hammam, 2008

On the other hand, the social aspect helps to promote the economic profile of the notable, boosting his reputation as a respectable and trustworthy merchant and providing him with the networks needed to market his merchandise.

In recent years, and prior to the January 25 revolution, the state began to realize the importance of co-opting those figures of lesser notability, acknowledging the crucial roles they play in local politics:

> Look at the most recent municipal elections in 2008. The majority of those that were pushed forward by the NDP belonged to this category ... Mostly illiterate or poorly educated local notables. They are the ones getting things done on the local/popular echelons, given their entrenchment within the community and their ability to capitalize upon the social networks they possess for the benefit of the party. For the popular *kbir* (notables) also, being in the MC is a great success that one should aspire for ... It gives them social honor and prestige, and for someone with such a socio-economic profile, this is a very important achievement that can't be overlooked.
>
> Hammam, 2008

According to several NDP-affiliated respondents, the role of the lesser notabilities was also apparent in the 2007 supplementary elections that brought Allam to parliament, where they succeeded in making a name for this virtually unknown figure in Misr al-Qadima over a relatively short period of time.

Alliances and interactions between the lesser notabilities and the NDP patrons

Hence, the lesser notabilities were indeed pivotal for NDP patrons such as Bahi or Allam for the purpose of networking with the grassroots level. Different lesser notabilities are usually co-opted by different patrons, and the reasons why certain lesser notables collude with certain patrons vary from case to case. For instance, Hajj Gad Megahed[27] collaborated with two NDP tycoons, Mamdouh Thabet Mekky and Ragab Mawhoub. Mawhoub had a stronger allegiance with Megahed as they both came from same *Sai`di* province – Sohag. Bahi was relatively new to the area compared with these well-established old guards of the NDP, whose networks of support had been implanted for decades. Therefore, getting through to these lesser notables was like a dream for people such as Ahmed or Hammam, as campaigners for parliamentary candidates. People like Megahed directed or influenced many voters, and had a certain pricing for their services in accordance with the number of votes they could direct for one MP candidate or another. Indeed, Ahmed cites how, in the course of Bahi's campaign for instance, the team succeeded in reaching some of them and gathered with them, introducing their plan and programme of action for development of the area. However, the soundness of their development plans was not exactly what such notables would be interested in. Instead, what was at stake was the amount of resources that could be dispersed to them by Bahi compared with the other political actors in the community:

> Let alone the fact that our candidate was also a woman, which somehow affected the way such people, usually with very traditional perspectives

concerning the role that should be played by women within the public sphere, received our campaign.

Ahmed, 2008

Despite the impact that Bahi and several other NDP patrons had at the popular level it was also apparent that, at the higher echelons of the NDP, they were not still as influential as the old guard of the party, which was often more capable of entrenchment through state institutions such as ministries, the police, etc. Yet most of the new-guard patrons still attempted to infiltrate those entities that were seemingly more supportive of the old -guard, such as police stations or the NDP party units:

> As intermediaries, we try to get through to these entities: sometimes through gifts of all sorts to the officers and policemen of the police station, and sometimes via offering funds to renovate or redecorate the headquarters of the station, and so forth. We also exerted a lot of effort in keeping our ties with the key-figures in the local Party Unit. But the problem was, more often than not, it was rather vague and difficult to pinpoint whether a certain person or office is on your side or not. They could accept the endowments and gifts that we provide pleasantly and help us out with some issues or permits when needed, but then comes the time of the elections and things get clearer.

NDP members and Social Workers, 2008

Thus, in the case of Misr al-Qadima, in spite of the attempts made by several figures to win over the police apparatus, it was almost a pattern that the police would support the candidates associated with the old guard of the party at election time.

Lesser notabilities against Bahi in 2007

Despite the fact that the state apparatus, spearheaded by Ezz, was not in favour of Bahi taking the parliamentary seat, there had to be a certain façade to cover up what was happening. In the elections, a considerable degree of forgery and manipulation was maintained to block any potential votes from getting through to Bahi. This electoral district has an estimated 120,000 registered votes, with typically only 15,000–20,000 of those who are registered deciding to vote. This time, the opposing candidate, Magdy Allam, won the elections with 14,000 votes. This was unreasonable in practical terms, given that, throughout the district's history, the average number of votes that went to the winner had always been between 4,000 and 5,000 (ibid). The police did everything possible to prevent people from voting in the first place, knowing that the votes would probably not favour their preferred candidate. The notables of the area, mainly co-opted by the leading cadres of the NDP, were also pivotal in this scheme. They helped spread negative rumours against Bahi among the populace, and, utilizing their influence, discouraged a lot of people from voting for her. In addition, Allam (the winning MP) was successful in getting through to the notables with the help of the NDP party unit, and certain promises were given regarding positions in the local MCs for the notables who would support him. This in fact occurred in the 2008 municipal elections, which, as mentioned earlier, brought forward a good number of the old-guard-affiliated lesser notabilities as members of the local MC (ibid, 2008).

Female lesser notabilities of Misr al-Qadima: Jamilla Abdelmajid – a success story?

As shown earlier, there are a few examples of NDP-associated female notabilities who played a multitude of sociopolitical roles in the polity of Misr al-Qadima, including figures such as Bahi and Al Saidi. Whereas the former did not really belong to the category of lesser notability, the latter, despite having socioeconomic and political features that fitted the lesser notable profile, was largely unsuccessful in competing with other lesser notabilities in the area due to a plethora of factors. The case of Jamilla Abdelmajid poses, however, an example of a female lesser notability who was, by and large, successful in cultivating an entrenched web of social and political networks within Misr al-Qadima.

Abdelmajid was one of the most influential NDP figures at the popular level in the area and was eventually elected as an MC member in 2008. She came from a working-class family: her mother was a housewife and her father a labourer in a local factory. Both of her parents were illiterate, and in fact Abdelmajid herself could barely read and write Arabic. However, she attests that, despite her parents' simple background, they were still ardent believers in the Nasserite project of Arab Socialism. Abdelmajid was a full-time politician; she was a member of the NDP's local Women's Secretariat and took pride in the fact that her main source of income came from the allocations she got from the NDP party unit and the local MC, as this meant that she made a living out of the thing she treasured most – 'serving her people' (Abdelmajid, 2008).

Abdelmajid's scope of activities with the NDP was quite rich. The primary post she held within the party was membership of the Women's Secretariat:

> One of the main duties of the Secretariat is to deliver specialized aid to women in all walks of life on the level of the governorate. Female doctors, lawyers, etc. are responsible for raising awareness among the women of the area. In the most recent municipal elections, political awareness had to be raised among the citizens of 'Ain Al Sirra and Misr al-Qadima proper. Women voters and candidates were trained to know more about their rights and duties in the electoral process. Our activities in the local community include educational services, illiteracy workshops, small and medium sized health clinics, vocational training courses and small and medium loans. These activities are implemented in partnership with a variety of local NGOs and businessmen.
>
> Abdelmajid, 2008

An example of such an NGO is the Mekky NGO, run by NDP strongman/businessman Mamdouh Mekky. In fact, such organizations were sometimes utilized by various lesser NDP figures, other than its owner or founder, in accordance with the alliances and networks that the lesser notables maintained with those big NDP names. For the most part, Abdelmajid was successful in sustaining a relatively sizeable web of networks with the key NDP figures in the area, in addition to her strong ties with relevant state institutions, such as government ministries, security apparatuses, etc., which subsequently facilitated her mission as a local notability and an MC member.

One of the success stories that Abdelmajid was proud of in the course of her sociopolitical activities related to her fruitful efforts in negotiating on behalf of 200 workers from the Electricity Company to get their jobs back after they had been laid off without retirement benefits. Within less than a week, she had ensured those workers' demands and secured their jobs. Abdelmajid was successful in lobbying the relevant ministries and drafted formal memos to the State Security, the Prime Minister and the Presidency. The intense level of her involvement antagonized the people higher up in the company and they threatened to harm her and her family if she did not withhold her efforts in the case, yet Abdelmajid said she was not really afraid as it was a very worthy venture as she thought: 'Those people were very simple workers mostly and they were in dire need … Getting these jobs back had to be accomplished' (Abdelmajid, 2008). Ultimately, the company agreed to return them to their jobs with better terms, thanks to the intervention of some key figures in the party and within government.

Such incidents reveal that, as a lesser notability, Abdelmajid was more successful in attaining her objectives as an MC member and an influential NDP cadre than, for example, Al Saidi, in spite of Al Saidi's seniority in the ranks of the NDP Women's Committee. The causes of these different degrees of success relate mainly to the kinds of alliances and networks that the lesser notability cultivates within his or her neighbourhood and also the kind of opposition that he or she might face from lesser notabilities or other notabilities higher up in the party. As opposed to Abdelmajid, Al Saidi was not fortunate on either account as she was clearly incapable of securing the needed networks and alliances that would enable her to infiltrate such state institutions as the government ministries or the police apparatus, while, at the same time, she also faced fierce competition and opposition from other powerful NDP notables.

Manifestations of lesser notability activities during the 18-day Tahrir sit-in

Also, as described earlier in this chapter, there was a great deal of connectedness and coordination between the lesser notabilities and the NDP cadres on the one side, and the police and other state apparatuses on the other, in many of Cairo's popular communities. Several lesser notabilities were reportedly involved in mobilizing *baltagiya* in various incidents after January 25, including the famous Camel Battle, yet the complete realities of these incidents have yet of course to be revealed, if they are to be revealed at all. However, the testimonies and findings of the initial reports issued by the different fact-finding missions mandated with investigating several acts of violence after January 25 reveal that the instigators of many of these were ex-NDP and regime cadres who depended on certain lesser notabilities to mobilize thugs from several popular areas (Fact-Finding Mission, 2011, and interviews).[28]

The prospects of the NDP-affiliated lesser notabilities in the post-January 25 phase

The observations pertaining to the NDP-affiliated lesser notabilities seem to suggest that, even after the January 25 uprising that put an end to Mubarak's regime and the subsequent dissolution of the NDP, the political prospects of the lesser notabilities are still present. The tendency of the lesser notables associated with the dissolved NDP to switch allegiances, and the fact there was no social or political agenda that unified them or tied them to the party, means that these notabilities are likely to remain in the political game despite the dissolution of the NDP. As opposed to big NDP names and figures who were or could be exposed to legal or disciplinary measures, lesser notabilities are present within the lower echelons of the polity, and it will be virtually impossible to try to track them down for illicit practices during the Mubarak regime owing to their sheer number and their entrenchment within low-income communities all over the country. Most of the ex-NDP cadres have either established new political parties or joined other already existing parties; as a result, the lesser notabilities associated with such cadres also moved with them and started functioning within the spheres of these different political entities (Ex-NDP cadres, 2011).

Of course, the status of many of the NDP-associated figures was negatively affected after the revolution. The dissolution of the NDP led to the disappearance of some of the venues that had previously been used by the lesser notabilities to channel services and resources to the populace, such as the party units and offices mentioned in this chapter. In addition, the image of some of these figures had been tarnished by their association with some of the bigger names that were found guilty or arrested after the revolution. However, for the most part, the disappearance of the NDP as an institutional entity did not exterminate the resources and networks maintained by the majority of these notabilities, which means that they are still ready to mobilize.

Conclusions: patronage politics, the dissolved NDP and the co-optation of the lesser notables

The NDP's symbiotic relationship with lesser notabilities

As shown in this chapter, ever since its inception as the state's ruling party in 1976, the NDP suffered from the detachment from the necessary popular or grassroots bases that could solidify its position in the popular polity *vis-à-vis* other political forces, particularly the MB and its affiliated ISIs. Hence, in order for it to establish and further consolidate its stature as a viable political actor in Cairo's popular quarters, the party was adamant on utilizing the lesser notabilities, which have been thriving in these areas as influential sociopolitical figures, especially since the adoption of the Open Door policies in the Sadat phase. In Misr al-Qadima, as well as in a multitude of other popular quarters in Cairo and elsewhere in Egypt, the MCs have served as a main area for creating the necessary alliances with those lesser notabilities, which constituted the majority of the MC's members and administrators, especially in the post-2005 phase, which witnessed a surge in the attention given by the NDP to the MCs. This co-optation of lesser notabilities has ensured their loyalty to the ruling party and guaranteed the NDP a venue that would, with relative ease, administer the affairs of the popular quarter in line with NDP guidelines. At the same time, the MCs also provided the ex-ruling party with an excellent setting for distributing resources and services among the residents of the popular quarters.

In Misr al-Qadima, the NDP succeeded in co-opting various lesser notabilities into its ranks. A chief factor that affected the ability of certain lesser notabilities to ascend within the ranks of the party was their propensity to generate a web of networks within the state institutions influential in the polity, namely the police apparatus and a wide variety of government ministries such as education, health, infrastructure and so forth. In addition, the lesser notabilities who had a range of sound networks and alliances with the big families of the area also succeeded in further promoting their socioeconomic and political profiles, especially in 'Ain al-Sirra, where a sizeable population of Upper Egyptian immigrants is present. The entrenchment within or influence upon these big families was crucial for the NDP, particularly during the time of the elections, when regional solidarity and traditional authority within the large family or clan could help to direct tens of thousands of votes towards one candidate or another.

The lesser notabilities of Misr al-Qadima have also played an essential role as intermediaries between other categories of notables on the higher echelons of the polity and the grassroots basis at the popular level. In order for that relationship to be attained, an amalgam of patron–client networks has had to be instated to ensure that the dissemination of resources, from the notable on the higher echelons to the lower strata within the popular community, would take place. For the most part, the older generation of NDP leadership, referred to in the course of this chapter as the old guard, was more successful in playing political patronage in Misr al-Qadima compared with the new guard represented by Gamal Mubarak and his neoliberal entourage. The new-guard generation of the NDP was predominantly incapable of cultivating the types of clientelist network necessary for entrenchment within the popular polity, as illustrated by the case of Ilham Bahi. In spite of holding a prime position in the party as a member of the Political Bureau, Bahi was still incapable of infiltrating the various state institutions, as opposed to the categories of lesser notabilities who were often better equipped to infiltrate the popular communities as well as the state institutions. In particular, institutions such as the police apparatus played an essential role in the political processes of the popular communities, as was observed in the 2007 elections, which witnessed some clear intervention from the police authorities for the benefit of NDP figures such as Magdy Allam.

Power structures within the NDP and the cooptation of the MCs

Hence, unlike the MB, which mainly operates in liaison with a wide scope of ISIs, the NDP, in addition to the NGOs that were virtually owned and operated by a wide variety of its members and affiliates in the popular communities, also tended to utilize various state institutions to help disseminate resources and services among the populace. NDP-affiliated state apparatuses, such as the municipalities and the police, provided the party with venues for exercising its power and influence over the populace. Of those institutions, the MCs were an essential venue for politicoeconomic co-optation.

In the few years that preceded its demise, the party acknowledged that there needed to be a more sound connectedness with the grassroots basis, and that this could be achieved via the consolidation of local governance entities such as the municipalities. On aggregate, the degree of autonomy of the local councils over their own affairs was quite limited, with decisions regarding the financial allocations and administrative affairs of the MCs typically stemming from the central party. In addition, virtually monopolizing the arena of issuing authorizations and permits for most of the everyday activities of the locals, the MCs were considered to be the powerhouses that enabled the NDP to exercise its power over the populace by bestowing certain advantages upon some individuals or groups. This turned the MCs into venues for rent-seeking activities undertaken by NDP officials and politicians. Such rent-seeking behaviour often meant that permits and authorizations would be issued, for instance, at a certain price or in return for political allegiance and support during elections.

With the advent of Gamal Mubarak's new guard, the local councils were the prime target for co-optation of the NDP. There is no unitary logic to suggest that the old-guard cadres were always dominant at the local level, whereas, at the central level, the new guard was more powerful. Tensions and competitions between these two main lines within the party existed on various levels and also with regard to the interest groups that were linked to them, i.e. in the realm of the business community. This was exemplified in the case of Ahmed Ezz, who succeeded in attaining his objectives concerning the elections owing to his prime position in the party and the extensive networks he maintained with the various state institutions, such as the police apparatus. On the other hand, the sizeable power that a figure like Ezz had was not matched, for instance, by that of the other businessmen who were involved with the skin tannery factories and who were faced with strong opposition when it came to relocating the skin tannery workshops.

This study reveals that, in the milieu of Misr al-Qadima, the lesser notabilities did not seem to harbour a particular preference for a certain NDP faction over the other. By and large, the lesser notabilities cooperated and allied with those NDP figures who acknowledged their role as popular notables in the low-income communities. As shown by the cases of Bahi and Al Saidi in Misr al-Qadima, and other cases all over Cairo as well, for example the case of the Qasr Al Nil district,[29] the cadres who were unsuccessful in the 2005 parliamentary elections were, by and large, incapable of consolidating the scope of socioeconomic and political networks maintained by their old-guard-affiliated counterparts.

Lesser notabilities ... why politics?

This chapter also argues that, overall, the factors affecting why the lesser notable chooses to enter the realm of politics in Cairo's popular quarters vary from one case to another. In fact, in the cases of a good proportion of the lesser notabilities that this study has attempted to scrutinize, there were not that many options a lesser notable could choose from with regard to his or her role in the community, yet the reasons for involvement of the lesser notable in politics vary. For example, Hajj Najar from the NDP Services Office and Hajj Khaled Abdelfattah from the Misr al-Qadima MC both virtually inherited their roles as community notabilities from their fathers. Other lesser notabilities such as Hannan Al-Saidi and Jamilla Abdelmajid had their own aspirations concerning their role in the community as societal leaders and politicians, and both, especially Abdelmajid, profiteered from their NDP association. The financial aspect also played an essential role with lesser notabilities such as Abdelhamid Shehata, who reportedly made hundreds of thousands of pounds from the votes that he helped in securing at election time.

The lesser notabilities and the post-NDP phase in Cairo's popular quarters

In the wake of the January 25 uprising, the NDP was disbanded and its assets were turned over to the government. Despite the dissolution, the majority of the cadres associated with the party – particularly those that operated in the lower and middle ranks in addition to a proportion of the high-ranking officials within it – were pretty much untouched by the court ruling that terminated the party and are likely to pursue their political activities in post-Mubarak Egypt. Several demands were put forward by the revolutionary forces to impose a ban on the political activities of the high-ranking NDP cadres, but even if this happens, the thousands of party cadres who were operational at the lower and middle echelons, and the lesser notabilities associated with them, are likely to pursue active roles in the political arena in the post-Mubarak phase.

Indeed, the dissolution of the NDP dealt a blow to the array of political patrons associated with the party, as opposed to the MB-affiliated cadres who arguably benefitted from the demise of the Mubarak regime owing to the removal of the state-sanctioned impositions that halted their activities and attempted to suffocate their networks of patronage. However, as portrayed throughout this research, the emergence of the lesser notabilities who were associated with the various political forces in the Cairene polity was directly related to the dominant socioeconomic conditions in Cairo's popular communities; this means that their survival as active sociopolitical actors is not necessarily tied to the existence of one political entity or another. The implications of the impact of the January 25 revolution on the overarching web of patron–client networks in the popular communities and the prospective sociopolitical role of the lesser notabilities will be tackled in the next chapter.

6 Conclusions

Reflections on the sociopolitical
agency and prospective role of lesser
notabilities in the Egyptian polity

Essentiality of the role of lesser notabilities in popular politics

As portrayed throughout this text, the political sphere enabled the notabilities to establish networks and symbiotic relationships with various state institutions in order for them to actualize their role in the popular community as mediators, arbitrators, powerful figures of authority, distributors of resources, etc. It could be argued that the competition over establishing alliances with the lesser notabilities is one of the main pillars of the ongoing struggle between the various political forces over the soul of Cairo's popular quarters. The lesser notable plays an important role at the grassroots level in determining electoral outcomes, administering local affairs and even affecting the street popularity and appeal of the political patrons associated with the various political forces. This chapter aims to draw together a multiplicity of findings and conclusions regarding the role of lesser notabilities in the popular polities of Cairo and the prospective sociopolitical agency of this category of popular figures post Mubarak.

The flexibility of the NDP platform, its co-optation machine and the new guard/old guard divide

In the case of the dissolved National Democratic Party (NDP), the absence of a rigid party platform helped in broadening the scope of the sociopolitical bases that were co-opted by the former ruling party. This gave the NDP more flexibility; for instance, as it had the versatility to collaborate with a variety of actors from different or even sometimes conflicting socioeconomic and political backgrounds. In doing so, the NDP mostly focused on collaborating with societal figures such as the lesser notabilities in order to utilize the wide scope of networks and the moral and material power and influence that such figures possess over the families and clans of the popular polity.

As stated in Chapter 5, in spite of the negative perception they were held in by the popular notables, some of the new-guard cadres of the NDP in Misr-al Qadima were willing, although not always able, to solidify their networks with the lesser notabilities in order to serve their political aspirations. However, these seemingly seasonal attempts to establish relationships and networks with the lesser notabilities were unsuccessful in consolidating sound ties with them. As shown in Chapters 4 and 5, these notabilities could play a tremendous role in either enhancing the prospects of a parliamentary or municipal candidate or, conversely, offsetting the chances of another.

On the other hand, the Muslim Brotherhood (MB) and its affiliated Islamic social institutions (ISIs) have been considerably successful in the realm of co-optation of lesser notabilities, thanks to the extensive webs of patron–client networks that they have orchestrated and that, by default, have required the presence of intermediary agents as such to ensure the consolidation of these patronage networks. The success that the MB and its affiliated ISIs have had in delivering much-needed resources and services to the popular quarters was predominantly unmatched by the NDP, especially in light of the incremental reduction in social welfare services provided by state institutions.[1]

Lesser notabilities and implications pertaining to state–society relations in the wider context of Cairo's popular quarters

The individual/state dichotomy and the power struggle of the state and lesser notabilities in the popular quarter

In Misr al-Qadima, the individual's loyalty to and conviction and realization of the goals and objectives of the ruling party and the state apparatus linked to it was, by and large, absent. The individual's basic needs for food stuffs, health-care services, etc. have hardly been met by such state apparatuses, and instead the NDP and MB-affiliated non-governmental organizations (NGOs) and powerful patrons have attempted to fill the gaps produced by the already diminishing role of the state. This has been actualized with the aid of lesser notabilities and other categories of sociopolitical agents who have been capable of playing several social, economic and political roles. In short, the gradually waning role of state institutions meant that the state had abdicated its responsibility as a welfare state. In this context, the legitimacy and popular acquiescence of one political entity or another, be it the MB or the dissolved NDP, were primarily attained through the intervention of local actors who provided services to the people and, as a result, gained power and influence within the sphere of the popular community. These local agents fulfil a variety of sociopolitical roles as figures of leadership, authority and sometimes even piety and good deeds, as manifested in some of the examples of lesser notabilities presented in Chapters 4 and 5.

Therefore, with the observation that lesser notabilities serve a plethora of personal and political interests, a question of power and also exercise and exploitation of influence by these notabilities over the popular polity has been firmly set in place. In fact, as shown in the example of Misr al-Qadima, the popular polity is incrementally morphing into a setting for ongoing contests over power and authority between state and societal/non-state actors, exemplified in this study

by the lesser notabilities. In addition to the crucial role played by the lesser notabilities as distributors of resources among the populace,[2] they have also fulfilled
other sociopolitical roles as intermediaries between locals and state authorities, as mediators and arbitrators in personal conflicts, as election-brokers and
campaigners, and sometimes even as coercive executors of order – in their own
terms – within the polity. Given their crucial role in administering the affairs
of the popular community, lesser notabilities have become a major target for
co-optation by state authorities, owing to their increasingly elevated stature as
powerful sociopolitical actors.

The lesser notable and contours of state–society interaction, collision and collusion: a state within the state? Al Hokouma and the alternative state

In the first chapter of this book, it was stated that the people's conceptualization
of the state at the popular level determines to a great extent the way they perceive
and deal with official state institutions. Practically speaking, for most of Cairo's
popular dwellers, the word 'state', in Arabic '*dawla*', is almost synonymous with
'*hokouma*', or 'government' in English. Yet, in the context of Cairo's popular
quarters, the main agent of governance is the police apparatus, and thus what
these people mean by *hokouma* is actually the police apparatus. Put simply, in
the eyes and minds of the majority of Cairo's popular quarter dwellers, the state
is the police.

Applying this model to the case of Misr al-Qadima, one can see that the
people's conceptualization of the state sheds some light on the role of the state
in the lives of Cairo's popular polity dwellers today. Equating the state with the
police apparatus and the sheer reduction in the state's perceived role to reflect
solely the coercive and enforcing institutions of the police reveals that the modern
Egyptian nation-state, as originally perceived by the Nasser regime after 1952 as
a service-based welfare entity, is perhaps in reality no more, particularly within
the popular communities. Logically, the gap that was created by the gradual
retreat of the welfare state had to be filled by a variety of actors, mostly from
within society, and this explains the rise of intermediaries, such as the lesser
notabilities, to prominence, and the increasing importance of their role in channelling a wide set of services and resources to the populace. Hence the ability
of such notabilities to have access to and circulate resources among potential
clients is a main determinant in shaping the scope and magnitude of the political
agency enjoyed by these intermediaries. This political agency also enhances their
propensity to fulfil the afore-mentioned multitude of social and political roles
they play as virtual administrators of the popular community.

As displayed in Misr al-Qadima, in fulfilling their roles as vital sociopolitical
actors in the popular polity, the lesser notabilities have virtually collectively,
albeit mostly unconsciously, engaged in a process of creating a societal structure
that has become increasingly capable of performing many of the functionalities of the waning and withdrawing state institutions. This process also entails
a crucial role for NGOs such as ISIs, within which the lesser notabilities have

also been quite pivotal, as seen in the case of al-Jamm'eyya al-Shar'eyya (JS; see Chapter 4). The mounting importance of the roles that such notabilities play in the popular community is reflected in the growing dependence of the 'formal' political actors, i.e. the MPs and the Municipal Council (MC) members, on these figures to consolidate their positions in and administer the affairs of the popular polity. This is reflected, for example, in arenas such as the parliamentary and municipal electoral processes in Misr al-Qadima, in which the informal networks maintained by the lesser notabilities have played a tremendous role in determining electoral outcomes.

Here, it could be argued that this lesser notability-influenced societal structure indeed echoes what was suggested in Chapter 1 regarding the process of cultivating an alternative state – a 'state-within-a-state', which is in a sense gradually encroaching upon the venues of the formal state, almost colonizing them. This is exemplified, for instance, in the networks that several notabilities have maintained with the police apparatus and their subsequent ability to act as intermediaries between the populace and such state institutions, as shown in Chapters 4 and 5. Hence it is safe to assume that a symbiotic relationship between the informal and the formal is in the making. In such a relation, the state benefits from the array of social networks possessed by figures such as the lesser notabilities and, in return, provides them with a plethora of benefits and privileges that empower them further and help to consolidate their positions as powerful sociopolitical actors in the popular community. This suggests that, almost coinciding with its withdrawal from the arena of administering the affairs of the popular polity, and in order for it to execute its policies and govern the populace, the 'formal' state is, in practice, becoming increasingly reliant on the sociopolitical agency of the lesser notabilities to fulfil a number of its previously ascribed functionalities. In fact, this process of 'informalization' through which the Egyptian state has been going exemplifies the state/society models introduced by analysts such as Joel Migdal and Salwa Ismail in Chapter 1. According to Migdal, there exists an ongoing process of dynamic interaction between the official venues of the state and the informal actors within society, which makes it unrealistic to attempt to perceive the state in isolation from society or vice versa.

The sovereignty of the Egyptian state in the popular polity has also been challenged on a regular basis. As shown in the case of Misr al-Qadima, the state finds itself in constant competition with other centres of sovereignty that tend to challenge its authority and sometimes create alternative venues in order to fulfil the functions that state institutions are supposed to perform. This echoes Thomas Hansen and Finn Stepputat's (2005) propositions concerning the limitations of the sovereignty enjoyed by the state. The incremental withdrawal of the state from administering the affairs of the populace in the popular communities of Cairo makes state sovereignty an arena for contestation with social groups such as the MB, or certain actors, like the lesser notabilities. As reviewed in several cases in this research, these entities often attempt to assert their claim to sovereignty via a plethora of socioeconomic and political venues. The case of the JS, which was represented in Chapter 4, is an example revealing that the influence of some of these non-state actors can sometimes exceed that of the state in the socioeconomic and political realms.

In addition, the dominant role that informal patron–client networks play in influencing the affairs and further shaping the ideologies and policies of various civil society organizations, such as the ISIs and the state-sponsored NGOs, suggests that the neoliberal model calling for the empowerment of civil society organizations as substitutes for the state is, in practice, unrealistic:

> Civil society is the area where political and social forces are most active and where political confrontations between these forces are forged. It is also where the state is a major political and economic player ... [It] should be seen as more than the sum of its organisations: it is the environment in which these organisations develop and interact. Civil society organisations are the product as well as the components of the society as a whole and their formation is an ongoing process which is born out of continuing changes in domestic social forces, the state, and the complex in which the two interact.
>
> Abdelrahman, 2002: 91

Indeed, the various examples of civil society organizations cited in this study show that the mainstream 'modernist' approaches that place civil society in opposition to the state and perceives the two as distinctively separate entities with clear-cut boundaries are, in reality, impractical. In addition to the wide array of NGOs and other types of civil society organizations that were directly or indirectly supported and sponsored by the state and the ex-ruling NDP, the heavy intervention of and considerable restrictions imposed by the Egyptian state on the civil society show that, more often that not, the state could be considered as a hegemonic actor in the arena of civil society organizations such as NGOs.

The NDP notabilities vis-à-vis the MB: political patronage and the role of the MCs

Whether it is attained via the overarching web of ISIs or the relatively more recently established NGOs that were affiliated to prominent NDP cadres, the competition between the various political forces over the co-optation of lesser notabilities was an ongoing reality in Cairo's popular quarters. Chapters 4 and 5 have revealed that, for most of the electoral campaigners and political cadres who were affiliated to the NDP and the MB alike, recruiting such notabilities and collaborating with them within the web of political patronage of the leading cadres of the NDP and MB was a prime target to be achieved. This is not to say that lesser notabilities are, in this context, merely passive objects who were on the receiving end of the NDP's and MB's activities. As manifested in various sections of this study, despite the fact that the gradual rise in the role of the lesser notable as a viable popular sociopolitical figure almost coincided with the launch of the Open Door and liberalization policies adopted by the state, the elevation of the lesser notabilities to the forefront of the popular polity was not a sheer byproduct of such policies. Lesser notabilities have indeed utilized and built upon on the opportunities created for filling in the gaps within the socioeconomic and political maps of the popular community.

As mentioned in Chapters 1 and 2, in the Middle Eastern polity, a plethora of categories of lesser notabilities have gone through a process of historical evolution that has situated them in a position allowing them to acquire considerable power and influence within the popular polity, even after the inception of the modern nation-state in the twentieth century. Chapters 2 and 3 argued that, post-*Infitah*, the sociopolitical agency of the lesser notabilities evolved in a way that enabled them to increasingly fulfil a variety of socioeconomic and political functionalities in the popular polity. It is thus worth noting that the sociopolitical agency of lesser notabilities appears to be an evolving, rather than a stagnant or a fixed, agency, which is affected by and interacts with the socioeconomic and political contexts within which the lesser notabilities thrive.

As far as most of the lesser notabilities are concerned, no particular political allegiances are necessarily constant or fixed. There are several examples of these notabilities switching their alliances between the NDP and the MB depending on the sociopolitical context and the benefits that they might be able to reap from prospective mutually beneficial relationships established and consolidated with the former ruling NDP or the MB at particular points in time.[3]

It is the observation of the researcher and a handful of those interviewed for the purpose of this study in the Misr al-Qadima community that the MB and its affiliated organizations were more capable of impacting the lives of Misr al-Qadima locals than was the ex-ruling party.[4] This comparative supremacy could be attributed to the prevalence of MB-affiliated grassroots and community-based socioeconomic and political services in the popular quarters over a very long time, compared with the relatively more recent awakening that brought the NDP and its affiliated personnel and NGOs to the forefront of popular mobilization. Other factors also added up to produce the comparative supremacy of the MB in the popular milieu, such as the presence of a plethora of ISIs with comparatively sizeable budgets, which sometimes exceeded those of the state itself in the realm of certain aspects of social services, as seen in the example of the JS.

The ISIs indeed constitute an integral part of the MB's Islamist project, which consists of an amalgam of socioeconomic and political networks, including MB-associated businesses, educational facilities, communal mosques, etc. Chapter 4 describes how this virtual state-within-a-state of the MB, which arguably aims to redefine state–society boundaries by establishing an alternative system to the failing state institutions, has played a considerable role in providing the populace with a wide scope of services that were largely unmatched by the NDP. Conversely, in the case of the NDP, the lack of such social institutions has left the ground open for the MB and its affiliated ISIs to reign supreme in this arena throughout the 1970s, 1980s and most of the 1990s, as this was the period that witnessed the gradual disappearance of the modern/secular state from the socioeconomic sphere.[5]

There are some mixed signals concerning the prospective scenarios pertaining to political patronage and lesser notability alliances in the post-Mubarak phase. The MB and its affiliated ISIs still appear to be an influential side of this equation, as we have seen in Misr al-Qadima. The exemplar case of the JS shows that it will be virtually impossible for the state apparatus to dismantle the multifaceted web of patron–client networks and resources maintained by the ISIs, unless it succeeds in substituting the socioeconomic roles that such ISIs seem to fulfil. In the meantime, this is somewhat impractical given the wide scope of activities sponsored by the ISIs and the subsequent inability of the state apparatuses to compete with them. The political orientation of the post-Mubarak state is still in the making, and it is not yet clear whether or not it will attempt to confront or compete with the MB and its affiliated ISIs. Irrespective of this, an arena that might hold some promise in this regard is the municipalities, the MCs,[6] which were virtually controlled by the NDP and its associated state apparatuses during the Mubarak regime, as has been mentioned in Chapters 4 and 5. It remains questionable whether this prospective domination over the municipalities will suffice to offset the entrenched network of political patronage that has been maintained by the MB and the ISIs. However, the municipalities appear to be a potential window of opportunity that could be capitalized on in the area of public participation.

NDP and MB notabilities post-January 25

Whereas the NDP and its grassroots levels were exposed to a massive blow after the January 25 revolution owing to the dissolution of the party and the imprisonment of a number of its leading figures, including Gamal Mubarak, the MB, on the other hand, first benefited to a great extent from the removal of the legal restrictions that had used to stifle its activities. Second, the scope of businesses that had played a crucial role in funding the MB's activities, as outlined in Chapter 4, was also freed from the firm scrutiny and surveillance imposed by the Mubarak regime, which means that the MB is expected to thrive further in the realm of amassing its networks of resources.

However, at the level of the patron–client networks in the middle and lower echelons of the polity, the NDP-affiliated lesser notabilities appear to be still considerably intact. As a party that was mainly dependent upon personal politics rather than organizational or institutional structure, those cadres who had previously been associated with the NDP have still been able to reign freely in the arena of socioeconomic and political networking. Even with the prospective ban on the political activities of the leading cadres of the NDP, it will be virtually impractical to halt the activities of the middle and lower-level notabilities. The vital role that was played by the cadres of the dissolved NDP and the lesser notabilities associated with them in mobilizing *balatagia* (thugs) from several popular quarters in order to instigate acts of violence in a plethora of incidents post January 25 shows the power and influence of the lesser notabilities within the popular communities and demonstrates their continuing ability to infiltrate such communities even after the downfall of the NDP.

154 *The role of lesser notabilities*

Summation: an attempt to answer the research questions posed in Chapter 1

One of the main questions posed earlier in the course of this study relates to the structural reconfiguration that has been taking place within the Egyptian polity in the early twenty-first century and the implications this reconfiguration might have with regard to reshaping the political map of Egypt. Put simply, with the mobilization of societal actors and sociopolitical classes that is taking place in the Egyptian polity, new categories of viable and politically meaningful actors who differ from the ones prevalent during the Nasser and Sadat eras are being created. For example, the 1980s and 1990s witnessed the increasing importance of the political agency of the business community as opposed to the military and technocratic classes, which had been somewhat dominant during the socialist heydays of Nasserite Egypt. So to what extent has this structural alteration – witnessed in the post-*Infitah* phase – empowered new classes of sociopolitical patrons and clients? And if it has, can one identify a certain set or sets of sociopolitical actors who are as a result likely to prevail within the Egyptian polity?

As noted in various parts of this study, it is safe to assume that, especially within Cairo's popular quarters, an increasingly noticeable role is being played by a variety of non-state sociopolitical actors, be these individuals or social entities/institutions, in most of the mundane and daily affairs of the people of the popular polity. The sociopolitical relevance and power and influence of those non-state actors have been directly proportional to the gradual, and sometimes abrupt, state withdrawal from the arena of social and economic services. For the most part, the category of the lesser notable stands out as one of the most visible and powerful categories of sociopolitical actors in the popular polity in the contemporary period.

As shown in Chapters 2 and 3, lesser notabilities have dwelt and thrived at various historical junctures within the Middle Eastern city, and it is not an entirely novel social phenomenon to see this grouping of sociopolitical actors rise to prominence in the popular quarters of Cairo in the early twenty-first century. However, it is still important to try to analyse the factors that led to the societal restructuring that brought those lesser notabilities to the forefront of the political setting of the popular polity. In aggregate, the typology of sociopolitical actors that this study refers to as 'lesser notables' are those societal figures who are characterized by their popular sociocultural personas and their ability to maintain and have access to extensive and multifaceted webs of socioeconomic and political networks, both within the community and at the level of state institutions. They are also noted for their piety and good deeds in the popular community,[7] being mediators in conflicts and intermediaries with state authorities and administrations. This research suggests that the failure or withdrawal of the welfare state created socioeconomic and political gaps of a sort that were almost necessarily filled by this category of notabilities.

There appears to be a directly proportional relationship between the withdrawal of the state and the rise of the lesser notabilities, whereby the sociopolitical agency of the lesser notable came into shape and was somewhat enhanced by the increasing retreat of the welfare state in the post-*Infitah* phase. In addition to the aforementioned characteristics of the lesser notable, the findings of this research also show that most of the lesser notabilities who were scrutinized in this study were becoming increasingly involved in formal or official state-sponsored venues of political action. Even the MB-affiliated notabilities are now becoming increasingly involved with state institutions, such as the police apparatus and government ministries, and state-sponsored political activities such as the municipal and parliamentary elections. This aspect of involvement is indeed crucial in order for the notability to fulfil his or her social function properly. Building alliances and networks within state institutions helps to elevate the sociopolitical stature of the notable, allowing him or her to actualize social roles such as mediator with the state and arbitrator at times of conflict.

With the dominance of political patronage, and the widespread role that patron–client networks have as an effective tool for circulating resources and cultivating political power and influence within the Egyptian polity, it has been logical for lesser notabilities to utilize such tactics of political patronage to establish and further consolidate their stature. The absence of the state and the ascent of the lesser notabilities mostly coincided with the resurgence of Islamists – mainly the MB – to the forefront of the political scene in Egypt. Particularly within the popular quarters, the Islamists' rise to political prominence was also in a major way attributed to the withdrawal of the state and its institutions, which were no longer capable of delivering the services needed by the people, especially those in low-income communities. The MB, which has been active in the realm of social work since its establishment, benefitted to a great deal from such state failures. The scope and magnitude of the services provided by the MB and the affiliated ISIs sometimes surpassed the services granted by the state in terms of quantity, quality and even promptness, as seen in the case of the 1992 earthquake.

The first chapter of this book described how the sociopolitical agency of the lesser notabilities has been identified as a social phenomenon by a variety of contributors and analysts. Diane Singerman (1995) and Janine Clark (2004) have argued that, in Cairo's popular quarters, informal networks play an important role in administering the affairs of the populace. In this sense, patron–client networks should be viewed as amalgams of reciprocal networks that represent a political resource as well as a political institution for the populace, rather than being seen as a mere embodiment of exploitative relationships. Thus, building upon this conceptualization, it is safe to assume that the role of the intermediaries who would facilitate the smooth exchange of resources and benefits between patrons and respective clients within such networks is crucial, as shown in various sections of this study. Salwa Ismail, in specific, has outlined the rise of the lesser notable figure in Cairo's popular quarters and drawn a general sketch summarising the main socioeconomic features of such personas. In doing so, Ismail has stated that the sociopolitical agency of the lesser notabilities is in the making and that one subsequently needs to analyse their modes of action, alliances and allegiances (Ismail, 2006).[8]

One of the main objectives of this research has been to build on the contributions of these analysts who have called for an alternative perception of the dynamics of informal networks in the popular polity, as opposed to the dominant focus on state-centered institutional politics that has characterized most of the literature dealing with Middle Eastern society and politics. In this regard, the study at hand has aimed to scrutinize the politics of the lesser notabilities and the possible directions that their involvement in local and national politics may take. The research findings suggest that, primarily due to the sizeable role they play in shaping the informal socioeconomic and political networks of the popular polity, the lesser notabilities help to reduce the already blurry boundaries between state and society and were thus key players in the political patronage of the NDP and MB alike. Indeed, lesser notabilities could be considered to be vital actors in the MB's project, which has succeeded in infiltrating the predominantly state-neglected popular communities.

As long as the socioeconomic setting that has favoured the flourishing of lesser notabilities as viable sociopolitical actors prevails, they are likely to remain active subjects who fulfil a plethora of social, economic and political roles in the popular communities of Cairo. The lack of a particular political agenda or ideology that gathers them, and the fact that these lesser notabilities sometimes also have a set of diverse social and cultural backgrounds, despite the fact that they also share an array of commonalities, made it possible for many of these lesser notabilities to collaborate with the NDP as well. This research argues that there appears to be no unitary logic why certain lesser notabilities have chosen to collaborate with the MB while others have allied with the NDP.

Yet, there are of course, as seen in Chapters 4 and 5, a multitude of factors that have driven the lesser notables in the direction of the NDP as opposed to the MB and vice versa. The scope and magnitude of such factors vary, depending mainly on the socioeconomic, political and cultural conditions of the community in which the lesser notable thrives and the sort of socioeconomic networks within which he or she operates. For example, in some professional middle-class-dominated Cairene polities, it has not been uncommon for a lesser notable to collaborate with the MB and not the NDP owing to the relatively influential socioeconomic and political roles played by the MB in some of these polities. Within the popular quarter, which is the subject area of this research, allegiances between lesser notabilities and the NDP or the MB have been, by and large, contingent on a diverse set of constantly changing socioeconomic and political rationales, which has made such alliances rather volatile and ever-changing, as asserted earlier. For example, within the popular areas in which the ISIs are active, it is likely that one will find a handful of MB-associated lesser notabilities. Conversely, and at certain junctures when the state attempted to, say, clamp down on the activities of Islamists in a certain neighbourhood, as noted in some areas of Misr al-Qadima, it would be logical for the lesser notabilities to alter their alliances away from the MB and towards the NDP and so forth. Overall, as manifested in the NDP's attempts to reinvigorate and co-opt the MCs, it appears as if the former ruling party was following in the footsteps of the MB.

Throughout this research, it has also been shown that the sociopolitical phenomenon of patronage is predominantly present among the various echelons of the Egyptian polity. The political regimes of Nasser, Sadat and Mubarak all attempted to benefit from this scope of patron–client networks in various ways. A set of common preconditions for political patronage was quite prevalent throughout the eras of Egypt's three chief regimes after 1952. First, the presence of a *shilla* or a clique of first-rate clients who are all linked to the ruling circles was a recurrent theme with Nasser, Sadat and Mubarak. The functioning of these *shillal* occurred in a horizontal manner among the various key players of the Egyptian polity. A vertical scope of patronage that stemmed from the patron(s) at the apex to the clients in a top-down approach was not uncommon throughout that period. Second, the existence of a specific category of clients, and a pool from which these clients emerged that was characterized by a bundle of sociopolitical inclinations and strata, was also crucial for patron–client networks to take shape and become actualized. As displayed in various sections of this writing, these 'classes' of patrons and clients have altered throughout the eras of Nasser, Sadat and Mubarak. Each of these eras was characterized by a particular taxonomy of relevant patrons and clients, which varied depending on the context within which the Egyptian political system existed at the time.

Building upon the observations regarding patron–client networks, it is safe to assume that the scheme of patronage politics, which operates within various societal and political echelons, has played a great role in shaping the features of the Egyptian polity at the ascent of the twenty-first century. Throughout this book, it has been apparent that the political regime was mainly reliant on this scheme of patronage politics in its attempts to build alliances with relevant political agents in the community. Bearing in mind that patronage is an outcome of interlinked processes of clientelism, the presence of a powerful group of patrons within the system is vital for this complex network to survive and prevail. It is essential to contextualize the phenomenon of political patronage and comprehend the factors that foster such a scheme as it would be somehow misleading if we stripped this socioeconomic phenomenon from the realities of the polity within which it is present.

Political patronage after Mubarak

So, in order to dissect political patronage, we have to examine its manifestations in line with the general politicoeconomic context within which it is present. Issues such as socioeconomic stratification, availability of resources, income distribution and the presence of venues of political participation or representation are among the main topics that need be addressed in order to scrutinize patronage politics. As reviewed in this study, the socioeconomic and political contexts of Egypt in the early twenty-first century seem to suggest that different categories of relevant patrons and clients are in place among the various echelons of the polity. Within the popular polity in particular, the lesser notabilities constitute the chief category of sociopolitical agents who shape and influence patron–client networks.

It is safe to assume that the features of the patron–client stratagem in the post-Mubarak phase will be affected by the social contract that will shape state–society relations after the Mubarak era. In other words, unless the calls for social justice and equality echoed by the social movements that spearheaded the massive uprisings are translated into clear-cut alterations in the socioeconomic policies adopted by the state, it will be highly unlikely that the machinations of patronage networks will be drastically changed in the foreseeable future. The people's dependence on informal networks of clientelism represents, in a way, an attempt to create and solidify an alterative set of socioeconomic and political institutions *vis-à-vis* the already existing yet failing 'formal' state institutions. And, as a result, the legitimacy of the state as a sovereign entity that is capable of maintaining law and order among its subjects has become questionable, especially in the low-income and popular communities. As seen in the case of Misr al-Qadima, the lesser notabilities lay at the core of these clientelistic structures that served a variety of social, economic and political functions in the aftermath of the state's withdrawal from the public sphere. It would be interesting to scrutinize the changes and potential roles that the lesser notabilities could play in the realm of popular and informal politics post Mubarak, for that is an area which is worthy of further research and analysis.

Postscript

Unsuccessful attempts at political ascent: alternative categories of notabilities – Ahmed Abdalla 'Rozza' and Al-Jeel Center

In the popular polity, the society notables who belonged to the well-educated or secular classes were mainly incapable of promoting their socioeconomic and political profiles as powerful political actors. In Misr al-Qadima, Ahmed Abdalla 'Rozza' provides a relevant example of this. In fact the experience of Rozza, who passed away in the aftermath of a shocking loss in the 2005 parliamentary elections, probably represents the counterexample of the lesser notable phenomenon. Rozza, who was a Cambridge graduate and had been a prominent activist and intellectual ever since he had been part of the student movement opposing the policies of President Sadat from around 1971 onwards, scored a surprisingly low number of votes when he decided to run in the parliamentary election.[1] He did not have well-known familial or clan ties to any of the major families of the area, and he certainly did not occupy any commercial or business roles that could enable him to channel resources and services to potential supporters. Instead, Rozza attempted to create an educational and cultural grassroots base within the Misr al-Qadima community by providing recreational and educational activities for its young people.[2]

Rozza's version of societal services came in the form of the Al-Jeel Center for Research and Youth Development. Established in 1995 by the prominent intellectual and activist as an initiative to serve the area he belonged to, by 2008 the centre had become home to a handful of old friends and acquaintances who were striving to keep it alive after the demise of its founder in 2006. Once established, the prime objective of the Al-Jeel Center was to act as a focal point of research pertaining to the Misr al-Qadima area. The centre had a depository of resources on a wide variety of social, economic and political issues relating to Misr al-Qadima and other urban and rural districts in Cairo and other governorates. It also issued a periodical that aimed to raise the awareness of the area's inhabitants regarding the major socioeconomic and political issues.

In addition, the centre paid special attention to the dilemmas facing the local children. The Misr al-Qadima area has one of the highest ratios of child labour all over Egypt,[3] and Rozza had a firm vision that some bond had to be set up between the young activists working at the centre and those children in order to provide them with an outlet to vent out their creative energy. Rozza's project depended on showcasing the talents of those children via some recreational activities that were not necessarily related to a rigid educational programme, so he constituted the activities unit at the Al-Jeel Center to serve this purpose. The outcome was to a degree successful, and eventually a considerable number of children started to participate in the weekly activities.

Furthermore, the centre provided a multitude of other services to the people of the A'in Sira community. A medium-sized library was available for reading and borrowing a wide variety of books related to almost all areas of life, and a few resident social workers were made available to help solve some of the social hardships faced by the area's inhabitants.

However, the centre also suffered from a multitude of hindrances that prevented it from creating a sound social base within the community. Mainly, there was a general lack of financial resources due to Rozza's tendency not to accept any funding or grants from abroad as he believed that this would inevitably infringe upon the centre's autonomy. Therefore, the main sources of funding were individual contributions from enthusiasts, primarily Rozza and the team working with him at the centre, and this by and large limited the sources of income available. Moreover, the mere nature of the activities and services provided by the centre, as a think-tank and an activities venue for the marginalized and voiceless segments of society, did not help in establishing any networks of support within the community. Thus, when compared with the other non-governmental organizations or Islamic social institutions that were mainly concerned with providing the people of the area with direct services and resources to aid them in their daily affairs, more often than not in return for political allegiance to and support for the leading figures within those organizations, the centre did not help in raising Rozza's prospects as an influential political figure.

Therefore, Rozza's comparatively poor results at the polling stations were not really a surprise. Overall, the scope of cultural and recreational activities for the marginalized population was not a viable asset that he could depend on to attain political popularity in an area like 'Ain al-Sirra. Compared with the lesser notabilities, Rozza did not have the financial capacities, the firm family or clan ties, or the prominent position within the community as a societal leader,[4] that were all essential for someone about to enter the realm of sociopolitical agency in the popular communities. Upon entering the political popularity contest, he could not compete with such figures on that level.

In actuality, the alternative example that Rozza attempted to provide further emphasizes the fact that such ventures cannot bring their originators to the forefront of political agency. An interesting question here is, what are the prospects of figures like Rozza for ascending within the political sphere in the post-Mubarak phase? Will the social movement that led to the demise of the Mubarak regime produce the socioeconomic, political and cultural changes that will allow societal figures such as Rozza to play a viable role in the Egyptian polity post-January 25? Only time will tell.

Appendix: Outline of interviews

The fieldwork upon which this study is based was conducted over a period of two years of field visits to Misr Al Qadima and other popular quarters in Cairo, which extended from 2007 to 2009. It consisted of more than 75 in-depth and open-ended interviews and focus-group discussions, mainly with the people of Misr al-Qadima and a few other popular areas, in addition to personal observations of everyday activities and interactions. During the same period, I also conducted a set of interviews with a variety of politicians, journalists and non-governmental organization (NGO) activists from all over Cairo. The names of most of the interviewees mentioned in this writing are real names, used of course with the permission of those interviewed. However, with some of the cited names, and due to the sensitive nature of the information they provided, I have used pseudonyms, in accordance with the interviewees' preferences.

Most of the interviews were carried out on a one-to-one basis, although some were held in small groups in a café, an NGO or a party office, or in the workplace, as stated in the research. The socioeconomic backgrounds and professional occupations of the majority of those with whom I conducted in-depth and one-to-one interviews are elaborated upon in the writing. However, this has not been the case with some of the respondents interviewed in small groups or on the street, and these were referred to in the course of the writing as Misr Al Qadima residents, National Democratic Party (NDP) members, etc. Therefore, in order to display an overall sketch of the socioeconomic biographies of the respondents, it is relevant to insert here Table A.1, which represents an overview of the genders and principal occupations of all of those interviewed for the purpose of this study.

Table A.1 Genders and principal occupations of interviewees

Job/sociopolitical occupation	Male	Female	Total
Doctor	2	1	3
Engineers	2		2
Journalist	3		3
al-Jamm'eyya al-Shar'eyya employee	5		5
Lawyer	1		1
Leather merchant	4		4
Merchant (other)	2	1	3
Municipal council member	4	1	5
MP	3		3
NDP employee (income solely form the NDP)	3	2	5
NGO chairperson	1	4	5
NGO employee	5	4	9
Peddler		3	3
Researcher	3		3
State employee	4		4
University student	3	1	4
Worker	6		6
Workshop owner	7		7
Total	58	17	75

Notes

1 Introduction, theoretical framework and methodology/approaches

1   Chapter 2 deals with this term in detail, contextualizing the notables and their lesser
    successors, and the role they have played within the Egyptian polity ever since the
    Ottoman period. Hana Batatu (1999) was one of the first contributors to use the term
    to describe a certain category of rural notability in Syria. The term 'lesser notable'
    was later used by Salwa Ismail (2006) to describe the type of notabilities that this
    research deals with.
2   Perhaps the Economic Reform and Structural Adjustment Program of a country like
    Egypt is a case in point, in which the upper echelons of the business community
    became empowered under the new realities to formulate a relatively new typology of
    patrons and clients in alliance with the governing regime.
3   See also S. Ismail (2006), on the *biytkabarluh* figure and the mixture of pragmatic
    and moral authorities he possesses within Cairo's popular neighbourhoods.
4   Ansari (1986) presents a few pointers regarding this aspect. He deals mainly with
    the sociopolitical diagnosis of the state structure in the post-1952 regime through an
    investigation of agricultural patterns and the role of the rural sector within the state.

2 Who are the lesser notables?

1   Note the similarities between the qualities of the *futuwwa* figure in Cairo's quarters
    in the early twentieth century and those of the contemporary urban lesser notabilities
    introduced in Chapter 1. In addition to the relevance of physical strength and courage
    as features of today's influential lesser notabilities, there are modern equivalents
    of such qualities that often characterize the twenty-first-century lesser notable. For
    instance, in this case, the power and influence that the contemporary lesser notability
    possesses and that often enable him to actualize certain objectives on the ground, for
    example by issuing a building licence or by granting a person an employment oppor-
    tunity, could be considered as equivalents. Furthermore, the financial capability of
    the contemporary lesser notabilities can be viewed as the modern-day equivalent of
    the physical strength that the *futuwwa* enjoyed in the past.
2   Here, the term 'lesser notables' connotes a sort of notability that is not necessarily
    linked to agrarian or land-owning privileges, as shown in the cases presented in
    Batatu's (1999) contributions on Syria, for example. Egypt's new typology of lesser
    notables includes a multiplicity of commercial agents: small to medium-sized busi-
    nessmen, contractors, shop-owners, etc. These figures have succeeded in estab-
    lishing a scope of political agency that pivots around their moral and social roles as
    community leaders who are mostly active within the popular quarters. Overall, there
    has been a significant surge in the role played by those lesser notables with the advent
    of the *Infitah* and then the Economic Reform and Structural Adjustment Program
    policies in 1974 and 1991, respectively.

3 Misr al-Qadima

1   Quote taken from the introduction to the film entitled *Misr Al Qadima: Legal and Political Participation*. Documentary, Legal and Political Participation Project in Misr Al Qadima, Cairo, 2006.
2   El Messiri (1978: 2–4) states that the *ibn al-balad* is characterized by 'Gaiety, good humor mixed with sarcasm and cynicism, and a tendency to live for the moment'. Other characteristics include 'simplicity and goodness'. *Ibn al-balad* should also be 'loyal to his country, love it and remain attached to it; unless a man is patriotic, he is not identified as a true ibn al balad ... [He] also sees himself as being direct and simple in speech, not sophisticated'.
3   Interviews with Misr al-Qadima residents from the old quarter; June–August 2008. In addition to the fact that most of the respondents considered themselves as '*awlad al-balad*', those respondents also echoed the observation that the majority of the residents of the old quarter also belong to the same category of inhabitants, meaning that their roots could be traced back to the same area within which they resided.
4   According to this study, in 1991 the informal economy constituted approximately 40 per cent of the total economy of Egypt. 'Furthermore, some surveys estimated that the volume of informal enterprises (entrepreneurs) in Egypt is 1.4 million with a percentage of 82 per cent of the total economic activities. The informal sector absorbs nearly 8.2 million workers with a percentage of 40 per cent of the total labor force' (Attia, 2009: 16).
5   Chapters 1 and 2 of this research deal with the concept of *infitah* and its effect on socioeconomic class stratification and social mobility.
6   Here, Assaad cites that, between 1988 and 2006, the construction sector also grew faster than average, at a rate of 5.9 per cent per annum, to capture an 8 per cent share of total employment in 2006.
7   The indicator of the degree of political awareness was measured according to the respondents' ability to answer a set of questions covering various political issues, at a local as well as an international level, in addition to a questionnaire on the main political institutions at governorate and country levels (the Municipal Councils, the parliament, the Cabinet, etc).
8   This national rate is much higher than the official figure released by the Mubarak regime for those who participated in the 2005 presidential elections (22 per cent of total eligible voters).
9   In a public poll conducted in September 2011 on a random sample of Egyptians from various age groups across Egypt, 97 per cent of respondents said that they had not been introduced to or approached by any political party since the demise of the Mubarak regime, and more than 50 per cent stated that if they were to participate in parliamentary elections, they would not vote for any political party. Source: *Analysis of Five IPSOS/NDI Surveys in Egypt: April-August 2011*, National Democratic Institute For International Affairs, September 2011.

4 The Muslim Brotherhood, al-Jammʿeyya al-Sharʿeyya and networks of support in Misr al-Qadima

1   The JS was established in 1912 with the primary objective of spreading Islamic awareness and *daʿwa*. In 1967, the JS was officially recognized as a civil society organization in accordance with the law issued in the same year to organize the affairs of civil society organizations.
2   By 1970, the year that witnessed Sadat's ascent into power, it was obvious that Egypt's five-year plans, which had targetted a reduction in the net value of imports and an improvement in the balance of payment, had failed to achieve their goals. In fact, in 1966, and even before the 1967 defeat, the value of net imports almost doubled, from 215 million LE in 1961, to 431 million LE in 1966. As a share of gross domestic

product (GDP), the value of net imports also increased from 15 per cent to 20 per cent of GDP within the same time period. Moreover, the deficit in balance of payments also increased, from 113 million LE to 166 million LE between 1961 and 1966.

3   As stated in Chapter 1, Sadat's empowerment of the Islamists (the MB and other militant groups) eventually brought about his own demise at the hands of Jihadist militants in 1981. By the time Mubarak took over, it was virtually impossible to counterbalance the huge spectrum of activities sponsored by the MB and other Islamists, and the regime was more or less forced to play stick-and-carrot negotiations and truces with the MB instead of confronting it. The regime's severe confrontation with 'Militant' Islam, represented by the groups that condoned violence against the regime, such as al-Jihad and al-Jamma'a al-Islamiya, as opposed to the 'moderate' Islamism of the MB, has nonetheless been ongoing since Sadat's demise. In 2005, the leaderships of 'militant' Islam renounced violence against the state and brokered a deal with the regime, securing the release of a large number of their cadres from state penitentiaries.

4   As opposed to the mosques that lie under the jurisdiction of the state, represented by the Ministry of Awqaf and Religious Affairs and the state-affiliated religious institution Al Azhar, these communal mosques are autonomous in terms of their sources of funding and also have their own *Imams* (priests), who are not supervised or monitored by Al Azhar or the aforementioned ministry. In its efforts to suppress the increasing influence of the Islamists, the police apparatus has been targetting a plethora of these communal mosques, shutting them down and arresting some of their *Imams*. However, due to their relatively small size and sometimes low profile, such mosques are often very hard to quantify, and consequently to target, which has to date made them rather influential, especially in the low-income communities of Cairo and elsewhere in the rural areas.

5   Most of these 'Islamic' businesses are similar to their secular counterparts, only with an 'Islamic' characterization to them represented by an Islamic dress code for the employees and/or an ethical/religious social and moral code. The owners and chief stakeholders of these Islamic ventures have been predominantly MB affiliates and sympathizers. A sizeable portion of the profits coming from these businesses constitutes a main source of income for various ISIs and the MB itself, and the channelling of such resources to these entities sometimes takes the form of sponsoring charitable activities, mostly also associated with the scope of services provided by ISIs.

6   Source: Naguib, S. (2005) *Al Ikhwan Al Moslemoun: Ro'eya Ishtirakeyya*, Cairo: Center for Socialist Studies, p.88. This aspect is of paramount importance in reaching out to the polity, noting the huge number of mosques that lie within the jurisdiction of the MB, which surpasses 5,000 mosques all over Egypt, as mentioned earlier.

7   In 1993, and in response to the successes of the opposition parties along with those of the MB and other Islamists within the professional syndicates, the state issued the Unified Syndicates Law; Law 100/93: Guaranteeing Democracy in Professional Syndicates. This was enforced upon all professional syndicates in order to place them under close state scrutiny and control. The provisions of Law 100/93 set particularly high electoral quorums, specifically 50 per cent + 1 of the eligible voters from each syndicate's general assembly. Election results were invalid if this quorum was not met.

8   There are other figures who do not necessarily belong to the category of lesser notabilities yet play an instrumental role in orchestrating the financial networks of the MB, such as engineer Khairat Al-Shater, the prominent businessman and Deputy Guide of the MB. Al-Shater was imprisoned by the Mubarak regime in 2005 in the wave of arrests that targetted the leading figures of the MB, and was released after the January 25 revolution.

9   See this chapter for an overview of the role of the communal mosques that operate outside the jurisdiction of Al Azhar and the Ministry of Awqaf and Religious Affairs. For the most part, the MB-affiliated *do'at* stand in opposition to the *Imams* and

religious cadres associated with Al Azhar, who are being increasingly portrayed by the MB and other Islamist forces as the mouthpieces of the regime and the government, rather than being independent religious scholars.

10 Hossam Tammam is a journalist and researcher, as well as the editor of Islam Online, a pioneering internet portal that presents and discusses the news and discourses of a plethora of Islamist movements around the globe. Tammam stressed that the office where we held our conversation also hosted a research centre dedicated mainly to studying the social and political implications of the phenomenon of political Islam.

11 Hassan Malek is a businessman who owns and operates one of the chief furniture stores in Cairo and is considered to be one of the main financiers of the MB.

12 Al Tawhid Wal Noor is a series of clothes stores that was owned and run by Al Swirky, a businessman and MB member. These shops scored an immense degree of success and popularity due to their wholesale prices, which were quite competitive when compared with those of similar stores. Its degree of success was so great that it expanded to virtually all of Cairo's popular quarters, almost driving all of its competitors out of business. Meanwhile, the state was irritated by Al Swirky owing to his growing profits and sound ties with the financing of the MB. Eventually, Al Swirky was condemned in a civil court on a charge of polygamy. According to the accusation, he had married a fifth wife prior to the conclusion of the 90-day interim period that is mandated by the Islamic *Shari'a* law after divorcing his fourth wife.

13 The list of accusations that the MB cadres were facing, as announced by the General Prosecutor, included money laundering, receiving financial transactions from abroad in order to finance the MB's activities and utilization of the profits generated by several domestic firms in funding the operations of the MB's committees in Egypt.

14 The reported relationship between some ISIs and petrodollars has been mentioned in some local pro-NDP newspapers and is, among the populace in places such as Misr al-Qadima, believed to exist, mainly at the level of individual contributions. However, the researcher has not seen any documented evidence to substantiate this claim.

15 The observation regarding the participation of MB affiliates in the funding of the Orphanage Sponsorship Program is also firmly in place at the local (municipal) level. In Misr al-Qadima, for instance, several MB affiliates have noted the linkage between some prominent Misr al-Qadima MB cadres and the funding of the programme at the level of the district.

16 In the office, there were three men, all bearded and dressed in traditional Arab-Islamic *Jalabiya*. The writer introduced himself as a researcher who was investigating the activities of the social organizations in the area, and he was of course met with some suspicion. The person in charge (Hajj Mohamed) said that he would not talk to me unless there was an official note from a 'national' research entity, indicating the nature of my research. However, after some effort, he reluctantly agreed to talk a bit about the goals, objectives and achievements of the society at a local level.

17 Indeed, the prime questions that needed to be asked with regard to maintaining the close connection between the JS and the MB and the sort of assistance that the JS provided for MB candidates in the parliamentary and the municipal elections could not be asked outright, in view of the sensitive nature of the issue and the fact that such a linkage is officially prohibited by law. Nonetheless, Hajj Mohamed tackled these points as he was presenting the case of the JS in the area, as he probably felt it was his duty to provide a proper portrayal of the scope and magnitude of the JS's activities.

18 Referring to the JS as a totally self-funded organization is not completely accurate. Just like all other local NGOs, the JS receives partial financial support from the state. This, in addition to the sizeable endowments that the JS receives from individual and entrepreneurial contributors – constitutes a source of funding that could be described as external sources that are not directly generated from the activities of the society.

19 In fact, most contributors would attempt to contact more than five additional donors, albeit not always being successful in persuading these prospective funders to donate. However, the mere attempt to contact such potential contributors is viewed as a religious duty and is often seconded and encouraged by the facilitators of the JS.

20 In this regard, Bahi's take on JS activities in Misr al-Qadima is a relevant testimony as she was subject to fierce competition from those JS/MB cadres, being a prominent Misr al-Qadima NDP cadre herself.

21 The post-1992 earthquake stand-off that took place between the state authorities and the ISIs in several parts of Cairo is described in Chapter 1.

22 See Chapter 3 for a detailed overview of the two main districts of Misr al-Qadima.

23 The new economic realities to which Hajj Abdelaal referred are mainly the neoliberal economic policies adopted by the government in the post-1991 era. This bundle of policies included, in addition to an overall emphasis on the reduction of the role of the state, a firm preference for private sector ventures at the expense of public ones, which had become incrementally less profitable. As the 'big' private skin tannery factories flourished in Misr al-Qadima, and in accordance with the 'economies of scale' rationale, there was only room for those mega-factories that pumped in sizeable investments – primarily in joint ventures with Italian foreign direct investment – and operated on a large scale to swallow the market. As a result, the smaller tanneries that Hajj Sayed and thousands of others were working in were almost entirely driven out of business, and only four or five businessmen were left in control of the skin tannery business in the area. This case will be looked at in more detail in Chapter 5 as the researcher further scrutinizes the association those businessmen had with the dissolved NDP.

24 In the 2000 and the 2005 parliamentary elections, the NDP adopted a certain tactic of co-opting the 'independent' candidates – those who were not running under the label of any official political party – who succeed in the elections after the electoral process is over. It is only via this tactic that the NDP was able to secure a majority in parliament in 2000 and 2005.

25 At 2009 exchange rates, 1 LE was almost equivalent to $US 0.2.

26 As will be discussed in Chapter 5, the arena of the municipalities was a prime target of consolidation for the NDP in order to solidify its presence at the popular level. One of the main tactics that were exercised by the NDP in this regard was to attempt to co-opt those figures of lesser notability onto its side in order to strengthen its patronage machine in the popular quarters.

5 The dissolved National Democratic Party-affiliated lesser notability in Misr al-Qadima

1 The bulk of the fieldwork used in this section was conducted between 2007 and 2009, almost two years before the eruption of the January 25 uprising.

2 The term 'neoliberal' here refers to the bundle of policies that had been adopted by the NDP and entailed a strong emphasis on trade liberalization, foreign direct investment and open market economic mechanisms as the main constituents of economic reform. According to these, social justice can be achieved through a 'trickle-down' effect. This also coincided with the type of economic thought championed by the Cabinet, which was headed by Ahmed Nazif from 2004 to 2011. On the other hand, those NDP cadres whom this study describes as the 'old guard' did not necessarily share unitary socioeconomic and political stances, yet they operated within an extensive web of patron–client networks that was linked to the key old-guard figures at the top of the NDP, as will be shown later.

3 The official NDP discourse that was often displayed in public meetings and the announcements of leading figures endorsed the Economic Reform and Structural Adjustment Program (ERSAP), which aimed to promote open-market economic policies by encouraging the private sector and undermining the role of the state.

However, when looking at the cadres who were associated with the NDP, and as displayed in Chapter 4 in the case of Misr al-Qadima's lesser notabilities, the picture becomes quite heterogeneous. In addition to the heritage of Nasserite pan-Arab socialism that is still alive among the older generation within the high and middle ranks of the party, one finds that, within the lower echelons, as seen in the example of the lesser notabilities, the promotion of a façade of Islamism also recurs among several NDP cadres.

4   Certain limitations indeed exist with regard to the scope of benefits that a person was expected to reap as a result of his or her NDP membership. The higher the rank of the person within the hierarchy of the party, the more he or she would be expected to gain in terms of resources and services, in accordance with the level of association that the person had with the leading figures in the NDP. For instance, the members of the party units (local offices) in the various neighbourhoods were considered to be better connected to the resources of patronage stemming from the party and its affiliated personnel – usually MPs – than, say, the ordinary members of the party that might not have any direct relationship with the MPs. Subsequently, the members of the specialized local secretariats – women, youth secretariats, etc. – were considered to be better linked to the decision-making circles of the party than the members of the party units owing to their closeness to the central decision-making bodies in the party, and so forth.

5   Safwat Sharif was the last General Secretary of the NDP and the Speaker of the Shura Council. He stayed in his position as Minister of Information for over 23 years until he was sacked and removed to the post of Speaker of the Shura Council in 2004. His post as speaker allowed him to broker deals with newly established opposition parties and newspapers in order to admit them into operation. Kamal Shazly was the Assistant Secretary General of the NDP. His close adherence to President Hosni Mubarak started in 1992 when he was appointed as Minister for Parliamentary and Shura Council Affairs after the assassination of previous speaker of parliament, Rifa'at Al Mahjoub. Shazly played an immense role in orchestrating the parliament and manipulating municipal and parliamentary elections. With sizeable networks with the security apparatus, Shazly acquired a multitude of 'classified' files on parliamentary as well as other governmental figures. He passed away in 2010. Zakaria Azmy was the Secretary of Administrative and Financial Affairs of the NDP. He was one of Mubarak's closest aides, mainly due to his role as the Head Officer of the President (*ra'is al-diwan*). He played an essential role in the parliament as devil's advocate of the government, voicing the opposition's opinion. This gave him appeal within the parliament. Sharif and Azmy were both arrested in the aftermath of the January 25 uprising.

6   See Chapter 1 for an overview of the history and current status of the MCs.

7   With its ascent into power in 2004, Ahmed Nazif's cabinet (central government) stressed that it represented the government of the party and not vice versa, i.e. it was a government mandated with a certain economic and political programme that had been set in accordance with the NDP's agenda. This central government (2004–2011) was primarily composed of Gamal Mubarak's close associates, who were strong advocates of the predominantly neoliberal programme that he was championing.

8   At 2008 prices, this amount of money could, more or less, provide over 500 medium-sized households (five people) with their daily needs of semi-subsidized basic goods (bread, butter, oil, sugar, rice, etc.) for nearly six months.

9   What is referred to as the process of socioeconomic development relates to Mubarak's Presidential Program, which was supposed to be implemented by the relevant central and local government entities. This programme was criticized for being unsuccessful owing to its failure in addressing, among other things, the major developmental issues of poverty alleviation, income distribution and corruption at the level of central/local government. Enhancing decentralization and empowering the MCs was supposed to be one of the main constituents of this programme.

10   Examples of the state's inability to secure the basic needs of the people of a popular community such as that of Misr al-Qadima vary, ranging from severe shortages of the supply of basic goods, such as the bread crisis outlined in Chapter 4, to the inadequacy of health, education and infrastructural services expressed by the majority of the Misr al-Qadima locals that the researcher met.

11   The pricing of permits is so common that the state itself has admitted that this phenomenon is a reality. Zakaria Azmi, ex-Chief of Staff of the President's Office, was famously quoted in parliament in 2007 as saying that 'Corruption in the municipalities has reached unprecedented degrees.'

12   See also comments in this chapter by Al Sai'di and Bahi on the same issue of relocation of the skin tannery workshops. The crisis of relocation of the skin tannery workshops is elaborated upon further in the section on the area's NGOs and their relationship with the NDP. In 2005, the state decided to relocate the skin tannery workshops, the chief economic activity for a sizeable bulk of Misr al-Qadima residents, to poorly prepared sites on the outskirts of Cairo, tens of miles away from where they had originally been located. This government plan was met with robust opposition from various societal actors, in addition to the owners and workers of these workshops, who perceived this plan as a mere uprooting of this industry from the locale without providing them with proper alternatives or compensation. The newly suggested sites were described to be unfit for relocation of the workshops and were quite remote from the areas in which the skin tannery community had lived and worked for decades.

13   Hannan Al-Saidi was the chairperson of the local Women's NDP Secretariat and the chairperson of the New Fostat NGO. This exemplar of Hannan Al-Saidi as an NDP cadre will be elaborated on more extensively later in this chapter.

14   In 2005, President Mubarak introduced a constitutional amendment stating that the President should be elected by a direct vote in which multiple presidential candidates would compete, instead of by a referendum, which had been the case since 1952. However, the prerequisites put forward for a nominee to be eligible for presidential candidacy were, in reality, very hard to meet if the candidate were not an NDP candidate. One of these conditions dictated that independent candidates (those not belonging to the senior rankings of an already existing political party) had to secure the approval of 250 MPs and MC members. Without the presence of an overwhelming majority of the NDP in these two entities, it would have been virtually impossible for any candidate not supported by the NDP to proceed in the presidential elections.

15   Note the Islamic characterization of the charitable activity despite the affiliation of Dr Shahin to the supposedly secular NDP. Such an Islamic façade was sometimes portrayed in order to compete with the NGOs affiliated to the MB.

16   Ahmed Ezz, one of the country's biggest business tycoons of industry and a virtual monopolizer of the steel industry through his megacorporation Ezz Steel, was arguably Egypt's most powerful regime crony from within the community of megabusinessmen. He was also the NDP Membership Secretary and the chair of the Parliamentarian Budgetary Committee. Ezz was sentenced to 10 years in jail after the January 25 uprising.

17   See Chapters 2 and 3 for detailed definitions of the terms *ibn al-balad* and *bent balad*. These terms reflect the moral goodness, helpfulness and supportive character of the people of a certain area or neighbourhood, especially in Cairo.

18   The decision, which was taken by the Ministry of Industry and encouraged by the Industrial Chamber, was to be implemented in 2007 upon completion of the newly designated areas; this did not, however take place, at that time because of the opposition mentioned here. Had the Ministry of Industry insisted on the relocation taking place in spite of the workers, a confrontation between the executive authorities – in this case the police, who would be mandated with closing down and evacuating the old workplace – and the people of the area would undoubtedly have erupted.

19   As described by several respondents, the workshops were, as designed, unfit for their purpose owing to a lack of proper space and ventilation.

20   In Misr al-Qadima, Mamdouh Mekky was often cited as an example of the NDP's manipulation of NGOs for the benefit of the party. Mekky, who was one of the five businessmen mentioned earlier in the chapter, was a local notable and an NDP veteran who established an NGO at the height of the relocation crisis in order to channel a multitude of resources and services to the people of the area in the name of the NDP. Prior to that, Mekky had had a virtually non-existent record of social work.

21   The researcher observed some of these NDP-sponsored medical caravans in rural and low-income urban communities. The caravans, organized and funded by the party along with some major financial corporations working under the umbrella of corporate social responsibility, usually provided the people with simple on-site medical services, such as blood pressure and blood sugar measurements, and swift treatments for flu and headaches. Some of these caravans also had a section for diagnosing and treating more chronic cases.

22   In the post-*Infitah* period, there were many similar cases that witnessed the rise of a construction worker or a builder to prominence thanks to the relatively high profitability of the constructional activities in the post-*Infitah* era in general, especially if this were in the 'trendy' neighbourhoods that flourished during that period.

23   Bakr Omar was introduced in Chapter 4 as a Misr al-Qadima MP. In spite of his official affiliation to the NDP, he has been dubbed an MB sympathizer and even been accused of being a MB member by some circles within the police.

24   In the 2005 elections, many incidents of vote-buying and other electoral irregularities were reported in the majority of the country's electoral circles. In most cases, the socioeconomic context of the area determined the price of the vote. For example, in the poorer neighbourhoods of Cairo, the price of one vote could be lunch and a soft drink.

25   Ahmed Ezz was in fact married to Shahinaz Al-Naggar. According to several respondents, there was some competition, and sometimes animosity, between Al-Naggar and Bahi owing to their competition in social and political leadership in the Misr al-Qadima and Manial areas. Ultimately, Ezz had to make sure that Bahi would not be the one taking Al-Naggar's place.

26   Manshiyet Nasser is one of Cairo's biggest and most populated popular quarters and lies in close proximity to Misr al-Qadima.

27   Hajj Gad Megahed was introduced in Chapter 4; he is one of the most powerful lesser notabilities in Misr al-Qadima.

28   According to the report, the accused NDP MPs subcontracted intermediary notabilities to hire thugs from several popular quarters in order to attack the protestors in Tahrir on 2 February (the day of the Camel Battle). Several respondents also asserted that lesser notabilities have mobilized such thugs in different neighbourhoods.

29   In 2005, the parliamentary seat in this district went to Hisham Khalil, whose ascent to parliament is an interesting one. He succeeded in winning his seat against Hossam Badrawy, one of the NDP's most powerful figures and a very close aide of and consultant to Gamal Mubarak. Khalil was in fact supported by the old-guard figures of the NDP such as Kamal Shazly, who was not fond of the idea of having the new-guard figures associated with Gamal Mubarak rise to prominence in the parliament.

6   Conclusions: reflections on the sociopolitical agency and prospective role of lesser notabilities in the Egyptian polity

1   On aggregate, the disengagement of the state from the arena of social and economic services is manifested in the virtual elimination of subsidies on foodstuffs and other basic goods, the increasing informalization of the economy and the ongoing privatization of the public sector. See Chapter 3 for an overview of the features of state

disengagement from the arena of social and economic services to the low-income communities.

2 Lesser notabilities and the political groups they are affiliated to engage predominantly in the distribution of resources and, to a lesser extent, in the production and acquisition of some commodities and products, as shown by the involvement of some popular notables in the skin tannery and construction industries. The main focus of this study has, however, been the role played by the lesser notabilities in distribution and circulation rather than production. This is due to the fact that, first, and as portrayed by Nazih Ayubi's contributions presented in Chapter 1, modes of circulation in the relatively nascent Middle Eastern polity of the modern state play a more important role than modes of production in determining the sociopolitical agency of individuals and institutions. This in part relates to the fact that most Middle Eastern and many other so-called Third World polities are still characterized by a class structure that, so far, has not been similar to that of modern Western, industrial, capitalist societies, where modes of production are far more influential than modes of circulation in determining socioeconomic and political outcomes.

3 Chapter 4 showed that one of the general characteristics of the lesser notabilities is their recurrent tendency to swing back and forth between the NDP and the MB. Examples such Hajj Bakr Omar and Hajj Sayyed Abdelaal show that the political convictions and allegiances of lesser notabilities were likely to be altered between the NDP and the MB.

4 There are no particular indicators for assessing the degree of influence of the NDP compared with the MB. The observation that the researcher and the respondents noted relates to the scope of services provided by MB-affiliated organizations, which was unmatched by NDP-affiliated entities. As asserted in different sections of the research, in areas like Misr al-Qadima and other popular communities in Cairo, and apart from some individual initiatives by one governor or MC member or another, the state has been only partially successful in terms of providing inhabitants with basic infrastructural services such as water, sanitation and electricity. This makes social services such as health care and educational facilities almost secondary on the agenda of the state and the ruling party, a virtual luxury that the state is hardly able to provide, and that is where such MB-affiliated organizations enter to fill in parts of this increasingly growing divide.

5 As one tries to assess the performance of political entities such as the NDP and the MB, they sometimes appear as external forces with exogenous resources facing passive recipients. However, it is crucial to note that the lesser notabilities and other sociopolitical figures have been also active subjects who have helped to stir up social and political change in the popular communities of Cairo.

6 See Chapters 1 and 5 for a discussion of the role of municipalities and the emphasis that the NDP placed on them.

7 The importance of lesser notabilities projecting an image of piety and benevolence is stressed in Chapters 1 and 2. This is exemplified in the case of various lesser notables acquiring the title 'Hajj', which connotes religious piety and moral goodness. See also Chapter 4, where Hajj Sayyed Abdelaal refers to the importance of the lesser notability figure maintaining a social or moral role as a pious notable, keeping a persona of helpfulness and giving, regardless of his MB or NDP affiliation. As seen in Chapter 4, this image of piety and good deeds is essential for almost all MB-affiliated notabilities. In Chapter 5 there were also examples of this related to several NDP-affiliated notabilities such as the NDP Services Office Secretary Hajj Najjar, and others like Hajj Abdelhamid Shaalan and Hajj Gad Megahed.

8 See Chapter 1 for an overview of the contributions of the second-generation of analysts who have tackled the issue of informal networks of politics in the modern Middle Eastern polity.

Postscript

1 According to his Al-Jeel co-workers, Rozza received approximately 250 votes, whereas the winning candidate amassed between 3,000 and 4,000.

2 As ascertained from interviews with founders and social workers of the Al-Jeel Center, Cairo, in July and August 2008.

3 According to the figures obtained by development practitioners affiliated to UNICEF and working within the Misr al-Qadima area, the Misr al-Qadima district has one of the highest rates of street children and child labour in all of Cairo, relative to its size and population. The figures suggest around 10,000–20,000 children. In addition, approximately 14,000 children were considered to be primary education drop-outs, as stated in the New Fostat documents.

4 See Chapters 2 and 3 for an elaborate discussion of the *ibn al-balad* figure and his or her role in the popular quarter.

Bibliography

Abdallah, A. and A. Siam (1996) *Al-Mosharaka Al-Sha'beya Fi Hay Ain Al Sira Bel Qahera*, Cairo: Al Jeel Center.

Abdelfattah, K. (2007) *The Political Participation and Awareness of The People of Misr Al Qadima and Dar Essalam*, Cairo: Political & Legal Awareness Project, New Fostat NGO.

Abu-Lughod, J. (2004) 'Cairo, an Islamic metropolis', in Bianca, S. and Jodidio, P. (eds.), *Cairo: Revitalising a Historic Metropolis,* Turin: Umberto Allemandi & C. for Aga Khan Trust for Culture, pp. 19–30.

Ali A.G. and A. Elbadawi (2002) 'Poverty and the labor market in the Arab world', in Handoussa, H. and Tzannatos, Z. (eds.), *Employment Creation and Social Protection in the Middle East and North Africa*, Cairo: Economic Research Forum, American University in Cairo Press.

Aly, A. (2004) *Al Ikhwan Al Moslemoun: Azmat Tayyar Al Tajdid*, Cairo: Al Mahroussa Center.

Amin, G. (2000) *Whatever Happened to the Egyptians?*, Cairo: American University in Cairo Press.

Amin, G. (2005) *'Asr Al Jamahir Al Ghafira: 1952–2002*, Cairo: Dar Al Shrouk.

Ansari, H. (1986) *Egypt, the Stalled Society*, Albany: State University of New York Press.

Assaad, R. (2002) *The Egyptian Labor Market in an Era of Reform*, Cairo: American University in Cairo Press.

Assaad, R. (2007) *Labor Supply, Employment, and Unemployment in the Egyptian Economy*, Working Paper 0701, Cairo: Economic Research Forum.

Attia, S. (2009) The Informal Economy as an Engine for Poverty Reduction and Development in Egypt, MPRA Paper No. 13034, Munich: Munich University Library.

Aulas, M.-C. (1982) *Sadat's Egypt: A Balance Sheet*, MERIP Report No. 107, Egypt in the New Middle East, Washington, DC: Middle East Research and Information Project.

Ayubi, N. (1991) *The State and Public Policies in Egypt since Sadat*, Reading: Ithaca Press.

Ayubi, N. (1995) *Overstating the Arab State: Politics and Society in the Arab World*, London: I.B.Tauris.

Batatu, H. (1999) *Syria's Peasantry: The Descendants of its Lesser Rural Notables, and Their Politics*, Princeton, NJ: Princeton University Press.

Beeri, E. (1970) *Dobat Al Jaish Fi Al Siassa Wa Al Mogtama' Al Arabi*, Praeger: Pall Mall.

Ben Nefissa, S. (2005) *NGOs and Governance in the Arab World*, Cairo: American University in Cairo Press.

Brown, N. and M. Dunn (2007) *Egypt's Controversial Constitutional Amendments: A Textual Analysis*, Washington, DC: Carnegie Endowment For International Peace.

Brynen, R., B. Korany and P. Noble (1995) *Political Liberalization and Democratization in the Arab World*, Boulder, CO: Lynne Rienner.

Cairo City (2001) *Cairo City Key Maps and Street Index of Greater Cairo*, Cairo: Elias Modern Press.

Central Agency for Public Mobilization and Statistics (2007) *The 2006 National Census of Egypt*, Cairo: CAPMAS.

Chalcraft, J. (2005) *The Striking Cabbies in Cairo: Crafts and Guilds in Egypt, 1863–1914*, New York: State University of New York Press.

Clapham, C. (1982) *Private Patronage and Public Power: Political Clientelism in the Modern State*, New York: St. Martin's Press.

Damasio, A. (2005) *Inching Towards Democracy: The Belief and Strategies of the Muslim Brotherhood in the Search for Political Inclusion*, Cairo: American University in Cairo Press.

Denoeux, G. (1991) Urban *Unrest in the Middle East: A Comparative Study of Informal Networks in Egypt, Iran, and Lebanon*, New York: State University of New York Press.

Egyptian Association for Community Participation Enhancement (2006) *Political Participation in the 2005 Parliamentary Elections*, Cairo: Egyptian Association for Community Participation Enhancement.

Eisenstadt, S.N. and L. Roniger (1984) *Patrons, Clients, and Friends*, Cambridge: Cambridge University Press.

El Messiri, S. (1977) 'The changing role of the *futuwwa* in the social structure of Cairo', in Gellner, E. and Waterbury, J (eds.), *Patrons and Clients*, London: Duckworth.

El Messiri, S. (1978) *Ibn Al-Balad: A Concept of Egyptian Identity*, Leiden: E.J. Brill.

Fact-Finding Mission (2011) *Synopsis of Fact-Finding Mission Report on The Camel Battle* [in Arabic], Cairo: Fact-Finding Mission.

Fawzy, M. (1993) *Abu Ghazala Wa Asrar Al Iqalla*, Cairo: Al Gedawy.

Al Gawady, M. (2001) *Al Nokhba Al Massriya Al Hakema*, Cairo: Madbouly.

Gellner, E. and J. Waterbury (1977) *Patrons and Clients in Mediterranean Societies*, London: Duckworth; Hanover, NH: Center for Mediterranean Studies of the American Universities Field Staff.

Handrell, A.W. (1989) *Patronage in Ancient Societies*, London: Routledge.

Hansen, T.B. and F. Stepputat (2005) *Sovereign Bodies*, Princeton, NJ: Princeton University Press.

Hathaway, J. (1997) *The Politics of Households in Ottoman Egypt: The Rise of Qazdalgis*, New York: Cambridge University Press.

Heydemann, S. (2004) *Networks of Privilege in the Middle East*, New York: Palgrave Macmillan.

Heywood, A. (1997) *Politics*, London: Palgrave Macmillan.

Hourani, A. (1970) *The Islamic City: A Colloquium*, Oxford: Bruno Cassirer.

Hourani, A. (1981) *The Emergence of the Modern Middle East*, Berkley, CA: University of California Press.

Hourani, A. (2001) *A History of the Arab Peoples*, London: Faber & Faber.

Hussein, M.F. (1965) *Potential Design For Mass Transportation in Egypt*, PhD Thesis, University of Michigan Industry Program.

Ibrahim, S.E. (1996) *Egypt, Islam, and Democracy*, Cairo: American University in Cairo Press.

Immam, A. (1983) *Qadiyat `Essmat Sadat: Mohakamat `Asr*, Cairo: Rose Al Youssif.

Immam, A. (1985) *Nasser wa `Amer*, Cairo: Rose Al Youssif.

Ismail, S. (2003) *Rethinking Islamist Politics: Culture, the State, and Islamism*, London: I.B. Tauris.

Ismail, S. (2006) *Political Life in Cairo's New Quarters: Encountering the Everyday State*. Minneapolis: University of Minnesota Press.

Jackson, R.H. and C.G. Rosberg (1981) *Personal Rule in Black Africa*, Los Angeles: University of California Press.

Jandora, J. (1997) *Militarism in Arab Society: An Historiographical and Bibliographical Sourcebook,* London: Greenwood Press.

Kassem, M. (1999) In *the Guise of Democracy: Governance in Contemporary Egypt*, Reading: Ithaca Press.

Kassem, M. (2004) *Egyptian Politics: The Dynamics of Authoritarian Rule*, Boulder, CO: Lynne Rienner.

Kavli, O.T. (2003) *On the Notion of Reform: Public Discourses and Reform Programs in a Changing World*, Cairo: Center for the Study of Developing Countries.

Levi, M. (1988) *Of Rule and Revenue*, London: University of California Press.

Martinussen, J. (1997) *Society, State and Market*, London: Zed Books.

Migdal, J. (2001) *State in Society*, Cambridge: Cambridge University Press.

Ministry of Planning (2006) *The Economic and Social Development Plan of Egypt 2005–2006*, Cairo: Ministry of Planning.

Mitchell, T. (2002) *Rule of Experts: Egypt, Techno-politics, Modernity*, Berkley, CA: University of California Press.

Moore, H.C. (1977) Gellner, E. and J. Waterbury (1977) *Patrons and Clients in Mediterranean Societies*, London: Duckworth; Hanover, NH: Center for Mediterranean Studies of the American Universities Field Staff.

Naguib, Sameh (2005) *Al Ikhwan Al Moslemoun: Ro'eya Ishtirakeyya*, Cairo: Center for Socialist Studies.

National Democratic Institute For International Affairs (2011) *Analysis of Five IPSOS/NDI Surveys in Egypt: April-August 2011*, Washington, DC: NDI.

Negm, I. (1996) *The Political Role of Islamic NGOs in Egypt: A Case Study of Al Jamm'eyya Al Shar'eyya*, PhD Thesis [in Arabic], Faculty of Economics & Political Science, Cairo University.

O'Donnell, G. and P.C. Schmitter (1986) *Transitions from Authoritarian Rule: Tentative Conclusions about Uncertain Democracies*, Baltimore: Johns Hopkins University Press.

Pariftt, T. (2002) *The End of Development?: Modernity, Post-Modernity, and Development*, London: Pluto Press.

Parfitt, T. and A. Hira (2004) *Development Projects for a New Millennium*, Westport, CT: Praeger.

Raymond, A. (2000) *Cairo*, Cambridge, MA: Harvard University Press.

Rizq, Y.L. (1993) *Misr Al-Madaniyyah: Fusul Fii Al-Nash'ah wa Al-Tatawor*, Cairo: Tiba.

Robinson, M. and G. White (1988) *The Democratic Developmental State: Politics and Institutional Design*, Oxford: Oxford University Press.

Roniger, L. and A. Güneş-Ayata (1994) *Democracy, Clientelism, and Civil Society*, Boulder, CO: Lynne Rienner.

Roussillon, A. (1998) 'Republican Egypt interpreted: Revolution and beyond,' in Daly, M.W. (ed.) *The Cambridge History of Egypt*, Cambridge: Cambridge University Press.

Sanders, P. (2008) *Creating Medieval Cairo*, Cairo: American University in Cairo Press.

Schwartzmantel, J. (1987) *Structures of Power: An Introduction to Politics*, Sussex: Wheatsheaf Books.

Shahin, E. (1997) *Political Ascent: Contemporary Islamic Movements in North Africa*. Boulder, CO: Westview Press.

Shiha, N. (2003) *The Accountability of NGOs Applied to Egypt: The Case of Al Jamm`eya Al Shar`eyya and Al Sa`id Cooperative for Education and Development*, PhD Thesis [in Arabic], Faculty of Economics and Political Science, Cairo University.

Singerman, D. (1995) *Avenues of Participation*, Princeton, NJ: Princeton University Press.

Soliman, S. (1998) *State and Industrial Capitalism in Egypt*. Cairo Papers in Social Science, Vol. 21, No. 2, Cairo: American University in Cairo Press.

Soliman, S. (2005) *Al Nizam Al Qawey Wa Al Dawla Al Da`ifa*, Cairo: Merit.

Soliman, S. (2006) *Al Mosharka Al Siassya Fel Intikhabat Al Niabiya*, Cairo: Egyptian Association for Community Participation Enhancement.

Springborg, R. (1988) 'Approaches to the understanding of Egypt', in Chelkowski P.J. and Pranger R.J. (eds.) *Ideology and Power in the Middle East*, Durham, NC: Duke University Press.

Springborg, R. (1989) *Mubarak's Egypt: Fragmentation of the Political Order*, Boulder, CO: Westview Press.

Springborg, R. and B. James (2000) *Politics of the Middle East*, New York: Longman.

Tal, N. (2005) *Radical Islam in Egypt and Jordan*, Brighton: Sussex Academic Press.

Tangri, R. (1999) *The Politics of Patronage in Africa: Parastatals, Privatization, and Private Enterprise in Africa*, Trenton: Africa World Press.

Verkaiik, O. (2004) *Migrants and Militants*, Princeton, NJ: Princeton University Press.

Waterbury, J. (1970) *Commander of the Faithful*, London: Weidenfeld & Nicolson.

Weber, M. (1994) *Political Writings*, Cambridge: Cambridge University Press.

World Bank and Maghrib Center (2008) *The Political Drivers of Spatial/Regional Disparities in the Middle East and North Africa: A Case Study of Egypt*, Washington, DC: World Bank and Maghrib Center, Georgetown University.

Zaalouk, M. (1989) *Power, Class, and Foreign Capital in Egypt: The Rise of the New Bourgeoisie*. London: Zed Books.

Journal articles

Abdelfatah, W. (2005) 'Hal Asbah Rijal Al Rais 'Eb'an Alaih?', *Al Fajr,* Vol. 1, No. 1.

Abdelrahman, M. (2002) 'The politics of un-civil society in Egypt', *Review of African Political Economy*, Vol. 29, No. 91.

Abdul Aziz, M. and Y. Hussein (2002) 'The President, the son, and the military: The question of succession in Egypt', *Arab Studies Journal,* Vol. 9, No. 2.

Abu-Lughod, J. (1987) 'The Islamic city – historic myth, Islamic essence, and contemporary relevance', *International Journal of Middle East Studies*, Vol. 19, No. 2.

Ashour, H. (1985) 'Al E`tessam yoshark fi Al Ihteffal Bzekra Al Za`eem', *Al E`tessam,* Vol. 46, No. 2–3.

Assaad, R. (1993) 'Formal and informal institutions in the labor market with application to the construction sector in Egypt', *World Development*, Vol. 21. No. 6.

Assaad, R. and M. Arntz (2005) 'Constrained geographical mobility and gendered labor market outcomes under structural adjustment: Evidence from Egypt', *World Development*, Vol. 33, No. 3.

Bayat, A. (1997) 'Un-civil society: The politics of the informal people', *Third World Quarterly,* Vol. 18, No. 1.

Bromley, S. and R. Bush (1994) 'Adjustment in Egypt?: The political economy of reform', *Review of African Political Economy*, Vol. 21, No. 60.

Clark, J. (2004) 'Social movement theory and patron-clientelism: Islamic social institutions and the middle class in Egypt, Jordan, & Yemen', *Comparative Political Studies*, Vol. 37, No. 8.

El Ghobashy, M. (2003) 'Egypt's summer of discontent', *Middle East Report*. Online. Available <http://www.labournet.net/world/0309/egyaw01.html> (accessed September 2012).

Harris, R. and M. Wahba (2002) 'The urban geography of low-income housing: Cairo (1947–96) exemplifies a model', *International Journal of Urban and Regional Research*, Vol. 26, No. 1.

Hashmi, M. (2000) 'Understanding Mamluk power: A survey of political rule using symbolic interactionism', Online. Available <http://unchicago.edu>.

Hilel, F. (2001) 'Guns and butter in the Egyptian army', *Middle East Review of International Affairs*, Vol. 5, No. 2.

Hunter, R. (2000) 'State–society relations in nineteenth century Egypt: The years of transition', *Middle Eastern Studies*, Vol. 36, No. 3.

Ismail, S. (1996) 'The politics of space in urban Cairo: Informal communities and the state', *Arab Studies Journal*, Fall.

Ismail, S. (2000) 'Popular movement dimensions of contemporary militant Islamism: Socio-spatial determinants in the Cairo urban setting', *Comparative Studies in Society and History*, Vol. 42, No. 2.

Ismail, W. (2006) 'Demystifying the fog: Oral history and structural analysis', *The Chronicles*, Vol. 2, No. 1.

Johnston, M. (1979) 'Patrons and clients, jobs and machines: A case study of the uses of patronage', *American Political Science Review*, Vol. 73, No. 2.

Khan, M. (2005) 'Markets, states, and development: Patron-client networks and the case for democracy in developing countries', *Democratization*, Vol. 2, No. 5.

Kotob, S. (1995) 'The accommodationists speak: Goals and strategies of the Muslim Brotherhood of Egypt', *International Journal of Middle East Studies*, Vol. 27, No. 3.

Lebon, J.H.G. (1970) 'The Islamic city in the Near East: A comparative study of Cairo, Alexandria and Istanbul', *Town Planning Review*, Vol. 41, No. 2.

Lemarchand, R. and K. Legg (1972) 'Political clientelism and development: A preliminary analysis', *Comparative Politics*, Vol. 4, No. 2.

Mahdi, K. (2007) 'Neoliberalism, conflict and an oil economy: The case of Iraq', *Arab Studies Quarterly*, Vol. 27, Winter.

Menochal, A. (2004) 'And if there was no state? Critical reflections on Bates, Polanyi and Evans on the role of the state in promoting development', *Third World Quarterly*, Vol. 25, No. 4.

Minissy, A. (1999) 'Rijal Al A'maal wa Al Parliament: Okzoubat Rijal Al A'mall, *Ahwal Massriya*, Vol. 6, No 2.

Mitchell, T. (1991) 'America's Egypt: Discourse of the development industry', *Middle East Report*, March–April.

Pearson, M.N (1982) 'Premodern Muslim political systems', Journal of the American Oriental Society, Vol. 102, No. 1.

Richards, A. (1984) 'Ten years of Infitah', *Journal of Development Studies*, Vol. 20, No. 4.

Rudolph, L. and S. Rudolph (1979) 'Authority and power in bureaucratic and patrimonial administration: A Revisionist interpretation of Weber on Bureaucracy', *World Politics*, Vol. 31, No. 2.

Shehata, S. and J. Stacher (2006) 'The Brotherhood goes to parliament', *Middle East Report*, Issue 240, Fall. Online. Available <www.merip.org/mer/mer240/brotherhood-goes-parliament> (accessed September, 2012).

Shehata, S. and J. Stacher (2007) 'Boxing in the Brothers', *Middle East Report*, August. Online. Available <www.merip.org/mero/mero080807.html> (accessed September, 2012).

Sidel, J. (1997) 'Philippine politics in town, district, and province', *Journal of Asian Studies*, Vol. 56, No. 4.

Springborg, R. (1978) 'Professional syndicates in Egyptian politics: 1952–1970', *International Journal of Middle East Studies*, Vol. 9, No. 3.

Stacher, J. (2009) 'The Brothers and the wars', *Middle East Report*, Issue 250, Spring. Online. Available <www.merip.org/mer/mer250/brothers-war> (accessed September, 2012).

Stepputat, F. (1997) 'Politics of displacement in Guatemala', *Journal of Historical Sociology*, Vol. 12, No. 1.

Weisman, I. (2005) 'The politics of popular religion: Sufis, Salafis, and Muslim Brothers in 20th century Hammah', *International Middle East Studies*, Vol. 37.

Wickham, C. (1994) 'Beyond democratization: Political change in the Arab world', *Political Science and Politics*, Vol. 27, No. 3.

Newspaper articles

Abo Talib, H. (5 December 2007) 'The Wanted Decentralization and Participation', *Al-Ahram*.

Al-Ahram (7 February 2007) Vol. 131, Issue 43892.

Al-Ahram (15 January 2007) Vol. 131, Issue 43869.

Blair, D. (2004) 'Mubarak's Half Welsh Son in Line to Succeed'. Online. Available http://news.telegraph.co.uk/news/main.jhtml?xml=/news/2004/09/24/wegyp24.xml.

Blair, D. (2004) 'Egyptians Spurn Mubarak's Son'. Online. Available <http://news telegraph.co.uk/news/main.jhtml?xml=/news/2004/01/27/wegypt27.xml>.

Butter, D. (28 April 1989) 'Mubarak Hits Army Power Base', *Middle East Digest*.

Al-Dastour (5 January 2007).

Essam El Din, G. (2002) 'NDP Looks to The Market', *Al-Ahram Weekly,* 26 September – 2 October.

Essam El Din, G. (2003) 'Egypt's Ruling Party', *Al-Ahram Weekly,* 22–28 May.

Al-Masry Al-Yom (20 December 2009) Vol. 6, Issue 2016.

Ziyyad, G. (4 November 2002) 'The Kiss of Life', *Jerusalem Report*.

Websites

Constitution of The Arab Republic of Egypt (2003) Online. Available.http:// www.sis.gov.eg/eginfnew/politics/parlim/html/pres0303.htm

Economist (2003) 'Surgery on Hardened Arteries'. Online. Available http://www. economist.com/ displayStory.cfm?story_id.

Egypt. Online. Available <http://countrystudies.us/egypt.edu>.

Government and Politics (2005) Online. Available <http://www.country-studies.com/egypt/government-and-politics.html>.

History of the Muslim Brotherhood in Egypt (2008) Official Website of the Muslim Brotherhood. Online. Available <http://www.ikhwanweb.com>.

National Democratic Party (2009) 'About Us'. Online. Available <http://www.ndp.org.eg/aboutus/en/aboutus_2_1.htm> (accessed June 2009).

Price, D. (2002) 'Unleashing Blood Meridian: Bush's War Threatens Egyptian Stability.' Online. Available <http://homepages.stmartin.edu/fac_staff/dprice/Egypt–2002.htm>.

Referendum Results. Online. Available <http://referendum.eg/referendum-results.html> (accessed 15 September 2011).

Smith, L. (2004) 'Egypt After Mubarak: Beware the Trust-Fundamentalists.' Online. Available <http://slate.msn.com/id/2103651/>.

Thawra News (2004) 'Democracy Digest'. Online. Available <www.thawraproject.com/index>.

Interviews

Abdelhamid Shehata, Cairo, May 2008.

Mr. Abdou, New Fostat NGO, Misr Qadima, Cairo, June 2008.

'Ain Al Sirra locals, Cairo, May–June 2008.

Ex-NDP cadres, September 2011.

Ms. Faten, New Fostat NGO, Misr Qadima, Cairo, June 2008.

Hajj Ahmed Najar, Cairo, 12 June 2008.

Hannan Al-Saidi, New Fostat NGO Chairperson and Misr Al Qadima NDP Member, Cairo, April 2008. l

Hisham Khalil, Cairo, July 2008.

Hossam Tammam, editor of *Islam Online*, Cairo, 3 August 2008.

Ilham Bibars, NDP, Cairo, 5 June 2008.

Jamilla Abdelmajid. Cairo, April 2008.

al-Jamm'eyya al-Shar'eyya members, Misr Qadima, Cairo, June, July and August 2008, 2009.

Jano Charbel, Human Rights Specialist, Cairo, July 2009.

JS members and Misr al-Qadima residents, 2009.

Kamal Zakher, Cairo, May 2008.

Khaled Abdelfattah, Researcher and Urban Politics Specialist, Cairo, July 2008.

Khaled Abdelfattah, Misr Qadima Municipal Council Member, Cairo, July 2008.

Khaled Abdelmalak, Cairo, 13 May 2008.

Madiha Ahmed, Cairo, 14 June 2008.

Magued Hammam. Cairo, 20 June 20th 2008.

Mahmoud Al-Khashab Cairo, July 2008.

Doctors' syndicate members, Cairo, July 2009.

Members of Ilham Bahi's electoral campaign, Cairo, March–April 2008.

Members of Magdy Allam's electoral campaign, Cairo, March–April 2008.

Misr al-Qadima locals, Cairo, June–August 2008, June–August 2009, June 2011.

Misr al-QadimaNDP members and social workers, Cairo, March–May 2008, June–August 2009, March–June 2011.

Misr al-Qadima residents, Rahraha Café, Cairo, May 2008, 2009.

Hajj Mohamed, Manager of al-Jamm'eyya al-Shar'eyya in Misr al–Qadima, Cairo, July 2008.

Muslim Brotherhood affiliates, Cairo, July–August 2008.

Muslim Brotherhood cadres, June–July 2008, June 2009.

National Democratic Party members, 2009.

Omar Abdalla, Cairo, December 2007.

Hajj Sayyed Ahmed Abdelaal, Cairo, January and February 2008.

Social workers, Al-Jeel Center, Cairo, July and August 2008.

Shobra locals, Cairo, June 2008.

Youssef Sidhom, Cairo, 23 April 2008.

Index

horizontal linkages 24
Hourani, A. 29, 31, 32, 33, 34, 35, 36
Hussein, M.F. 48

ibn al-balad 51–2
Ibn Toulun 48
identity, local 21
iltizam system 35
IMF *see* International Monetary Fund
immigration 66, 96, 126–7, 138
income, foreign 40
India 18
industrial investment 40
Infitah (Open Door policy): dissolution of
   ASU 112; expansion of construction
   sector 64; and foreign income 40;
   revival of MB 74, 75–6; and state
   withdrawal 8, 10, 44, 60, 66
informal networks, patron-client 3–5
informal sector 60, 62–5
'informalism' 55
infrastructure 60
International Monetary Fund (IMF) 15, 111
interventionism 18
intimidation, electoral 113
Iran 20
ISIs (Islamic social institutions):
   academic focus 24; as alternative
   system 79; banned 93; funding 85–6;
   and Islamist identity 77; and middle
   class 24; and MB 74; nationalization
   of 73; popularity in `Ain Al-Sirra 96;
   resurgence of 90; and rise of NGOs
   100; services 110
Islamic Societies for the Placement of
   Funds *see* ISPF
Islamic Solidarity Committee 86
Islamic Unity (NGO) 123
Ismail, Khedive 35, 36, 53
Ismail, S. 5, 10–11, 15, 20, 24, 25, 42, 43,
   44
Ismail, W. 26
Ismailia 71
ISPF (Islamic Societies for the Placement
   of Funds) 45

Jordan 24
JS (al-Jamm`eyya al-Sharr`eyya)
   71–99, 86–9, 90–9; banning of 73;
   board dissolved Mubarak regime
   89; decentralization 86; funding as
   local 86, 88; General Assembly 87;
   headquarters, and electoral campaigns
   100; as hierarchical 87; ideology that of
   MB 89; membership 74; organization

87–8, 89; political activities banned 90;
   political role 89, 90; popularity poor
   areas Cairo 96; services 95–6; welfare
   services 93

kbir 101, 138, 139
Khan, M. 22
Al-Khashab, Mahmoud 115, 116

Labor party 82
land reform laws 40
Lapidus, Ira 29
lesser notables 28–46, 138–41;
   backgrounds 24–5; categorization 100;
   change of allegiance after 25 Jan 142;
   co-optation 45; contemporary 42–4;
   and employment 102, 103; financial
   arm 83–4; *futuuwa* 36–9; growing
   importance of 43; and MB 103; middle
   class 79–81; Misr al-Qadima 101–2;
   NDP affiliated 124–6; and networks
   139; revolution 1952 39–42; rise of 76–9
liberalization 10, 15, 60, 64, 75, 76
liberal/pluralist analysis 11
linkages, importance of 131
lower echelons, rise of 7–8, 9
loyalty, to state 41

Mamluk period 30, 48
Mamluk states 32, 33, 35, 36
Marcais, George 28
Marcais, William 28
Martinussen, John 3
Marxism 13
Mawhoub, Ragab 139
MB (Muslim Brotherhood) 71–99; aims
   of 78–9; banning of 85; candidates
   successful in election 11; class
   and ideology 82–3; consolidation
   76; co-optation NDP 97–9;
   decentralization 72; expansion 72;
   financial arm 83–4; funding 85–6; as
   grassroots movement 71–2, 73, 80;
   Guidance Council 72; importance
   of rural cadres 83; and ISIs 74; legal
   ban removed 71; middle class 79–81;
   in Misr al-Qadima 90–9; mosques
   74; as movement of middle class 24;
   MPs 81–2; Mubarak regime campaign
   against 45; network of Islamic
   institutions 8; as opposition force
   113; patronage networks 16; patron-
   client networks 74–5; placement in
   oppositional spaces 10–11; popular in
   poor areas 69; popularity 93, 96; post